Restoring the Soul of a Church

Healing Congregations Wounded by Clergy Sexual Misconduct

Contributors

Nils Friberg
Darlene K. Haskin
Harold Hopkins
Nancy Myer Hopkins
Richard Irons
Chilton Knudsen
Mark Laaser

Mary Lou Lavallee
Ann and Derek Legg
Margo Maris
Kevin McDonough
Katherine Roberts
Roxanne Moore Saucier
Phyllis A. Willerscheidt

Editors

Nancy Myer Hopkins
Mark Laaser

Published in association with the
Interfaith Sexual Trauma Institute,
Collegeville, Minnesota

A Liturgical Press Book

 THE LITURGICAL PRESS
Collegeville, Minnesota

Cover design by Greg Becker

1   2   3   4   5   6   7   8

Library of Congress Cataloging-in-Publication Data

Restoring the soul of a church : healing congregations wounded by
    clergy sexual misconduct / contributors, Nils Friberg . . . [et al.] ;
    editors, Nancy Myer Hopkins, Mark Laaser.
        p.   cm.
    "Published in association with the Interfaith Sexual Trauma
Institute, Collegeville, Minnesota."
    Includes bibliographical references.
    ISBN 0-8146-2333-6
    1. Sexual misconduct by clergy.   2. Sexual abuse victims—Pastoral
counseling of.   3. Reconciliation—Religious aspects—Christianity.
I. Friberg, Nils, 1935– .   II. Hopkins, Nancy Myer.   III. Laaser,
Mark R.   IV. Interfaith Sexual Trauma Institute (Collegeville,
Minn.)
    BV4392.5.H43   1995
    261.8'32—dc20   95-24145
                                                                          CIP

Contents

Foreword   v

Introduction   vii

Acknowledgments   xv

Part One: Primary Victim-Survivors and Offenders

" . . . that which is hidden will be revealed" (Luke 12:2)   3
Margo Maris

Healing for Victims   23
Phyllis A. Willerscheidt

The Unhealed Wounders   33
Richard Irons and Katherine Roberts

Part Two: Secondary Victims

Wounded Congregations   55
Nils Friberg

Understanding Congregational Dynamics   75
Chilton Knudsen

The Effects of the Misconduct Crisis on
Non-offending Clergy   102
Kevin McDonough

The Effects of Clergy Sexual Misconduct on
the Wider Church   116
Harold Hopkins

The Offender's Family   140
Ann Legg and Derek Legg

Afterpastors in Troubled Congregations   155
Darlene K. Haskin

Further Issues for Afterpastors   165
Nancy Myer Hopkins

Communicating with the Wider Community   173
Mary Lou Lavallee

One Reporter's Story   184
Roxanne Moore Saucier

Part Three: Intervention and Long-Term Healing

Living Through the Crisis   201
Nancy Myer Hopkins

Long-Term Healing   232
Mark Laaser

Conclusion   251

Contributors   254

Foreword

We welcome this volume as the first publication under the sponsorship of the Interfaith Sexual Trauma Institute. ISTI was created in May 1994 by St. John's University and Abbey as a means of providing leadership in addressing issues within ministry of sexual abuse, exploitation, and harassment through research, education, and publication.

In its statement of purpose for the institute, the ISTI board, which represents some fifteen Jewish and Christian traditions, strongly affirms the goodness of human sexuality and advocates respectful relationship through the appropriate use of power within communities of all religious traditions. Everyone stands to gain by examining openly together whatever we discover are the issues and by providing the means to confidently promote an informed awareness of our common failure. We must look critically at history, sexuality, human relationships, and our collective struggle to develop sexual meaning.

ISTI believes that human sexuality is sacred; misuse of power underlies all forms of sexual compromise, compromise that violates human dignity and harms individuals and communities both emotionally and spiritually. Healing and restoration are possible for survivors, offenders, and their communities through a complex and painful process. However, truth telling and justice making are integral to change and healing in individuals and institutions.

The goals of ISTI are to

- collect and disseminate accurate information about issues of sexual misconduct;

- develop models of intervention, psychological and spiritual healing, restitution, and recovery of community trust in collaboration with such persons as victims, offenders, religious leaders, and those in the helping professions;
- advance research on sexual abuse, exploitation, harassment, and their prevention;
- publish materials regarding victims and healing, offenders and rehabilitation, and spiritual communities and their transformation;
- encourage understanding of sexual misconduct through interdisciplinary seminars, conferences, and seminary instruction;
- support the systematic study of and theological reflection on healthy human sexuality and appropriate use of power;
- network with other professional organizations and agencies that deal with issues of sexual misconduct.

Roman Paur, O.S.B.
Executive Director
Interfaith Sexual Trauma Institute

We welcome comments and suggestions of how ISTI can be a resource. Please address correspondence to

Executive Director
Interfaith Sexual Trauma Institute
St. John's University and Abbey
Collegeville, MN 56321
U.S.A.
Phone: 612-363-3931
Fax: 612-363-2115

Introduction

The work and inspiration for this book began in the fall of 1989. At that time Mark Laaser taught a course at the Institute for Behavioral Medicine of the Golden Valley Health Center entitled "Healing the Wounds." The course was designed to educate attendees about sexual addiction and its effects on clergy.

Mark had been a pastor and is himself a recovering sexual addict. His energy for this course came from his history of acting out, offending against a number of women in his pastoral counseling practice, and the damage he had done to various people in his community and church. His concern was for others who suffered with similar problems, and he felt that if he could help it might be a small way of repaying a debt.

Nancy Myer Hopkins and her husband, Episcopal bishop Harold Hopkins, were in attendance at that first seminar. Nancy had often worked with churches and pastoral couples. She came out of growing concern for the incidence of sexual abuse in the Church and its victims. We struck up a friendship around mutual interest in these topics.

While one of us had background with sexually addicted and offending clergy and one with family systems and congregational life, we began to ask the question: What happens to the congregations in which sexual abuse by a pastor has taken place? We discovered that at that time little work had been done about it.

The obvious answer to us in our Protestant background was "form a committee to study the problem." The many people we talked to about our questions all seemed interested and enthused about it, and gradually we assembled a group of them who donated their time to come to regular meetings. This was the beginning of what we came to call the Parish Consultation Service.

From the start we felt it would be important to include people from various experience in the area of clergy sexual abuse. Harold Hopkins was a vital part of this early group. In his position as director of the Office of Pastoral Development of the Episcopal Church he had been consulting with more and more bishops who were dealing with cases of sexual misconduct among priests. The "Healing the Wounds" seminar contained a panel of recovering clergy who had sexually offended and who told their stories in a powerfully healing way. They were invited to participate in our committee and two of them accepted.

Nancy was familiar with those who were working in the field of helping victims. Among these, the Rev. Margo Maris agreed to come. Margo had been working over ten years to develop an approach to victims' advocacy. Dr. Nils Friberg, a professor of pastoral care who had worked on sexual-abuse investigations for his evangelical denomination, came. Derek and Ann Legg, a couple who counsels with clergy couples, were enthused about participating. Darlene Haskin, who is on the board of the Alban Institute, joined us. Thus, we brought our various perspectives as Lutherans, Roman Catholics, Episcopalians, and Evangelicals. Since 1989 this group has been faithfully meeting. All have contributed to this volume either publicly by authoring one of our articles or anonymously by helping with the research and writing of others.

We had an obvious area of tension in those early days. How do those who have offended talk to those who work with victims? For some, like Mark, being honest with some members of the group, mainly those coming from a victim's perspective, didn't come easily, and he had to be confronted about telling his whole story. With some pain, all of us began sharing our stories and paths with each other. We found that there is great healing in being honest. We also found many places of common pain and concern. The issues between offenders and victims didn't seem so black and white, both groups having experienced damaged and wounded emotions and spirits. All of us genuinely wanted to find ways to help others and give back to the Church. From that early meeting we continued to check in with each other at the start of each meeting. It has been this mutual and honest sharing that has formed the bond of dedication, friendship, and energy that got much of our work done.

Our first year was spent in a research phase. We felt that we needed to talk to as many churches as we could that had lived through the experience of losing their pastor due to sexual misconduct. Although there were plenty of churches around that fit this description, we had to be careful to seek only those in which the knowledge of it was public. We didn't want to expose or re-open raw wounds. Several denominations cooperated with us in finding these churches. Gradually we began to accumulate experience with Catholic, Protestant, and Jewish congregations.

In each case we assembled a group of leaders from the congregation who had been involved when the events had first gone public. We spent many fascinating hours with these honest and hurting people as they told their stories to us. We had many questions. What happened? What was the history of the congregation before the offending pastor came? Had there been other offenders before the latest case? What had been helpful and hurtful? What could have happened during the crisis time that would have helped? What was the nature of current feelings? What still needed to be done to help with a healing process? Many of the answers to these questions will be in the articles in this volume. For some it was a relief just to have someone listen to their pent-up feelings. We hope that it was healing for them to talk to us in this way, and we owe them a great debt of gratitude for their willingness to be open with us.

Those early meetings led to many ideas about what happened in those churches and what was the nature of the current need for work. In most cases we found that little had been done to help the churches get through their crisis, much less plan any long-term strategies for healing. In several of our research congregations we became involved helping committees do some of this delayed planning. In one case we were able to hold a series of congregational meetings to discuss the still-festering issues. An overpowering lesson to us was that congregants are stronger and more able to deal with the issues of sexual misconduct than most denominations ever gave them credit for. Providing a forum for truth telling and an atmosphere of ongoing honesty was the essential key in discovering the potential for healing.

From that initial research phase we started formulating the results of our work into policies and strategies. Churches began inviting some of us to come and tell them what we knew and to help them with current and past situations. We have now had experience with congregations of various denominations around the country, and we have encountered other friends in this process along the way like Chilton Knudsen, who writes for this volume. We also began inviting interested groups to the Institute for Behavioral Medicine for informal seminars. This included many denominational leaders like Fr. Kevin McDonough, another of our authors.

Some of our most poignant and compelling information has come from afterpastors. These are men and women who have been successor pastors in congregations that have experienced a betrayal of trust. A group of them spent time with us at the Institute. It was helpful for them to begin to share their stories and find strength in talking to others going through a similar experience. Their pain convinced us that we were on the right track. Darlene Haskin's article describes some of our learnings in following up with afterpastors.

The original group, based in Minneapolis, continues now under the sponsorship of the Minnesota Council of Churches. We now span the continental United States, with branch offices in Maine and Oregon.

Our work has been challenging and vastly rewarding. Many of us have gone to various religious groups, ministerial associations, and denominational gatherings around the country to share our work and strategies of healing. It has become obvious that it was time to share this with others in a concentrated and written way. It is the synergy of our concentrated work that forms the foundation of the articles in this volume.

Often, we have found ourselves engaged in lively conversation about words that are used to define the dynamics of which we write. In this field it is not uncommon for words to inspire emotional and dramatic reactions. For example, when does a "victim" become a "survivor"? What exactly do those terms mean, and when does the transformation take place? How comfortable are we with words like "offender" as opposed to "perpetrator"? When does a "victim" become an "offender" (since most offenders have been sexually victimized), and how does that transformation take place? Can you be a "victim-offender-survivor"? Several of our authors address these questions.

It is important to define four terms for sexual misconduct used in this volume:[1]

Sexual abuse is sexual involvement or contact by one person with a minor or one who is legally incompetent to consent. Sexual abuse of a minor or of one who is legally incompetent to consent is a criminal offense and must be reported to law-enforcement officials, as specified in state law.

Sexual coercion is the use of force—physical, emotional, spiritual, supervisory—to gain sexual gratification.

Sexual exploitation is a betrayal of trust in pastoral relationship by the development or the attempted development of a sexual or romantic relationship between a church worker and a person with whom that worker has a pastoral relationship. Sexual exploitation includes activity during the course of a pastoral relationship such as intercouse, erotic kissing, touching of breasts or genitals, verbal suggestions of sexual involvement, or sexually demeaning comments.

The apparent consent of a victim to the sexual or romantic relationship seldom determines whether there has been sexual exploitation because the imbalance of power between the church worker and the person in a pastoral relationship may undermine the validity of such consent. The fact that sexual activity is initiated by someone other than the church worker does not relieve that worker of responsibility, nor does it make sexual activity under those circumstances acceptable.

Sexual harassment includes but is not limited to unwelcome sexually oriented humor or language; questions or comments about sexual behavior or preference unrelated to employment qualifications; undesired physical contact; inappropriate comments about clothing or physical appearance; or repeated requests for

---

[1]We are using with permission the definitions written by the Committee on Sexual Exploitation of the National Episcopal Church. These are part of a larger document, "Respecting the Dignity of Every Human Being: A Manual for the Help of the Church and Its People in Response to the Possible Sexual Misconduct of Its Leaders," 1994.

social engagements in a situation where there is an employment, mentor, or colleague relationship between the persons involved.

Two other terms that will be used often are "primary victim" and "secondary victim." By "primary victim" we mean those people who have actually had sexual contact with a church worker. By "secondary victim" we mean all those others whose trust has been betrayed by the sexual misconduct.

This volume is presented in three parts. Part one, on primary victim-survivors and offenders, begins with an article by Margo Maris, " ' . . . that which is hidden will be revealed' (Luke 12:2)." The victim's loss of power is compellingly described, as is the process whereby she or he regains power in the process of confronting the Church as well as the abuser. The voice of the victim is often not heard or understood. It is imperative that everyone who is impacted by clergy sexual misconduct understand that there *are* direct victims, that their wounds are the most profound of all.

"Healing for Victims" by Phillis A. Willerscheidt describes the victims' advocate program she coordinates and the victims' support group she works with. Rebuilding trust and self-esteem, learning assertiveness, and developing healthy boundaries, as well as facing the spiritual void left by a spiritual leader's betrayal of trust, are all tasks that result in empowerment for the survivor. Willerscheidt also covers the practical aspects of forming support groups.

"The Unhealed Wounders" by Richard Irons and Katherine Roberts discusses issues of assessment, diagnosis, and treatment of offenders as well as indications for possible restoration. These authors provide a typology that will be helpful for both professionals and nonprofessionals in understanding the behavioral categories that offenders fit into.

Part two, on secondary victims, beings with Nils Friberg's "Wounded Congregations," in which he summarizes elements of the congregational system that are impacted and discusses theological, spiritual, and polity differences, both personal and denominational, that may cause the response to clergy sexual misconduct to vary.

Chilton Knudsen, in "Understanding Congregational Dynamics," describes universal patterns of organizational distress in congregations where clergy sexual misconduct has occurred, whether in the recent or distant past. Knudsen's method emphasizes the power of group dynamics from the very beginning of the healing process; it calls for bringing the congregation together for disclosure of the misconduct as the first step toward congregational recovery.

Kevin McDonough discusses the impact of the continuing scandal of clerical abuse in "The Effects of the Misconduct Crisis on Non-offending Clergy." McDonough describes the "signs of death" in the perceptions these clergy have of themselves, their vocation, and the broader Church and follows with emerging "signs of life," as they are reexamining their own personal health issues and recognizing the preventative dimension of self-care and peer support.

Harold Hopkins, in "The Effects of Clergy Sexual Misconduct on the Wider Church," discusses the various entities that are impacted within a denominational system or congregational setting. He addresses the need for better screening and evaluation of candidates for ministry as well as for health maintenance for clergy; and he concludes by emphasizing that a systems problem requires a systems analysis and a systemic response.

Ann Legg and Derek Legg write with great sensitivity about those who are most often the forgotten victims in these issues, the wives and children of the offenders. The effects on these victims are truly devastating, as we see in the examples taken from follow-up interviews. If there is still an area that needs much work, this is it.

"Afterpastors in Troubled Congregations" by Darlene K. Haskin and "Further Issues for Afterpastors" by Nancy Myer Hopkins address the difficult issues that must be dealt with by those who follow an offending clergyperson in a particular congregation. These issues include not only healing for a congregation that has become dysfunctional—perhaps remained so for years—but also the very difficult task of maintaining physical and emotional health for themselves and their families.

The next two articles, by Mary Lou Lavallee and Roxanne Moore Saucier respectively, discuss press releases and, more generally, maintaining a good relationship between Church and secular media. "Communicating with the Wider Community" speaks from the perspective of the church community and "One Reporter's

Story" from that of the news media. A common theme emerges that openness and mutual respect increase cooperation and serve well all parties involved.

Part three, on intervention and long-term healing, begins with Nancy Myer Hopkins' article "Living Through the Crisis," in which she presents a detailed model for working in a congregation during the crisis phase. Important here is the comparison between "open" and "closed" congregational systems, which can be used as an assessment tool by consultants and, later, by congregational leaders.

"Long-Term Healing" by Mark Laaser describes the stages of grief as they apply to situations of clerical abuse. Just as congregations experience long-term effects of clergy sexual misconduct, so also is healing a long-term process. And ultimately, "the long-term healing of a congregation is an act of reconciliation with God."

Acknowledgments

A project like this requires the help, support, and encouragement of many people along the way. Chief among our supporters have been the authors of this volume. Our friendship with them has been a major inspiration to us.

Sarah Sandberg of the Institute for Behavioral Medicine of Golden Valley Health Center shared her wisdom and the resources of the Institute. Without many of the support services that Sarah provided we would never have gotten off the ground.

Bishop Margaret Thomas of the Minnesota Council of Churches has been extremely insightful and helpful to us. The Parish Consultation Service, which inspired this volume, continues to be a part of the Minnesota Council of Churches under her wise leadership.

Fr. Michael Naughton of The Liturgical Press has been both gracious and understanding. He is a reflection of the gentle spirit that pervades St. John's University in Collegeville.

Most of all, our families and spouses have been sources of strength and encouragement for us, and we are extremely grateful to them.

There are others who contributed to this volume who can't be mentioned publicly. They are the victims, offenders, and church members whose advice, stories, strength, and hope weave the fabric of what we have to say. We continue to marvel at the courage in healing that they have modeled to us.

Part One:
Primary Victim-Survivors and Offenders

" . . . that which is hidden will be revealed" (Luke 12:2)

Margo Maris

Is it safe? Will I be believed? These are two questions I am always asked by victims of clergy sexual abuse, exploitation, or harassment. Ten years ago I would have answered no to both questions. In 1994 I can give a qualified yes to both questions. In some places it *is* safer to expose the wounds suffered by victims of clergy sexual misconduct. For so many years the silence and disbelief of these allegations was deafening, but now there are those who do listen and act when allegations are brought forward and proved to be true. And there are a small but growing number of people who have been trained to be advocates for those who have suffered as a result of clerical power abuse and the mishandling of cases by church leaders.

The advocate's job is to act as a bridge builder for Church and complainant. Advocates will be most effective if they are practicing church members who will therefore understand the power the Church has in a complainant's life. Because of possible boundary issues, however, it is best if advocates are of a different denomination or jurisdiction from that of complainants. A good advocate can assist in bringing forward a case and help to reach a satisfactory resolution at a fraction of the cost in time, money, and aggravation that a case generates once it goes to litigation; however, the best argument for an advocacy system is that it is not adversarial and is a much more humane way for cases to proceed.

The primary role of the advocate is to help the complainant speak the truth about his or her victimization. A complainant

asking for assistance might be anywhere on a continuum from recent recognition of one's victimization to nearly complete healing. Eventually, it is hoped that a victim will move beyond just
surviving to thriving. A sensitive, fair, and faithful response from
the Church will do much to ensure that happens.

The gravest loss suffered by victims of clergy abuse is often
that of their spiritual grounding. Therefore confrontation is
often necessary in order to restore meaning and healing to their
lives. The hope is to develop once again an open pathway to
God, a pathway that may or may not include an organized religion as a source of ongoing spiritual nurturing.

What Does an Advocate Do?

Very simply, an advocate is someone who helps the victim discover the still, small voice inside, which has been unable for a variety of reasons to speak with courage and force, and ask for what
that person needs in order to heal. An advocate does not speak
for others but rather helps and encourages them to make decisions for themselves. When anyone, male or female, adult or
child, has been betrayed by a clergyperson so that vulnerability
and innocence are lost or stolen, the ability to trust deeply is
gravely undermined. It is hard for a victim to believe once again
in many of the fundamental spiritual values. An understanding of
reconciliation, forgiveness, peace, justice, and mercy has to be restored. It is in the process of healing that hope will return.

Telling the Story

The use of the stained-glass window was an ancient way of
telling a story to people who were illiterate. Stories in stained
glass were a way of touching people's hearts and spirits, a way of
asking them to join the believers. It was also an inspiring way of
keeping spiritual education alive for those who had already pro-
fessed their beliefs.

The image and symbol of the stained-glass window provides a
metaphor to help describe and understand what happens to a
person hurt or wounded by clergy sexual misconduct as well as
what happens in the healing process. As a religious and spiritual

person, I believe that everyone is born to tell a story and to learn many lessons from that story. Each story is multidimensional and in some way points us to a deeper understanding of the divine as we discover the meaning of our incarnated nature.

The victim-survivors of clergy sexual abuse, exploitation, and harassment are offering their stories in the hope that hearts will be transformed. It is necessary to understand the profound pain of sexual abuse in order to arrive at the firm conclusion that this behavior is wrong and cannot be tolerated any longer in Church or synagogue or anywhere else.

The Story of Stained-Glass Windows During World War II

June 6, 1994, marked the beginning of the fifty-year celebration of the end of World War II in England and Europe. There are some striking analogies between the European war stories of the efforts at window preservation and the internal war we are now struggling with in the Church.

The first time I visited England and Europe, in 1966, I heard stories coming from tour guides as I visited church after church and cathedral after cathedral. Many of the stained-glass windows, having been declared national treasures, had been removed during the bombings. These windows were preserved at all costs. After there was a cease-fire and a treaty had been signed it was declared safe for national treasures to once again be brought out of hiding. The rebuilding of churches and cathedrals could begin, and the stained glass, the stories of God's people, could be restored to the light of day. Once again it was safe to tell the stories, the stories in fragile glass.

In the image of glass that is so easily shattered into a hundred or a thousand pieces, we find the initial breakage in a person wounded by clergy abuse and exploitation. The world of the person who has suffered the ultimate betrayal by a trusted adult who also at some level embodies the divine falls into a million pieces. It is only when the person is able to pick up those pieces and begin to place them side by side in some recognizable form that there will be hope of restoration and wholeness—holiness. I believe that each person has the status of a national treasure to the

Church. And the Church needs to pay attention, as did the governments of Europe and England, to its treasures. Church leaders must take an active part in assuring that congregations are safer places as well as in providing a process of healing and restoration for those who have been damaged.

Ruth's Story

Ruth's story is illustrative of one voice in stained glass. Late one afternoon I received a phone call from Ruth. She had been referred to me by a local therapist. The therapist had told her that emotionally she had rebuilt her life enough to begin to weave the spiritual parts of her story into the rest of her life. The therapist had indicated that the healing of her soul could be more elusive than picking up the pieces of events remembered and especially the feelings attached to those memories. But now it was time for her to try. I asked Ruth a few questions to clarify whether I was a person who would be helpful to her. Here are some sample questions and Ruth's responses:

1. Had the offender been a clergyperson? Yes.
2. Had Ruth made a complaint to the denomination? Yes, but not formally.
3. Did she feel ready to tell another person her story? Yes.
4. Did she know my background? No. I briefly told her my background and experience of doing advocacy in cases of clergy sexual misconduct.
5. Did she know I was a priest? Yes.
6. Did she need someone to come with her to see me? No.
7. Did she want to make an appointment to call back or make an appointment to see me next week? She wanted to see me next week.

After scheduling an hour-and-a-half appointment for the following week, I wondered how the pieces of Ruth's story would have to be washed, cleaned off, and chipped away before the glass could once again hold the light so that she could see out and would allow others to see in.

Ruth came in the following week. She was still a little unclear about why she was here and what we would do, but she knew that when she heard any kind of music related to the Church it made her weep profusely. She also knew that hearing anything quoted from the Bible enraged her. The music and the spoken words either reflected her deep sadness or uncontrollable rage. Ruth told me she wanted to be free of these burdens. She knew that what had once given her energy and joy now deprived her of any sense of freedom and lightness. That which once was light was now dark.

Over the next few sessions Ruth revealed the story of a young woman for whom religion had played a primary part in her life. She had been raised in a strong mainline denomination and had participated in Sunday school, youth group, choir, campus ministry. Later she was a Sunday school teacher, youth group leader, and finally there was the big church wedding. These events and activities had shaped her life. Unlike her home, where she had experienced sexual abuse at the hands of an uncle who lived with the family for five years, the Church and its leaders had always been safe. The Church had been a sanctuary.

Ruth especially remembers how, during times of confusion and questioning, she could walk into any church and receive comfort and peace just from being there—smelling the smells, touching and feeling the well-worn pews, gazing at the stained-glass windows. Here is where she found her solace.

Ruth, with her husband and two children, had moved to a large city in the Midwest from the West Coast. It was the first time she had been away from her family. Her parents were killed in a car accident within months of this move. After the funerals, Ruth turned for comfort to the Church and her local pastor. She wanted to understand how this tragedy could have happened. When she returned from the distribution of her parents' possessions she sought counsel from Father Jim, who was the preacher and celebrant on her first Sunday back.

Ruth met with Father Jim once or twice a week over the following months. He encouraged her to become active in the congregation. She taught an adult class and sang in the choir. These activities brought them together often, and it was not long before their relationship became first emotionally, then physically intimate. Hugging turned into kissing, which escalated to petting and finally to meetings that included sexual intercourse. All this time Father Jim was telling Ruth how special she was to him and how he could not possibly manage his difficult job without her.

The relationship with Father Jim became Ruth's primary source of spiritual comfort, while the other activities that had always fed her spiritually faded into insignificance. Then one day, everything fell apart. Ruth's life shattered into a million pieces. She realized that this relationship was wrong, and she blamed herself. She was filled with shame and guilt. She soon went into a deep depression and was hospitalized.

Ruth was taken to the same hospital where her parents had been taken after their accident. Once again she returned to the chapel that had been such a source of peace when she was facing the tragedy of their deaths. She set one foot in the chapel and the pieces in the stained-glass window over the altar felt like they were cutting her arms off and her heart out, and the old familiar smells made her nauseated. When she attempted to steady herself on the back of a pew, the wood seemed to be driving deep splinters into her fingers. At that moment, Ruth vowed never to return to see those windows, smell those smells, or touch or be touched by the Church again.

Ruth turned away, went back to her room, and closed the door on her life with God. She said her voice also changed and she no longer felt like singing to express joy, no matter what the context. When she left the hospital the following week, she felt that as long as she stayed away from the Church, she could never be hurt by it again. The relationship with Father Jim would remain a secret, and only she and God would know the truth.

I asked if anyone from the congregation had called her and asked about her well-being. She said no one, not the secretary, not Father Jim, not the choir director, not even the stewardship chair; no one seemed to care. Ruth did realize that she had managed a quick escape from the congregation, however, and for that she was grateful. She said that her children had actually welcomed the other Sunday activities in which the family became involved.

Two years passed. Then Ruth received a phone call from her siblings asking her and her family to return to the West Coast for the dedication of the stained-glass window in her parent's memory. The window depicted several of the gospel stories of healing and forgiveness.

When Ruth hung up from her sister's call, she could see the image of a door with steam coming out around the sides; the wood was vibrating as if ready to blow. The old feelings that had emerged in the hospital came back and dragged her down. She just sat in a heap with the telephone receiver cradled next to her breast, and all she remembers saying is no! no! no! no! no! This is how her husband found her, and once again she was hospitalized.

Apparently it was time to let the spirit back into her life. It was time to tell the doctor and the therapist that it was not her parents' deaths but the death of her trust in the Church that had caused her to fall apart. The therapist helped her identify many of the pieces of her life that had been shattered by so many events. Ruth said she could not remember the things that had happened to her without experiencing intense pain.

I asked her to imagine each of the traumatic events of her life as shattered pieces of glass that were hidden behind that closed and locked door. The stained-glass windows that had been constructed in her parents' memory were included. I again assured Ruth that stained-glass windows were supposed to bring her peace and not pain. It was in hearing Ruth's story that I was able to see more clearly how helpful the symbol of stained glass could be in a healing process. In most victims' stories of exploitation and abuse, the sacred and the profane become hopelessly confused. In Ruth's case the sin of her exploitation had taken on a spirit of evil, which was made much worse by the fact that the Church had done nothing to help. But now Ruth was going to give the Church a different kind of window—a window of opportunity.

I am thankful that Ruth came to me for assistance with her own private war in confronting the Church. She had already done a lot of work with her therapist in order to confront the family abuse, which was probably a necessary prior step for her, and she would continue to explore the connections between the two episodes as her healing progressed.

Even in the best of circumstances and with the most sensitive handling by church officials, doing the work of bringing forward a complaint is very difficult for victims. This is not a venture to be undertaken lightly, and advocates will do well to make this clear to anyone who asks for assistance. There is, however, a fine line between giving complainants some idea of what they might run into and making a complainant feel that the advocate does not really want to take on a case.

As an advocate, I have found that there are certain things each wounded person needs to hear over and over again as she or he enters into a healing process. These are (1) to know that the advocate believes the story (if an advocate finds that the complainant's story doesn't seem credible, then she or he ought to immediately suggest that the complainant get another advocate); (2) to be told that sexual involvement with one's pastor is wrong and that it is always the clergyperson's job to maintain the boundaries; (3) to know that the Church does not sanction this kind of behavior on the part of its leaders.

These first three pieces of knowledge are repeated over and over again in the process of advocacy and healing. But until a person can erase and replace the messages of the offender the healing will not take place. Following are some examples of the messages offenders who fall into predatory categories[1] often use to keep their victims under control: "If you tell, who will believe you anyway?" "This is a special relationship, sanctioned by God, so of course it is not wrong." "No, you must not tell anyone because they would not understand, and they might be jealous." "If you do report me, I will just tell people you seduced me." "I will tell people that you are having problems so that you are not to be believed."

Another message that is most likely given to the victim is that he or she is very special to the offender and somehow needed by him or her. In fact, we now know that a red flag is raised the minute a clergyperson's emotional needs begin to intrude on any pastoral relationship. The idea of being special and needed is extremely seductive, especially for a person who has been previously abused. This is because child sexual abuse creates certain core beliefs in a victim, not least of which is the belief that the only way she or he can experience intimacy and feel a sense of self-worth is through sexual expression. This is why people who are victims of earlier abuse are so vulnerable to abuse by clerical figures who, through the process of transference, often unconsciously represent the earlier family member who abused them.

[1]See Richard Irons and Katherine Roberts, "The Unhealed Wounders," p. 33 of this volume.

Still another message that often needs challenging is connected with another subtle form of power abuse. In all exploitative relationships there are usually a number of sources of power imbalance present. Role power imbalance as well as age and gender power imbalance are commonly found in such relationships, so that mutual consent is not possible even if the victim at the time felt differently. But there is also the power invoked by the requirement for secrecy. This is connected to the issue of specialness and functions to keep victims from escaping the relationship or doing any whistle blowing. Once this power is broken, other steps will be open to the victim. An advocate has the responsibility for continuing to remind victims that they are no longer bound by the need to keep the secret. A caveat, however, is that one has to be selective in deciding who hears a victim's newfound truth.

Ruth and I began to meet weekly for an hour. During these appointments the focus was kept on the need to once again trust that still, small voice within her rather than the voice of Father Jim or other authority figures in her life. That voice was telling Ruth what was necessary for her healing. Finally Ruth was able to distinguish all those other voices, which had long clamored for attention, from her own.

What I noticed with Ruth and with many others was that when her own voice did begin to speak, it was at first small and tentative. The voice of many victims is often that of a young child, typically of a five- or six-year-old. Gradually Ruth was able to find her adult voice, which told her what she needed in order to heal. Each person's needs are different and will be expressed differently, but when there is a sense of trust established, I will show a complainant a list of options and ask how I can help with her or his needs.

Below are listed fourteen options. There are many variations of this list, but this is a good place to begin:

1. File a criminal complaint. States differ on this as an available option for people who were adult victims. However, if the victim was a minor at the time of the abuse, there will be no doubt about the necessity to do this.
2. File a civil suit for damages.

3. Report to church bodies.
4. Report to Adult Protection. This is especially important if the person is a vulnerable adult according to state law. This usually and especially includes persons who are institutionalized or of limited intelligence.
5. File a complaint to an ethical standards or licensing board.
6. Write or call a former counselor's supervisor.
7. Engage in additional therapy.
8. Tell extended family or close friends.
9. Enter a support group that deals specifically with clergy sexual abuse, exploitation, or harassment.
10. File a complaint with the local Equal Opportunity Employment Commission.
11. Report to a judicatory official.
12. Ask for reimbursement of therapy costs from the Church.
13. Ask for confrontation and/or processing sessions with the offender.
14. Do nothing.[2]

I explain to all victim-survivors, as I did to Ruth, that she was not bound by these options but could be guided by them. What she would do would be based on the discovery of what she needed to heal rather than on a recipe handed out by her denomination. If she chose to go the legal route and hire a lawyer for the purposes of initiating litigation, that would likely end my involvement as advocate, but I would have helped her up to that point. Many of the victims I have worked with over the past ten years have discussed their case with a lawyer but ultimately have chosen not to pursue a legal course of action. Of those who have, it has been largely because they were not able to get satisfaction from the Church through the advocacy process.

What I believe I was doing with Ruth was giving her several pieces of colored glass and asking her to shape the pieces, pick out the colors, and begin to design her own window of opportunity—to let it speak first to her and then to the rest of the world. Ruth's design for healing would then become a one-of-a-kind work of art, her vehicle for healing.

After reviewing the list of options and knowing she could add others later, Ruth chose to do six things: (1) to tell her extended family, (2) to formally tell the denomination and to bring a charge, (3) to ask for reimbursement for expenses of therapy for her and her family, (4) to request that all congregations where Father Jim had served be told, (5) to see a lawyer, (6) to ask for a meeting with Father Jim.

By this time, having already met weekly with Ruth for five months, I began meeting with her every two to three weeks. She needed more time to put her thoughts in place and to return to her therapist as new feelings emerged. Ruth now had a team helping her discover her options, which included her physician, therapist, advocate, and lawyer. All helped her keep the focus on her healing. At this time Ruth told her sisters about the abuse, and all siblings flew in to listen, support, and assure her of their love for her as she tearfully and often haltingly told of Father Jim's exploitation of her vulnerability during the years after her parents' deaths. New understanding was created among them.

By the time Ruth had reached the point of choosing options she had progressed to the intermediate stage of the healing process. The lawyer she consulted knew her role was to give information and not to start litigation immediately. However, telling the judicatory head, meeting with Father Jim, and getting reimbursed for her expenses were all far more complicated steps.

One of the temptations a victim faces once she has broken the silence is to want to tell everyone. Although it is important to break the bonds of secrecy, it is also important to be careful to distinguish between private information, secrets, and confidential matters. People whose boundaries have been broken need help in learning, maybe for the first time, what appropriate and healthy boundaries are.

I always make the distinction for victims between confidentiality and secret keeping. I explain that for me, keeping a story in confidence is not keeping it a secret. A secret has an implication of power, whereas confidentiality implies information held out of care and honor. One of my jobs is therefore helping a person understand that what has happened to her is personal and private and that she needs to know that the people she shares her story with are safe and honorable people. This knowledge helps a client learn about her own power and the authority she is receiving as her inner voice grows.

Bringing a Complaint Forward

The meeting that takes place between the judicatory official and the complainant is a key ingredient in the healing process for all parties concerned. Those present at this first meeting will include the judicatory official; a church lawyer and/or deputy, who are both only there as witnesses; the complainant and his or her advocate; and a therapist, if desired. However, different denominations have different disciplinary laws for bringing complaints forward, and the appropriate local policy and procedures should be faithfully followed. Another thing that varies considerably from place to place and denomination to denomination is the statute of limitations. Even if the statute has run out on a case, it may be possible to get some needs met but perhaps not all.

Following is a brief outline to help conduct such a meeting: (1) The complainant tells in detail the role the Church has played in her or his life. (2) The complainant develops a chronology of events with attention to dates, times, places, and names of people who might also know about or verify the misconduct. It is important to remember that this is a reporting, not an investigation. Cross-examination or the challenging of information is inappropriate at this point. The judicatory official is asked to listen and to limit questions at the end of the session to those needed for clarification. (3) The complainant outlines the effects the abuse has had on his or her life—physical, emotional, financial, sexual, economic, family, spiritual, and church life. (4) The complainant gives a list of needs for healing.

Ruth told her bishop, with his assistant in attendance, how from early childhood the Church had occupied a special place in her life. Much of what I outlined in the beginning she elaborated to the bishop. She then, with difficulty, retold several but not all of the sexual encounters. She gave times, places, dates, with a great deal of accuracy, since like many victims, she had kept a journal as well as all the cards and letters Father Jim had sent her.

Ruth needed a break at this point. Her therapist and I accompanied her to a separate room. We returned after about ten minutes, and Ruth told the bishop what she needed for her own healing. These were Ruth's needs:

1. To know what the Church's stand was on these issues. She also asked for a copy of its policy and procedures.
2. To know if the bishop believed her.
3. To know if this behavior had ever been reported about Father Jim by anyone else.
4. She requested that Father Jim be evaluated, receive therapy, and be disciplined so he would not hurt anyone else.
5. She requested that his congregation be told as well as any other congregation he had ever served. Ruth also wanted the denomination to provide help for the congregation in dealing with the truth of Father Jim's behavior.
6. Ruth wanted eventually to meet with Father Jim in a safe setting so she could tell him in person what effect his behavior had had on her.
7. If there were other victims, she wanted them assisted to come forward and receive help also.
8. Ruth requested reimbursement for all past, present, and future therapy costs.

As expected, these requests met with mixed results. But Ruth was so empowered by the process of identifying her own needs and asking that they be met she did not feel revictimized just because she did not get everything she had asked for. A major help at this point was that the bishop was able to explain to Ruth's satisfaction why every request she made could not be immediately granted.

The first request, for a copy of policy and procedure, was easily filled, as the church body had recently completed new and updated ones. The bishop and his assistant also clarified the policy verbally.

The second question, that Ruth would be believed by the bishop, was not possible for him to grant immediately to her. He explained that while his job was to take her complaint very seriously, he had to suspend belief until there was further investigation. This was necessary for the time being so that due process and fairness would be assured for all parties involved.

The third request, that Ruth be told if anyone else had ever reported such behavior, was also not immediately within the bishop's power to grant. He did, however, assure Ruth that he would certainly be looking carefully at Father Jim's file, because the bishop was relatively new and had not yet reviewed all files. He also stated that they would do a background check on Father Jim with other judicatory officials from all the places he had previously served.

Requests 4 and 5 were immediately promised, because as part of the district's new policy anyone having a complaint made against him or her would be given a thorough multidisciplinary evaluation and receive the recommended therapy. Further, all clergy in the district knew that if allegations were found to be true there would be appropriate discipline meted out. In addition, all clergy knew that as a consequence of such behavior, their congregations would be informed and would be offered a process for healing. This was also written into the new policy, and clergy were required to document that they had read it and understood it.

The requested meeting with Father Jim was put on hold until it could be determined that everyone was ready for such a meeting. The request for reimbursement was also put on hold. Pending an investigation, some reimbursement would probably be possible, but this would also require further documentation by Ruth about costs. For a more detailed discussion of investigative interview issues and techniques, see two papers by Anne Underwood, available from Alban Institute.[3]

The Meeting with Jim

About ten months after the initial meeting, Ruth's meeting with Jim did take place. By this time Jim had confessed to the essential facts of the story as Ruth had presented them, but he continued to minimize and deny that there was a power imbalance in their relationship. He had been suspended indefinitely

---

[3]Anne Underwood, "Consideration for Conducting an Investigation of Alleged Clergy Sexual Misconduct" and "An Attorney Looks at Clergy Sexual Misconduct," Papers on Demand (Washington: Alban Institute, 1994).

and was probably going to lose his credentials. His wife had sued for divorce, and he was seeing a local therapist twice a week. Two other victims had surfaced.

Such a meeting between victim and offender will only happen if it is at the request of the victim and only if both parties are judged strong enough and far enough into recovery by their respective therapists. Sometimes a meeting can never happen. But for there to be any possibility at all, an offender will have moved to the point of at least partially understanding the effects of his behavior on the victim, and the victim will no longer be primarily thinking of herself as a victim and will not be consumed by rage. Here again, as in the first meeting, the survivor's continued recovery must not hinge on having her hear everything she would like to hear. The empowerment comes from having clarity about what was done to her and being able to express that. The offender's response is out of her control and does not make or break the meeting. But sometimes remarkable things happen.

No matter how much preparation has been done in advance, neither person is fully prepared to meet the other. Each seems to believe they will be meeting the same person they were involved with at the time of the exploitation. Generally, but not always, the power balance has switched between victim and offender. The victim is often in the stronger position, having become at last a survivor, thus beginning to thrive in a newfound sense of self-worth.

The meeting had been scheduled and postponed twice because Jim was still judged by his therapist to be in so much denial that any meeting would be counterproductive for both Jim and Ruth. But finally the day arrived. The meeting was scheduled to begin at 10:00 A.M. and end at about 11:30. Ruth knew in her head, because we had discussed it, that Jim would be different. He was older and dowdier looking than she remembered. What she reflected on afterward was that he did not even have the graciousness to wear a clean shirt.

The bishop opened the meeting with prayer, having first asked Ruth if she wanted them to pray. Ruth's and Father Jim's therapists and I were present with them. I asked people not to interrupt Ruth until she had finished and stated that there would be time for a response. Ruth carefully outlined events, going into even greater detail than she had ten months earlier. Next she outlined what the costs had been to her and her family. Last, she spoke of her spiritual and community losses. Ruth was eloquent in her description of loss of faith, biblical stories, theology, ethics, and the memories of the Church and of her relationship with God as being special.

Ruth spoke in a clear voice of power and authority and with such frankness and truth that her words tore apart the veil of denial that had surrounded Jim's heart and soul. His crying, then deep sobbing, interrupted the meeting. We took a break while he composed himself. Not always, but many times, the truth told by a survivor is the most powerful contribution to an offender's recovery.

Ruth did discover later on in the meeting that she had really been special to Jim, and he was able at some level to apologize to her. But he had a long way to go before all she had given him would feel like a gift.

Ruth was getting some of what she needed to continue healing that day. She recognized the power shift and that she was now living out of the voice of her own inner authority. She was no longer speaking from the place of a victim but as a survivor, and she knew it. The bishop also updated Ruth at this meeting on the healing process being offered to the congregation and the status of the other victims. The issue of reimbursement for therapy was working its way through the system, and things looked hopeful for at least some assistance. Throughout the process the bishop's pastoral response to Ruth had been helpful. He had not promised her anything that could not be delivered; he had kept in touch with her regularly; and he had given her careful explanations if there were any delays. Once it became clear that Ruth was to be believed, the bishop told her so, and he also thanked her for her courage in bringing the case forward.

After the meeting with Jim, Ruth was exhausted. Yet she was surprised by her reaction. She exhibited a kind of excitement generally observed in young children when they have accomplished a task they had previously been incapable of. It was like riding a bicycle for the first time without training wheels or parental support. Ruth then knew she could go on telling her own truth. She had broken the power of the negative energy symbolized by the locked door in the hospital chapel.

Suddenly it became clear that everything was possible. There was the possibility of entering the chapel again, hearing the words, listening to music and singing, sitting in the pews, receiving the sacraments. But what of the stained-glass windows? Would she be able to see a new light through them? Would she trust others to see the new light in her?

Each step was a painful one for Ruth. She decided to try taking one thing at a time. She thought the music and stained-glass windows would have to wait a while longer, so she called her sisters and asked them to put off the dedication. They assured her there was no hurry.

After the meeting with Jim I reduced our remaining sessions to a few every six to eight weeks. It was time for me to fade out of the picture except for an occasional follow-up call. I referred Ruth to a spiritual director, who would help her wrestle with the in-depth understanding of her faith, her theology, and the practice of her spirituality. During our last session Ruth told me that she had integrated the image of the stained-glass window into her own spiritual journey. She especially liked the idea of the English and European cathedrals having hidden their treasures— the stained-glass windows—until it was safe to replace them.

Time, Energy, Resources

By now the reader must be wondering how much of an advocate's time typically goes into the successful resolution of one of these cases. The range is anywhere from one phone call and a referral to someone else to countless hours, many of them on the telephone and after business hours. It is not unusual for the total time spent to exceed one hundred hours of combined phone, in-person, and meeting time. In addition, there is a considerable expenditure of energy. But the work is immensely rewarding. I have been doing this work for over ten years, and seeing the breakthrough and the profound healing that happens is what keeps me renewed.

However, my situation has been somewhat unique. Until recently, I have been fully employed on an Episcopal Church diocesan staff, and while much of my advocacy time was volunteered after hours, the Diocese of Minnesota was generous in allowing me to function as a victims' advocate for many other regions and denominations, at least partially on their time. They realized that in doing this they were contributing to the development of a vital service that would benefit the whole Church.

We have had two ecumenical advocates' week-long trainings, sponsored by the Minnesota Council of Churches, and have drawn participants from around the United States. Yet we need to select, screen, train, supervise, and compensate many, many more victims' advocates.

It has been difficult to get grants to do this. Denominations are reluctant to set aside moneys for paying advocates, let alone to compensate victims for therapy. However, this too is a justice issue. There are many forms of exploitation, and if we are not careful, the Church will take advantage of advocates, many of whom are women, in the time-honored way that the Church and the culture has often exploited women's time, considering it essential—but not valuable in terms of funding.

There are also boundary issues to be considered. If a certain denomination in a certain region decided to train and compensate its own advocates, those advocates might be in danger of perceived or real conflicts of interest, for example, in being paid by the organization that was being challenged by a victim. This complication probably dictates that any funds earmarked for advocacy must come out of a larger pool, which would also have available a pool of advocates chosen ecumenically and trained to serve a particular region.

The screening of advocates is important. While an advocate may have at one time been a victim of sexual abuse, it is absolutely essential that she or he will have long been in a recovery process and have become a survivor. I would rule out anyone who has a history of having been an offender. Good training is essential; this also costs money. Supervision is another very necessary component and should also be compensated for.

Perhaps a national and ecumenical organization such as the Interfaith Sexual Trauma Institute, sponsored by St. John's Abbey and University in Collegeville, Minnesota, might be an appropriate place to manage a fund. It is possible that recovering offenders who wish to make amends but cannot do so directly might welcome a chance to contribute to such a fund.

It will cost the Church money to do this well. However, as has already been pointed out, the potential cost of *not* having advocates available is far greater, and not just in monetary terms. Ruth's case is instructive on this point. If she had not had an advocate most likely she would have asked a lawyer to help her file a civil suit. It doesn't take much imagination to figure out that the monetary outlay could have been huge and that a lot of third parties would have taken their cut. Furthermore, the process would have been far more adversarial, and the eventual attempt at reconciliation between Ruth and Jim would probably never have happened. It is a great tragedy whenever the Church loses a chance for forgiveness and reconciliation because, after all, that is what we are about.

To return to the image of the stained-glass window, we can now look at the final stages of restoration. Ruth was learning to discern who was safe to tell her story to. She wanted someone to know that the war was over and the pieces of glass could be returned to their rightful place. Her story has been brought out of hiding.

The pieces that were broken or chipped or had just fallen out have been identified. Most have been repaired. They have been washed and polished. The old lead has been discarded and new lead ordered. The pieces are assembled, but Ruth can't yet see the full story they tell. Some of the pieces are still too far apart. She feels that if some of the pieces touch other pieces, it will still hurt too much. Ruth prays for the moment of grace when the pieces are pulled together and the story becomes clear. She knows that when this happens the great risks she took and her faith in the future will be revealed. She trusts that one day the window will illumine many inner spaces and transform the darkness into light. Ruth's story will give hope and power to others who are struggling to heal from sexual abuse perpetrated by trusted adults.

Ruth's imagery helps me to see this work as a picture never completed but as a process in which there are possibilities for growth and change. She is blessed because she has surrounded herself with people who believe that healing is possible. They have been there to assist, not to take over her healing.

I can see Ruth's stained-glass window, filled with shades of yellow, blue, red, and green but with some being clear, white, and black. In my imagining the pieces are laid out on a warm wood floor basking in sunlight. These pieces are loosely lying in a frame waiting for the strength of the lead to draw them together. When the time is right, I believe her window will stand as a symbol of forgiveness and reconciliation, of justice, peace, and mercy for all the wounded souls of the Church.

I pray daily for Ruth and all other victim-survivors, but I also pray for the soul of the Church, which has had its veil of denial torn apart by the truth tellers.

Healing for Victims

Phyllis A. Willerscheidt

Introduction

I have co-facilitated a support group for women who have been sexually exploited by clergy from a number of different denominations for five years. I am still learning from all the women in the group. It is important for me to recognize that I continue to grow in knowledge with regard to sexual abuse and exploitation.

Just as faith is something we cannot give to another, so too the journey of healing is something one does for oneself. But what are the elements that help heal a broken individual into a whole person? What are his or her needs? What are the stages of healing? How does the situation affect the victim's family? What is justice? Is reconciliation with the Church possible? These are the questions that are helpful to ask any time we set out to consider what the Church—or anyone—can do to minister to a victim who is suffering from the pain of sexual abuse or exploitation.

While we will be speaking in generalities about this issue, we all know that no two people are alike, whether they be female or male; thus it follows that the healing process will be different for different people. There are, however, some similarities that we can begin to talk about.

First and most importantly, victims need to say, "Yes, this is what happened to me." Regardless of the mental and emotional needs of individuals, this is the first step that begins the process of healing. Once they recognize that they have been victims of abuse or exploitation and that they need help, the quest for wholeness begins. Yet they still may be in various stages of denial. With the help of a support group that hears and responds to each person's story, they will begin to work through this first step.

At the initial stages of their journey victims often feel as though they were responsible for what happened to them. Many times the victims come to a support group still caring for and protecting the perpetrators. Some think and feel they are still in love with the clergyman and come with the hope that he will leave the ministry or divorce his wife and marry them.

The first step for those who are laboring under the illusion that they will marry their perpetrator must be to recognize that they have been exploited and that there is no hope for a marriage to happen. The damage done physically and emotionally is both real and devastating. Many are under a doctor's care for serious physical problems. Many have carried the emotional scars of their exploitation for years and have buried them deeply within their psyche. For these victims the road is longer and often takes many years before they can unravel their feelings and deal with the issues.

The Healing Process

What is involved in the healing process when a woman or man is a victim of sexual exploitation? What happens to the body and soul of the person?

The process of healing is a slow and painful journey known only to a few. Often the victim is not able to talk about his or her pain because of the difficulty of articulating what it is. A support group will assist in bringing some of the pain out in the open.

Women may join support groups for a variety of reasons, for example, to further the cause of justice, a goal that often seems insurmountable. Yet in many cases it is the healing of the soul that takes the longest time to accept and recognize.

The first few meetings for support groups are important steps in building trust among the members and the facilitator. In the very first session, the group leaders often ask for words that describe how the women are feeling and what some of the effects have been on them. Words such as anger, rage, fear, hatred, pain, shame, guilt, depression, panic, loss of self-esteem, and lack of trust readily come to mind. The amazing thing is that they all say, "Yes, that's how I feel," to practically every one of these characteristics.

The experience of being a victim seems to consume their very beings. The following statements are typical:

> I feel he has essentially destroyed my life, and because of that, I felt I was at fault . . . continually feeling flawed without being able to name the horrible thing that I did. Now, with greater knowledge, I feel that I can begin to reclaim my life.

> I was stalked by my perpetrator in the eighth grade, abused in the ninth; raped in the tenth, and continually exploited for another twenty-seven years, until finally I was able to get out from under his power and [I] broke from him. He continued to stalk me and make threatening phone calls to me and my family for another twenty years

The impact the abuse has had on the person emotionally, physically, and spiritually varies from individual to individual. To describe this, here are a few examples, all from victims of clergy, in their own words:

> [It] destroyed my spirituality; I am currently depressed, with a slight tendency to somatize. Emotionally, the damage is second only to the lack of spirituality. The greatest thing was the feeling of being flawed, stupid for letting him manipulate me.

> Since realization [of the abuse], I have contemplated suicide, become extremely depressed, required psychiatric intervention with medication, had problems with my job, experienced insomnia, and no longer go to church.

> The abuse I have experienced has colored every aspect of my life! To cope with the severity of [it], I developed multiple personalities. As the abuse continued and increased, so did my alter personalities. At this point, there have been thirty-five to forty alters or "fragments" identified. I lived my life from a state of detachment, completely unaware of what it was to feel any emotion or instinct. I observed those around me and did what it seemed was the "appropriate" thing to do, projecting the behavior "as if" I had actually experienced some kind of feeling, thought, or conscious awareness of choice. I tried to project what I believed to be the anticipated behavior of any other person in the same situation.

I was raped physically, spiritually, emotionally, and mentally by my perpetrator and my Church! My self-esteem, self-confidence, and carefree youth were stolen from me, to name just a few of the negative impacts. Intimacy and communication in my marriage have suffered greatly. The abuse and exploitation created a dysfunctional home scene in which my younger sister grew up. To this day she is experiencing the negative residue caused by my perpetrator.

Victims' Needs

Margo Maris, who also writes in this volume, cites several needs that victims have:

1. To be believed by the Church.
2. To hear stated that it is not the victim's fault. For officials to believe that it is the behavior of the perpetrator that is wrong, not the fact that the victim reported the behavior.
3. To hear that others won't be hurt by the perpetrator and that other victims will get help.
4. To hear an apology. Most victims will accept it whenever it comes.
5. To be advised that they should not go to congregational meetings in which the exploitation will be disclosed.
6. To have justice for themselves, to know that what happened was wrong.
7. To be considered courageous, not troublemakers.
8. To heal.
9. To be accepted within the community and know they are loved by God.

Most victims should be compensated by the Church for their therapy costs and their suffering. But most are not as interested in getting money as they are in getting well. Only when the Church does not respond to them in a fair and equitable way do they resort to hiring attorneys.

Stages of Healing

The stages of healing are similar to Kübler-Ross's stages of dying: anger, denial, depression, bargaining, and acceptance. The victim may go through these stages in varying degrees as well as in a different order. Often people slip in and out of them. Some of the victims' own comments include the following:

> . . . anger, denial, overwhelming sadness and pain. Memories surfacing through nightmares, flashbacks, or hypnosis.

> Healing is just beginning. At first, [it] was disbelief, followed by recognition, rage, and now grieving for lost potential of the person I could have been. But also activism stirring, so others won't have to go through what I did.

> Sometimes I still blame myself. Sometimes I feel angry—angry enough that I fantasize killing him. Often I feel sad, depressed, and overwhelmed. Sometimes I try and pretend it never happened. I keep trying to tell myself it wasn't my fault. It just seems endless.

> Opening the can of worms; breaking silence; feeling naked and alone in the middle of a sleet storm; wanting to run away from, instead of dealing with, the pain of healing; guilt changing to anger as I realized I was a victim abused by an evil man of power; regressing into deep black holes; surviving; wanting now to live and not to die; connecting more with nature spirituality; trusting *me* a bit more. [I'm] still scared of the child within and terrified of buried feelings. Forgiveness? Never!

Predictable Stages of Recovery

Each person heals at a different pace. One of the pieces that needs to fall in place is working through the initial stage of anger, if there is evidence of anger. If there is no sign of anger, it is best to find out if a person has already gone through it. Contrary to popular belief that all victims are extremely rageful, a common problem we observe in the early stages of recovery is that victims are not angry enough. One needs to experience this step and work through it in order to move on.

It is important also to start to look at self-esteem issues; also, most victims have trouble maintaining physical and emotional boundaries. Many times this begins with realizing that they have been socialized all their lives to be "nice." They have experienced being vulnerable for one reason or another and never knew how to be assertive and take care of their own needs. Some emotionally dependent women exhibit behavior established in childhood during interactions with those in positions of power and authority. It has paid for them to be agreeable, conforming, and "nice." Once children learn such habits of compliance it is hard to break them, and these interactive habits often continue into adulthood. If, through therapy and the support of friends, they can learn to recognize when they are being nice only for the purpose of pleasing others, they have begun the process of healing.

Another important step for victims is to feel empowered by making small and good decisions that are successful. Then they begin to feel as though they are worth something and start to become proactive with regard to taking control of their actions and their lives.

Many victims lose their spirituality when they experience clergy sexual abuse. They blame themselves, but they also blame God for what happened to them. It is crucial to their spirituality to separate God and their faith from the institutional Church. We ask questions like Who was God for you before the exploitation; How did you experience or image God during the exploitation; What is God like for you now? The purpose of asking these questions is to focus on integrating a new image of God and to let go of older, more paternalistic ones. Once victims are able to distinguish between the God of their childhood and the newer God of their adulthood, they will be able to communicate with God in ways that are more spiritually energizing and fulfilling. Freedom to experience God as an adult in a way that is enriching is a major goal of spiritual healing.

Once an individual has gone through many of the healing stages, it may be time to think about holding a confrontation with the perpetrator. This takes place between the victim, the perpetrator, and any supportive people that the victim would like to include in the meeting. The purpose of this is to return the feelings of guilt and shame to the perpetrator and to regain the power the victim—now a survivor—lost during the exploitation. This should be strongly encouraged, although many victims will be very resistant in the beginning. The process may take years before this meeting is achieved. Confrontation will bring final closure, and the survivor's life can move on.

Issues for Family Members of the Victim

Just as the victim has a hard time dealing with all the issues surrounding sexual exploitation, family members have their own way of dealing with their pain. Not all families react in the same way. Some find the victim's story difficult to believe, based on their own love for the Church, and thus they do not understand the pain the victim is experiencing. Other family members who do understand the victim's pain find it hard to forgive or understand the Church.

Family members often have a particularly hard time dealing with the emotional fallout. They must stand by and watch while their loved one experiences severe physical and emotional pain. They also must hear the story over and over again, which can be exasperating. Some younger members of the family may not understand what happened, but they know that something is wrong and that the family isn't telling them what it is. The secret continues.

Family members are secondary victims of the exploitation, and they need to be helped through their own anger, disgust, and frustration. Many, however, do not seek help from others and thus either bury the feelings or act them out in inappropriate ways. Sometimes family members become obsessed by their child's or spouse's victimization and hang onto their own rage far longer than is healthy. In cases like this, the direct victim may be ready to get on with life only to be hampered by a family member's obsessive and continuing rage.

Justice for Victims

The idea of justice for the victim has to come from the victims themselves. I believe that each person has her or his own concept of what justice might be. While the needs of both victim and perpetrator are important, it is imperative to the healing of the victim to find out what they think would be fair or just accountability for the perpetrator. Victims' feelings about justice will change according to the various stages they are in. In the very early stages, victims cannot ask for much for themselves because they have been so thoroughly devalued. They typically ask that the perpetrator get help and that others will be safe. Later on, however, as their anger kicks in, restitution for themselves and consequences for the perpetrator take on much more importance. The idea of restoring a perpetrator is usually one that victims don't tolerate in early stages, but this can change as they come to forgiveness later on. Some will never come to this kind of acceptance.

Based on an informal survey we conducted with victim members of our support group, it appears that many feel the Church offers no justice. As long as some Churches continue to leave perpetrators in positions of parish ministry, there is no acceptance of the events as exploitation and therefore no justice. Not only is the victim's pain not accepted in these situations but prevention of future harm is not accomplished.

Many feel that justice happens when the pastor is removed from active ministry of any kind and publicly exposed. Others feel that a monetary award helps ease the pain and is an admission of guilt by the Church of the harm caused. For some victims to become survivors and feel whole again, this kind of justice must take place.

According to Marie Fortune,[1] justice begins with these elements:

1. Truth telling. Giving voice to the reality of the abuse is important for the victim to do in order to break the silence surrounding the issue.
2. Acknowledging the violation. Hearing the truth, naming the abuse, and condemning it as wrong are essential elements of acknowledgment.
3. Compassion. Listening to and suffering with the victim by the Church is a critical step in justice making.
4. Protecting the vulnerable. Taking steps to prevent further abuse to the victim and others is a necessary step toward justice from the Church.
5. Accountability. Confronting the abuser and imposing some consequences helps make repentance possible. It is important for the Church to hold clergy accountable for their actions.
6. Restitution. The Church should make symbolic restoration of what was lost and give a tangible means to acknowledge

---

[1] Marie Fortune, *Is Nothing Sacred? When Sex Invades the Pastoral Relationship* (San Francisco: Harper & Row, 1989).

the wrongfulness of the abuse and the harm done, such as paying for counseling.

7. Vindication. This helps set the victim free from the suffering caused by the abuse. Finally, when the other steps have happened, the victim can be set free from the multiple layers of suffering, thus becoming a survivor who does not merely survive, but thrives.

Restoration and Reconciliation to the Church

After months and sometimes years of grappling with the issues of the exploitation the victim-survivor is thinking about regaining spirituality, even though her spirituality never really left her. A victim often feels as though God has let her down, in addition to her feelings of unworthiness. She goes through a phase of anger at God for letting this happen and wonders what she did to cause this kind of response from God. For these reasons it may be a long time before she even considers returning to active church participation. Many will go to church, sit in the back of the sanctuary, and cry. Many will look at any clergyperson and wonder, Can I trust you? Others may ask, Are you going to exploit someone? It may take years for them to allow themselves to belong again to a community of faith.

It is important for the Church and for pastors to be patient with this process. A victim has already been pressured into doing things she didn't want to do. Coming back to the Church must be her own choice.

Probably one who has been a victim will never completely let go of the anger. However, it is to be hoped that anger and rage will recede to the point that it does not rule the person's life. Sometimes a conscious choice must be made by the survivor to let go of the experience of pain and anger. With this can come empowerment, through God's grace.

Operating a Support Group

Our support groups are ecumenical and are sponsored by the Commission on Women of the Roman Catholic Archdiocese of Saint Paul and Minneapolis. Because I am paid by the Church, and since the abuse is identified by the victims with the Church in cases of clergy sexual abuse, I am sometimes viewed as suspect by new members of the group, and often I must work very hard to build their trust. I must also be aware of my own potential boundary issues in working for the Church on behalf of these victims.

We offer twelve-week facilitated sessions three times a year. The attendance is limited to between five and ten members. So far, all the groups have been for women. We have had some interest from men, and when we get enough to have a group, a men's group will be offered, with a male facilitator. We advertise in the *Catholic Bulletin* and the *Women's Press*. Often, local therapists will refer their clients to our groups.

Meetings last from 5:30 to 7:00 P.M. As the meeting begins each person chooses how much time she needs to discuss her current issues. One person will have volunteered the week before to tell her story in some depth that night. The group sometimes chooses topics and speakers to address them. If we are incorporating new members, we do it at least two at a time. We have some ground rules: (1) Call the office if you are not going to be there. (2) Everything is confidential. (3) No direct advice is given; we express our thoughts about another by beginning with "My wish for you is. . . ." (4) We start and end on time.

Conclusion

What would I say to anyone wanting to start a victims' support group? Just do it!

When healing has finally happened, a survivor feels strong and can move on to a fuller life. Memories will still be there, but these do not control her like they once did. The survivor experiences forgiveness and begins to trust and love again. This is truly a process of God's grace. Many of us have the honor to walk beside survivors. When victims become survivors it is truly a miracle of God's restorative power.

The Unhealed Wounders

Richard Irons
Katherine Roberts

The spiritual, healing potential in the relationship between clergy and those they serve is empowered by inherent disparity in position, education, and power. Each congregant attempts to muster courage and faith to trust the minister and the Church and implement the instructions, traditions, and counsel given. Since the beginning of recorded history, standards of conduct and ethical codes have been established in every religious tradition. Yet clergy are human and subject to the same maladies and shortcomings as those they serve. Although held to a higher moral and ethical standard, they sometimes fail to remain faithful to ordination vows and perfect in the discharge of duties. Abuse of power and position in the ministerial profession has been present since its origin, and sexual misconduct and offense are among the most common and egregious transgressions.

Professional sexual misconduct is defined as overt or covert expression by the clergyperson toward the congregational member of erotic or romantic thoughts, feelings, or gestures that are sexual or may be reasonably construed by the congregant as sexual. Sexual offense is a direct or indirect attempt by the cleric to inappropriately touch or make contact with any anatomic area of the congregant's body commonly considered reproductive or sexual. Offenses also include any efforts made to have the congregational member make contact with these same anatomic areas on the cleric. The array of conduct that is considered exploitation

33

includes sexual innuendo, derogatory comments, verbal or physical improprieties (such as nontherapeutic hugs), erotically charged encounters with present or former congregants in or out of the sanctuary or office, overt sexual activity, and abuse through perpetration analogous with rape or molestation. This is a highly charged emotional, moral, and legal terrain that is quite irregular and filled with many ambiguities and gray zones.

The purpose of this article is to provide a basic cartography to help one negotiate in this arena. It is based on our experiences as medical director and chaplain of hospital inpatient professional assessment programs that have formally evaluated over two hundred religious and medical professionals facing allegations of professional sexual misconduct or offense.

The incidence and prevalence of professional sexual exploitation and sexual disorders in ordained ministers, professional staff, and other church workers is not precisely known. To date, within the particular field of ordained clergy, there have been no definitive studies completed. Limited statistical information can be found buried within the narrative-related literature. Such information remains inconsistent and often anecdotal. Its utility is further eroded by divergent denominational positions that rarely agree on the definition of professional sexual exploitation or on the theology concerning such conduct. Studies completed on other types of professionals suggest a significant rate of sexual exploitation in psychiatrists, psychologists, medical doctors, and teachers. Estimates vary considerably within and between professions, depending on the type of survey studies utilized and the methodology, yet commonly a lifetime prevalence of 7 percent or more is quoted. All these professions have in common with church professionals a fiduciary responsibility to those they serve as well as a privileged relationship characterized by a covenant of trust. At this time we have no reason to expect the prevalence of sexual misconduct to be any less in ordained ministers.

Despite this lack of authoritative data, it is commonly accepted that mental-health professionals, ordained ministers, and pastoral counselors (particularly those who offer assistance with relationship or sexual matters) are at increased risk for engaging in professional sexual exploitation. Others will have allegations of such conduct or of sexual harassment brought forward against them.

Transference is ubiquitous in the relationship between a clergy-person and any congregational member. It is commonly defined as an idealized projected image of the professional (clergyperson) by the patient (congregant) that is positively or negatively charged emotionally. Feelings, reactions, expectations, and unresolved conflicts from past experience with one's parents, family, and other authority figures are often "transferred" into the current relationship with the clergyperson. Another form of transference is the corporate social and cultural projections that attach deep symbolic moral authenticity and power to the role of ordained professional. Countertransference, the image of the patient (congregant) held by the professional (clergyperson), is also ubiquitous in these relationships, though commonly denied, especially when it is negative or sexualized.

Rutter describes forbidden-zone relationships as exploitation occurring between "a man in a position in power and a woman under his care" in 96 percent of cases involving exploitation.[1] Experience shows that although women professionals can and do exploit, it is statistically far less common. In our sample of two hundred professionals, only five were women. The model presented here is based on male professionals, therefore male pronouns and titles will be used in depicting the sexually exploitive professional. False accusations occur but, despite the temptation of financial reward, remain uncommon. We believe this is in part because the process of reporting sexual exploitation and pursuing civil litigation is abusive and traumatic for the parishioner in and of itself. False or induced memories from childhood of sexual exploitation by clergy has emerged as an additional issue of growing concern within Churches.

Many sexually exploitive clergy will be found to have a paraphilia, or sexual disorder, as defined in the *Diagnostic and Statistical Manual of Mental Disorders (DSMIV)*. Paraphilia is considered to be deviant sexual behavior such as that seen in pedophilia, voyeurism, and fetishism. Others do not meet these diagnostic criteria, and sexual misconduct or offense may be categorized as a work- and stress-related problem involving boundary violation. Commonly psychopathology or addictive disease coexists, further

[1] P. Rutter, *Sex in the Forbidden Zone* (Los Angeles: Taracher, 1989).

complicating the picture. This makes it difficult to determine if professional sexual exploitation is primary or if the conduct is a symptom or complication of a psychiatric disorder, addiction, or medical illness. At some point these conundrums become academic, for once the Church and its regulatory body has determined that professional sexual misconduct has occurred, they are obli-gated to decide on an appropriate course of action. We list four questions of immediate relevance:

1. Who is this sexually exploitive minister, and how does this person differ from the vast majority of trusted servants in the Church who have not engaged in impropriety?
2. Why did this exploitation occur, and what dynamics and vulnerabilities were involved?
3. Is the professional impaired (unable to engage in ministry with reasonable skill and safety)? Can this clergyperson ever safely return to ministry and, if so, under what conditions?
4. Should the professional misconduct be addressed with treatment, disciplinary action, or a combination of both? How should these actions be explained to the congregation and especially to the victims and their families?

We believe that comprehensive assessment by a multidisciplinary team that seeks to understand the total professional can best answer these questions. The importance of considering the vast array of mental disorders, addictive diseases, medical illnesses, mitigating circumstances, and spiritual factors that may be operative in any given situation where professional sexual exploitation is alleged to have occurred cannot be overemphasized. In each case assessment should continue until a reasonable causality hypothesis is determined. This postulation is often unique to each professional and should be based on information and observations accumulated by a multidisciplinary team. It provides an adequate explanation but not an excuse or rationalization for the exploitive behavior. The hypothesis should represent a dynamic formulation of the complex admixture of developmental and situational factors faced in the clergy's personal, spiritual, and professional life as well as complimentary factors seen in the complainants. The hypothesis is crucial in defining an appropriate plan for corrective action, prevention of further exploitation, personal as well as congregational healing, and, when appropriate, rehabilitation with possible return to ministry.

The initial steps to professional sexual misconduct or offense usually occur during childhood development, before one even considers a call to ministry. For many, personal vulnerability or woundedness comes about with male separation and individuation. Normal male sexual and emotional development is associated with disidentification from mother and counteridentification with father, as classically described by Greeson.[2] A young boy's relationship with mother must undergo fundamental change in childhood to establish an effective relationship with father and other male role models. He may then develop secure self-concept as a male and sexual being. Disruptions or failures in this process lead to vulnerabilities and shortcomings expressed years later as personal insensitivity, ambivalence toward complex and sexual relationships, and misogyny.[3] Often feelings of masculine inadequacy can be identified as well as fears of never being fully accepted by others, especially women, as a man apart from his ministry.

And so, many a psychological wounding unique to the individual takes shape in response to these developmental flaws. Once formed, it has an autonomous life and is carried into adolescence and adulthood. It is characteristic that this wound

- remains a central feature of male mental architecture,
- is a source of unresolved tension,
- exerts a formative influence on imaginative needs the male subsequently experiences,
- imparts a characteristic bias or spin to the expression of those needs,
- is evident by a loose-knit group of telltale signs,
- has effects that can be temporarily overridden but that tend to emerge again over time,
- exhibits a variety of forms of expression in the adult that are both creative and destructive.

[2]R. Greeson, "Dis-identifying from Mother: Its Special Importance for the Boy," *International Journal of Psychoanalysis* 49 (1968) 370.

[3]R. Stoller, "Symbiosis Anxiety and the Development of Masculinity," *Archives of General Psychiatry* 30 (1974) 164.

Such wounds affect personal development and have profound influence on intellect, intimacy, and erotic imagination, as eloquently outlined by Hudson and Jacot.[4]

The developmental process for females suggests that they will often anchor their individual identity in a vocation that expresses relational connection. The female child does not disidentify from mother, in contrast to the male child. She continues in a pattern that reflects the caring and assumption of responsibility for caregiving taught and experienced through mother and other maternal figures. Failure to feel acceptance or appreciation by father or paternal figures may supplement or exacerbate identification with mother, increasing inner conflict, shame, and worthlessness, creating wounds that may be repressed but persist into adulthood. In our limited sample of clergywomen who were assessed in our program, the ability to be appropriately responsible while maintaining personal boundaries had become distorted during the developmental process and was later seen as a significant factor in their pattern of professional sexual exploitation.

Over 80 percent of sexually exploitive professionals we assessed were victims of physical, emotional, or sexual abuse, emotional incest, or profound abandonment as children or adolescents. Due to the cultural expectation that adults should be tough and capable of repressing the abuse, neglect, and wounds suffered in early life, most never discuss these traumas or undergo personal healing. Sometimes, under circumstances unique to the individual, wounds may be reopened. This may result in progression through the transition from victim to victimizer in order to protect oneself and maintain personal power and control. Only later does one discover the personal and professional crisis that results from his or her exploitation of power and position.

Metaphorical Classification

These exploitive clergy usually sexually act out in a ritualized pattern with vulnerable congregational members or other carefully selected individuals. Characteristically, patterns can fall into one of the following categories: professional incest, "rape" of

[4]L. Hudson and B. Jacot, *The Way Men Think* (Yale Univ. Press, 1991).

victims, and rarely, molestation of those individuals unable to offer effective resistance.

Metaphorical Incest

Sexual exploitation often parallels in some ways the relationship between an incestuous father and his abused child (see table below). These dynamics were defined by Luepker[5] and modified by Blanchard.[6] Sexually exploitive clergy, like incestuous fathers, appear to be psychiatrically and psychologically normal in most respects. They are seen by their congregation, family, friends, and peers as basically normal until a formal complaint surfaces. With this pattern of metaphorical incest, sexual addiction, as classically defined by Carnes[7] and later diagnostically categorized by Goodman,[8] is frequent. With commitment to definitive treatment and a personal recovery program, prognosis for personal healing is good for such clergy. Approximately 70 percent of our assessment study population fit into this category.

Incest offenders are generally considered to have the highest response rate to treatment and the best success with long-term rehabilitation of any group of sexual offenders. A parallel pattern in this category of clergy sexual offense and misconduct would be expected.

Metaphorical Rape

A clergyman in a position of power may advance his sexual agenda on a congregational member by exerting physical force, through intimidation, blackmail, or by utilizing direct coercion. Such offenses feel similar to criminal rape. Masters and Johnson first used this metaphorical concept when they were discussing

[5]E. Leukper, "Sexual Exploitation of Clients by Therapists: Parallels with Parent-Child Incest," *It's Never OK: A Handbook for Professionals on Sexual Exploitation by Counselors and Therapists*, B. Sanderson (St. Paul: Department of Corrections, 1989).

[6]G. Blanchard, "The Role of Sexual Addiction in the Sexual Exploitation of Patients by Male Psychiatrists," *American Journal of Preventive Psychology and Neurology* 3 (1991) 24.

[7]P. Carnes, *Out of the Shadows* (Minneapolis: CompCare, 1983).

[8]A. Goodman, "Addiction: Definition and Implications," *British Journal of Addiction* 85 (1990) 1403–08.

Incest and Exploitive Professional Relationships
A Comparative Analysis

Incestuous Relationship (Father-Daughter)	*Exploitive Relationship* (Clergyman-Congregant)
Age difference	Professional generally ten or more years older than congregant-victim
Intrinsic trust of father's role	Intrinsic trust of clergyman and his intentions
Intrinsic and unequal power of father's position	Intrinsic and unequal power of clergyman in congregation
Authoritative qualities of father	Authoritative qualities and liturgical power of the ministry
Intellectual and educational differences	Intellectual and educational differences
Natural desire to obediently please father	Natural tendency for the congregant to obey and to please the clergyman
Psychological vulnerability in childhood	Psychological vulnerability of congregant, especially when in personal crisis
Father's woundedness and vulnerability	Clergyman's own woundedness and vulnerability, often exacerbated by stress

physician exploitation of patients. Many clergy who act out sexually with patients are portrayed in the media as rapists of the soul, increasing public fear and distrust. The belief is perpetuated that all clergy who exploit and seduce parishioners are sexual deviants consumed by evil who, because of their positions and the desire of the Church to hide them, are never brought to criminal justice. Within this category the recovery prognosis and rehabilitation potential varies but at best is considered only fair, and return to ministry is in general not usually possible. Approximately 22 percent of our assessment population fit into this category. Some of the clergy in this category have committed sexual offenses that are criminal in nature and will be subject to prosecution; rape may be literally as well as metaphorically present.

Molestation

A small number of ministers act out sexually with congregants who are children or adults who are severely psychotic, physically disabled, senile, or developmentally disabled. The victim may be seriously ill, vulnerable, and fearful of death. These congregational members are often defenseless, and revulsion and disgust with clergy who exploit them is understandable. Most clergy who fall in this category have serious paraphilias that are difficult to treat. The prospect of professional rehabilitation is remote. About 8 percent of our assessment professionals fell into this classification, which we feel represents or has features of sexual molestation.

Archetypal Categorization

It has been helpful in our assessment program to categorize professionals who have abused power and position to exploit those they serve through the utilization of an archetypal framework that separates them prognostically. Although these are not classic Jungian archetypes, they possess some of their flavor and utility. They are of considerable benefit as a therapeutic language to successfully convey to the exploitive clergyperson, congregants, and all other concerned parties the nature of the misconduct or offense.

The Naive Prince

Early in his ministry, this man feels the power of his newly ordained status and feels invulnerable. He meets one or a few congregational members with whom he develops close and unique relationships in which he attempts to fill multiple personal and professional roles. Commonly, congregants are women with challenging or difficult personal problems who possess a specific psychodynamic profile the clergyman finds challenging, provocative, intoxicating, and intriguing. Interaction intensifies and exposes vulnerabilities in each of them, to which each responds. Subsequently, a blurring of appropriate professional boundaries leads to sexual misconduct or offense. The clergyman comes to recognize he is involved with a congregant in a relationship far more complex and problematic than he had intended or anticipated, and within a short period of time the sexual nature is discovered or reported by one of the involved parties. The clergyman is usually psychologically healthy and exhibits limited neurotic conflicts. He demonstrates only partially formed professional boundaries and can in retrospect realize he violated ethical standards. He may have been poorly or incompletely trained, especially in the area of pastoral counseling and the phenomena of transference and countertransference. He characteristically exhibits features of social inexperience with personal naiveté. His spirituality and self-image are highly defined by how others see him, especially by the external authority of the Church. His ability to maintain appropriate boundaries in relational life with others and God is limited by an underdeveloped and idealized sense of appropriate action within ordained ministry. Exploitation is infrequently associated with substance abuse or chemical dependency in this category. If the Naive Prince recognizes he violated professional boundaries, acknowledges shortcomings in professional training and education, and exhibits genuine remorse, his prognosis for recovery and professional rehabilitation is excellent. Such clergy respond well to education, counseling, and monitoring. Those confronted at this stage are fortunate, for most avoid progressing to other archetypal categories. Princes may be naive but not innocent, and they must learn to appreciate the responsibility of power and the hazards and consequences of its abuse.

The Wounded Warrior

Following completion of training and ordination, a clergyperson in this category usually commits much effort and energy to serving his congregation and Church. He ventures into the world and becomes engrossed in a demanding ministry. Social life and personal needs are relegated to secondary status, as they were during seminary matriculation. He may be married with children, but his personal validation and self-worth come from this Church-endowed mantle, coupled with a personal drive to serve others as a means to maintain self-worth and repress personal shame. He comes to experience existential conflict, and repressed wounds from his past emerge and manifest in new expressions of vulnerability. Professional and social demands combine with internal struggles and lead him to become sexually or romantically involved with one or more congregants or professional staff. He becomes progressively more isolated and wounded by his continued secret interactions. His exploits serve as a temporary escape from pain and profound shame but resolve nothing. He covertly bears the burdens from this hidden life and may actually feel relieved when confronted. The Warrior presents in spiritual crisis. Internal struggles originating from the paradox inherent in the disparity between the ideals and traditions of his ministry and his own hypocritical actions contribute to existential conflict. The perception that God is absent exacerbates guilt, shame, and feelings of worthlessness.

Wounded Warriors are often relatively healthy psychologically with limited neurotic conflicts and may have symptoms of situational depression. When they are discovered early enough in their careers and remain sufficiently invested in maintaining their professional status to successfully respond to therapy and treatment, their prognosis is favorable. Addictive disease, including early- or middle-stage chemical dependency admixed with sexual addiction, may be found. Successful completion of primary treatment with peer professionals is often a crucial necessary prerequisite prior to consideration of possible return to ministry. In our experience, Warriors usually do well following confrontation, boundary education, and completion of primary treatment. Rehabilitation potential is good in the majority of cases. Professional reentry is possible if such clergy remain in a structured and closely monitored recovery program under a contract that includes provisions for defined limits and boundaries, psychotherapy, and direct supervision during the early and middle stages of recovery.[9]

[9]R. R. Irons, "Contractual Provisions for Reentry," *American Journal of Preventive Psychiatry and Neurology* 3:1 (1991) 57–59.

The Self-Serving Martyr

Clergymen in this category have progressed to middle or late career stages and in the process have sacrificed personal growth and family involvement for ministry and service in the Church and community. Work becomes the primary life activity and the only way to meet personal needs for affirmation and validation. Over time, innate woundedness becomes expressed in sexual and/or romantic relationships within the congregation. The Martyr views himself as a suffering servant of others who do not appreciate how consumed he has become in his professional duties and his service to Church and community. His lament can often be heard in words such as "I've done so much for so many for so long that I deserve something for me." He becomes angry, resentful, and isolated, often taking on the self-anointed role of prophet-victim. He makes rationalized and justified exceptions to ethical standards and professional boundaries with "special" people, characterized by emotional enmeshment and a blurring of the roles he plays in their lives. Ritualistic grooming progresses to sexual misconduct and offense, often with a series of congregants over significant periods. A highly developed narcissistic self-idolatry may develop, associated with the belief that he has the ability to understand and appreciate a special ministry that God has created for him. By the time confrontation occurs, he may be exhausted physically, emotionally, and intellectually as well as being spiritually bankrupt. He may be experiencing considerable existential sadness and feel stuck. God is perceived as a distant, remote, and judgmental force who has not provided the boons and affirmation he has expected in return for all that he has sacrificed for others.

Martyrs have significant neurotic conflicts, are often withdrawn or melancholy, and may have unattended physical maladies. Addictive disease is common, often in a pattern of controlled chemical use associated with covert unmanageability mixed with sexual addiction, compulsive eating or gambling, and used in an attempt to escape pain. Characterological pathology may be seen with obsessive-compulsive, narcissistic, dependent, or hysterical features. Martyrs are almost always professionally impaired by the time they present for assessment. Withdrawal from ministry and

intensive treatment are usually required. Recovery often progresses slowly, and further primary treatment in an extended-care
facility dedicated to professional patients may be helpful. Civil litigation and marital discord are common, and disciplinary action
by the church regulatory agency is almost certain. If the clergyman commits himself to a recovery program and successfully
completes primary treatment, his prognosis and rehabilitation is
fair but varies considerably from case to case. Professional reentry
is often delayed and even when feasible is usually severely re-
stricted. Career transition may be desired or necessary due to the
treatment demands and expenses as well as the length of time required out of work to pursue rehabilitation.

The False Lover

In reaching adulthood and then attaining professional success,
a man may advance his desire to live a life of intensity and continuous high drama. While maintaining professional status and
social respectability, the clergyman indulges in the loves and appe-
tites of his body and mind, enjoying life on the edge and the thrill
of seducing another in the fulfillment of passion and conquest.
Although he may be dramatic, perfectionistic, and enthusiastic in
his ministry, he may often be seen to represent a *puer aeternus*,[10]
one who has remained too long in adolescent psychology. He becomes captivated by a series of women, each of whom appears for
a while to meet his image of perfection. But each is soon found
to be ordinary and mundane. His preoccupation with one dissi-
pates, and he moves on to project his ideals and desires on another, hoping she might satisfy his every need. False Lovers are
charming, creative, energetic, idealistic, and romantic. "Love"
may become the word used to express the signs and symptoms of
addiction, as described by Carnes.[11] Hunger for adventure and
notoriety may lead to high-risk behavior and a desire to have it
all—fortune, fame, ministerial distinction, and a Dionysian life-
style. Inevitably conflicts arise in personal and professional life.
Chemical dependency in middle or late stage is frequent. Sexual
indiscretion takes place in and out of the congregation. Religious

[10]M. Franz, *Puer Aeternus* (Sigo, 1981).
[11]P. Carnes, *Don't Call It Love* (New York: Bantam, 1991).

beliefs and practices, rites, and rituals are used compulsively to convince others that he is close to God and thus worthy of admiration and trust. Loss of control and unmanageability are often reflected in a pattern of divorces, job changes, failed geographic cures, accidents, and legal problems.

False Lovers usually present with extreme denial and in genuine crisis. They generally meet the criteria for a sexual disorder with addictive and exploitive features and at least one other active addictive disease. Characterologic pathology is common and may include obsessive-compulsive, narcissistic, adolescent, and dependent features. A characterological disorder may be present as a primary diagnosis, complicating treatment of other problems. Impulse control is often of major concern and may be a significant complicating factor.

These clergymen are usually professionally impaired by the time they present for a formal assessment. Withdrawal from practice and intensive treatment are required, usually in an inpatient setting with peer professionals. Successful treatment and recovery require rigorous honesty and a commitment to growth and change in order to overcome denial, develop increased compassion for others, and maintain commitment to a lifelong recovery program.

This group is usually best understood and treated by addiction specialists and chemical dependency counselors. Their sexual acting out represents a facet of addictive disease as classically described in the Big Book.[12] Paraphiliac disorders require treatment in specialized treatment centers by experienced therapists.

Professional rehabilitation may be possible for some clergy after sufficient therapy and treatment but is by no means assured. Those who attain genuine recovery often do so through substantial personal change and a genuine spiritual awakening. Others will comply with treatment and superficially express re-morse and a desire to change while harboring characterological pathology or an impulse-control disorder that cannot be easily overcome. These defects make professional reentry difficult and potentially hazardous. A favorable response to therapy over time and a specific contract for monitoring the clergyman from a multi-disci-

---

[12] *Alcoholics Anonymous* (A.A. World Services, 1976) 68–71.

plinary team of experienced professionals who will continue to be involved in this rehabilitation may be required before such a one is permitted to attempt a return to ministry.

The Dark King

This clergyman is adept in the exploitation of power for personal aggrandizement and gain. Socially skilled and verbally facile, he appears charming and charismatic. Using rational and refined arguments, he convinces those he serves that he possesses special abilities. He is dynastic and driven by grandiosity and a pathological need to control and dominate. Once confronted and exposed, he is someone you will never forget.

He initially experiences professional success and renown. With experience and greater resources at his disposal he becomes more deliberate, cunning, and manipulative. Sexual exploitation represents an expression of power, superiority, and dominance. Victims are carefully chosen to meet his sexual agenda and interests. He may be a Dr. Jekyll/Mr. Hyde figure with episodic acting out that appears superficially out of character. Or he may present as a refined persona with many friends and supporters who attest to his virtues and good moral character.

The Dark King will often expend considerable effort to prove his innocence and to justify his personal and professional actions at all costs. He often believes that the allegations that have been brought forward against him are the result of a conspiracy fomented by a small faction of the congregation who are out to discredit him. Expect him to be therapy wise, psychologically well defended, and legally informed. Some Dark Kings present disenfranchised, broken, and embittered. In exerting their need to subjugate others they have lost power when allegations against them were found to be true, and they are discovered to be in abject spiritual poverty. Spiritual assessment will often reveal a clergyman who holds a primal image of a capricious and malevolent God that was acquired from the significant adults in his life. This may have been compartmentalized, utilizing rageful disillusionment during adolescence or early adulthood.

Although Dark Kings are rare, they are the professional exploiters most frequently portrayed in the media. They are the clergy society loves to hate. Many fear that all sexually exploitive clergy are Dark Kings and that in time they will all be found to be sociopathic. Possessing a rich and pathologic array of narcissistic, antisocial, borderline, and schizoid personality disorders, often with superior intellectual gifts, they are the material from which books are made. Paraphilia, if present, is difficult to treat. Addictive disease is relatively uncommon. Professional impairment is a risk to public safety and usually requires summary suspension or removal from ministry. Civil litigation and criminal prosecution is common. Treatment is prolonged and difficult and is often not attempted until loss of vocation or incarceration. Nearly all are unable to return to their ministry.

The Wild Card

These clergymen have an erratic, unpredictable course in personal and professional life. At some point in their career, usually prior to allegations of sexual impropriety, they experience significant difficulty functioning effectively, seek professional help, and are diagnosed with a major mental-health disorder on Axis 1 in the DSM 4.[13] Subsequent treatment often brings improvement, and the clergyman may perform well for period of time before there is a return to mental illness. Following this relapse, the clergyman is found to have engaged in sexual impropriety.

Sexual acting out occurs when management of the primary disorder is not optimal and is often associated with poor social judgment and loose professional boundaries. The dynamics of exploitation are often less ritualized, premeditated, or easily defined. Usually, the professional does not meet the diagnostic criteria for psychosexual disorder or paraphilia. Sexual misconduct or offense is associated with disinhibition, lack of impulse control, cognitive distortion, dissociative states, psychotic thinking, or dementia. The clergyman is able to maintain a veneer of religious faith, but spirituality may be genuine. During the exacerbations of his mental disorder the language of faith becomes as distorted as the patterns of thought that characterize his illness.

In our program, the most common diagnoses are major depression with psychotic features, bipolar affective disorder, atypi-

---

[13] *Diagnostic and Statistical Manual of Mental Disorders,* 4th ed. (American Psychiatric Association, 1994).

cal psychosis, dissociative disorder, and organic mental disorders associated with medical conditions of unknown etiology. Chemical dependency is a complicating problem that is fortunately not common.

The Wild Card is categorized by the inconsistent and unpredictable nature of sexual impropriety and the uncertain risk of recurrence. Accurate prognostic predictions depend on precise and appropriate diagnoses. Documentation of compliance with treatment of medical or psychiatric disorders is required to determine if the illness is responsive to medication and therapy. It is then possible to make cogent recommendations concerning the risk of disease recurrence, further episodes of sexual misconduct or offense, and the wisdom and safety of return to ministry. Clergy in this category may be considered for return to their congregation if the professional undergoes successful treatment and complies with ongoing therapy, medication (if needed), structured practice boundaries, and a continuing care contract.

Spiritual Reconciliation

Within each human being is the need to know that he or she is uniquely loved and affirmed. The foundational environment for this to occur is placed in the early developmental years. As reported previously, over 80 percent of sexually exploitive professionals experienced psychological wounding in their formational environments. The theological tasks for the exploitive clergyman are to ask for and accept the forgiveness of God and others and to reestablish a relational quality of life that reflects a personal relationship with God that influences and frames his life. The movement is marked as a passage from self-doubt, fear, denial, and anger to a humble perception of oneself as acceptable and worthy to be a beloved child of God.

The journey toward healing and reconciliation begins with the honest assessment of the level of spiritual development present, regardless of the clergyperson's chronological age. The goal of treatment is revitalization of the God-given gifts of faith and hope. For some the lost vision of being acceptable and beloved of God will be difficult, as their spiritual life is marked by estrangement or feelings of abandonment rather than by a personal relationship with God. Clergy that present in crisis usually demonstrate a high level of denial. Denial precedes a healthy recognition of guilt and anger, which may, in the grace of a moment, evolve into true remorse and genuine spiritual awakening.

Guilt and anger may serve as the catalytic agents of healing. Exploitive clergy tend to espouse a theology that rationalizes greed and competition; this is intended to remove guilt from their lives as it brings dis-ease. The Christian gospel points toward a way where guilt is redeemed for love, health, and humanity.

Guilt may well be the Christian's shadow. Mortals cannot be aware that they cast a shadow unless they understand that they walk in the light. Here we speak of the "Word that was the real light that gives light to everyone" (John 1:9). The marvel becomes the understanding that the shadow of guilt affirms the presence of God in each life. As the exploitive clergy come to understand that guilt need not mean rejection and condemnation but may become an occasion for sanctification, they let the acknowledged guilt press them forward toward a healing they have yet to know. Guilt can inflame compassion and love for God and others.

Anger based on resentments, bitterness, and hatred is destructive. Destructive anger articulated by clergy in crisis bears the marks of resentment, and it manifests itself in attacks against themselves and others. The good news of the gospel points instead toward a righteous anger that is part of love and is present to defend and protect the God-given gifts of life and dignity. The healing of exploitive clergy depends in part on their willingness to seek the roots of their anger. Demonstrating the courage to risk confrontation with their anger, they may discover that the anger is caused by feelings generated by their own earlier victimization as well as unrealistic expectations of their chosen vocation. In addition, their anger can be fueled by feelings of helplessness caused by witnessing innocent suffering, the unjust presence of evil, and the heartbreaking tragedies of human lives. The redemptive movement toward healing for impaired clergy comes as they utilize their freedom to address anger and aggression. Seductive and sexually exploitive clergy can be offered the hope of healing when they seek their own wholeness and authenticity.

In the Professional Assessment Program we have emphasized an environment of truth and honesty that welcomes "unhealed wounders" in their brokenness. The environment is unique, as it articulates the Christian hospitality of welcome and does not stress acceptance as the norm for welcome. Acceptance carries with it an interpretation that might suggest the patient's behavior is acceptable. The welcome the Church may offer in a moment of judgment sets forth an unspoken realization that each individual is affirmed in their essence while not confusing their existence with their essence. This is close to Paul Tillich's understanding of the existential being. When acceptance is substituted for forgiveness it lowers the hope for awareness of the patient's essential nature as a child of God to the level of control of behavior. Mere acceptance in the process is treatment that amputates the individual's hope and freedom. It is necessary to face the consequences of one's actions and experience remorse in order to know the grace of forgiveness and the blessing of spiritual healing.

Conclusion

We have attempted to provide an overview of sexually exploitive clergy. These metaphorical classifications and archetypal categorizations have been helpful to our assessment team. They provide a nontechnical framework useful in coming to terms with a clergyman who presents with allegations of sexual exploitation and in providing conclusions and recommended courses of action to him, his peers, congregation, and family. Every clergyman does not fit into a convenient niche, and elements from several of these brief sketches may need to be combined to provide a composite personal portrait. A great deal of work is needed to refine assessment approaches and to provide specific, appropriate, and effective treatment that can more frequently lead to recovery and rehabilitation. It remains our ethical responsibility to assist potentially exploitive clergy, though the prospect is at times daunting. If we cannot or will not provide compassionate, responsible intervention for a clergyman engaging in sexual impropriety, how can we address this or other pertinent issues of abuse and victimization in those we serve?

Part Two:
Secondary Victims

Wounded Congregations

Nils Friberg

When clergy sexual misconduct occurs, the impact on different people depends on a number of variables. Three major ones are the nature of congregants' relationship to the Church, to the perpetrator, and the level of fiduciary trust placed in the clergy-person. This is analogous to those who have experienced bereavement, whose grief depends upon the kind of relationship they have had with the deceased. Those who are closest in relationship to the perpetrating clergy are usually hit the hardest because the ties and interrelationships are inevitably more intense. However, beyond the degree of relationship the impact depends also on the process involved in the revelation and the way this happens over time. One's personal history will also be a factor. I will describe several areas of impact and examine these areas from structural, relational, personal, or processing perspectives.

Spiritual Impact

The spiritual impact is closely linked to the meaning of ministry and the particular denominational or congregational expectations for the involvement of ordained ministers in members' lives. For example, if the view of ministry leans more toward sacramental presence, this will mean that misconduct may powerfully affect the areas of their own spirituality involving sacraments such as baptism, Eucharist, or marriage. For those who emphasize the primacy of the Word, as historically most Protestants do, sexual misconduct might affect more strongly their receptivity and feelings about the preaching event and Scripture. For people from either side of the spectrum, worship is certainly affected. For attenders who focus on the ethical and moral issues in life, the abuse of power on the one hand and breaking of rules regarding sexual behavior on the other would affect feelings and convictions about ethical and moral norms they learned in this particular setting.

It is interesting to note that clergy ethics writers like Lebacqz and Barton, and Fortune[1] place most emphasis upon the breaking of the fiduciary relationship, which is defined as a relationship of trust such that a clergyperson must put the interests of the congregant above his or her own. Other writers stress spiritually or psychologically focused factors. This illustrates the principle that the way we experience our faith has much to say about what will be affected by these cases.

For example, Winebrenner and Frazier take a theologically conservative and highly spiritualized view of sexual misconduct.[2] They speak of "people lying at the bottom of the heap, crushed by the weight of another's sin," needing to be "restored to a faithful stance." In the annotations on their bibliography they recommend one particular book very highly because they know many of their readers will have to deal with the abuse of spiritual authority by certain conservative religious leaders and—for church members—the resultant mistrust of religious systems. The particular book they reference, by Johnson and Van Vonderen, titled *The Subtle Power of Spiritual Abuse,* does this very well.[3] These writers assume that readers will use their faith to deal with the problem not so much through intellectual categories as through a rearrangement of inner loyalties and spiritual investment of self.

If we focus on the involvement of persons who find regular worship a meaningful and intensely personal experience (Gordon

[1]Karen Lebacqz and Ronald Barton, *Sex in the Parish* (Louisville, Ky.: Westminster/John Knox, 1991); Marie Fortune, *Is Nothing Sacred? When Sex Invades the Pastoral Relationship* (San Francisco: Harper & Row, 1987).

[2]Winebrenner and Frazier, *When a Leader Falls: What Happens to Everyone Else?* (Bethany, 1993).

[3]See David Johnson and Jeff Van Vonderen, *The Subtle Power of Spiritual Abuse* (Bethany, 1991).

Allport would say "intrinsic orientation to religious life"),[4] we see clergy as lifting people up to God in prayer, often leading congregational music and worship. Clergy are often associated with God's own person and will, since their preaching, liturgical leadership, and pastoral care is powerfully representational of the divine. The clerical role and persona has been tightly associated week by week with our holiest moments. To accept the possibility that this person is one who is capable of serious violation of sexual boundaries creates for us emotional and theological dissonance of the highest order.

Conversely, for the person with an extrinsic orientation who attends worship basically out of a need for social affirmation and belonging, the above elements would not be in focus. Rather, there would be more importance attached to one's group identity, sense of security as a person, and the usefulness of congregational life to social status. Obviously the two categories of intrinsic and extrinsic orientations are not mutually exclusive, but degrees of each can be found together in one person. Most of us lean more strongly one way or the other.

One could also postulate that varying levels of the development of moral and ethical reasoning would influence reactions to clergy sexual misconduct. For example, if we follow a schema such as Lawrence Kohlberg's, we could expect that persons with a more rigid black-and-white moral stage would react differently than those with a more open stance toward the grays of life. The call for harsh penalties, high-handed authoritarian "gate-keepers," might result from an earlier stage, whereas, with a later or more mature developmental achievement, persons would be capable of patiently working with a longer-range process of healing and reconciliation.[5]

---

[4]A thorough discussion of this issue is conducted by John T. Chirban, *Human Growth and Faith: Intrinsic and Extrinsic Motivation in Human Development* (University Press of America, 1981). Following Allport, he defines intrinsic religious motivation as the striving of religious experience that stems from within the individual. Such a person's creed is part of his or her personality, is implicit, and is personal. Extrinsic religious motivation stems from external needs or concerns such as security, affiliation, power, or self-aggrandizement (cf. p. 5).

[5]Bonnidell Clouse, "Church Conflict and Moral Stages," *Journal of Psychology and Christianity* 5(3) (1986) 14–19.

Because clergy participate with us in our own personal and family crises and needs, they are there when we are at the height of joy or the depths of sorrow. In some cases clergy know our most precious thoughts and feelings. They lead and influence us in significant spiritual experiences such as conversion, moral self-examination, confession, and repentance before God, as well as spiritual renewal. They attend to us in life-marking events of various kinds, so that the feeling of personal and spiritual betrayal or treason when things unravel is huge. The basic fabric of life gets torn. God seems to have let us down, since God was perceived to be palpably absent during those negative events of life. In the battle between good and evil, evil seems at the moment to be winning.

In addition to these personally meaningful experiences, if we have also entrusted our children or young people into their care, hoping and praying for the spiritual transformation and formation of those precious lives as we did so, and then find out the clergyperson has crossed sexual boundaries by misusing his or her position and attacking our families at their most vulnerable level, the effects are incalculable. Reactions to such basic assaults to our being can run the gamut from murderous feelings to disillusionment, throwing our spiritual moorings into chaotic unrest. The fact that a book published about child sexual abuse by priests has a title such as *Slayer of the Soul*[6] reveals how one group of authors sees the impact of such misconduct upon spiritual life.

Reactions by people to the revelation of clergy abuse in their own congregation are strong, whatever the focus. Often, disbelief pours out: "I can't believe this! You had better be sure you're right! If this is true, this hits us harder than anything else can!" "How can we be sure this really happened?" "Why didn't I see this coming?" "Who could have stopped this?" "What is *real* truth in this situation?" "How can I trust clergy again?" "That deceiver!" "I *thought* something was wrong!" "What will become of our congregation?" There's an emotional tearing: fear mixed with shame, disillusionment and grim-faced anger, a bodily sensation of shock and pain, disbelief. In the face of such powerful incursions, all sorts

[6]Stephen Rossetti, *Slayer of the Soul: Child Sexual Abuse and the Catholic Church* (Mystic, Conn.: Twenty-third, 1990).

of defenses rise up. In some cases there is simply a profound sadness, tending toward temporary depression and withdrawal. One church secretary told of a stream of tearful, pain-filled telephone calls to the church office that lasted over a period of nine months after the clergyman's behavior came to light.

The most vulnerable might be the young people. The fragile nose of their idealism is cruelly rubbed in harsh realism. Anyone in the congregation who depends on the support and modeling of other adults may be impacted more powerfully for evil. When I was a young person, my own home church was the scene not only of clergy sexual malfeasance but of mean-spirited conflict over long periods of time. Only the steadily positive model of my own father kept me from throwing out the whole idea of belonging to the body of Christ. Many youth do not have a stabilizing positive or supportive model to follow. A wide variety of clerical abuses of power, not just sexual in nature, can be occasions for "throwing in the spiritual towel." One child scratched the picture of the pastor out of the church directory in her home. We can only surmise the damages she suffered and how they might endure in her soul to this day.

In congregations pastors often take on a familial parent role. David Brubaker spells this out in an article in *Christianity Today.*[7] Offending pastors get looked at like incestuous fathers. They have been surrogate father figures to some people, put on a pedestal, called man or woman of God, with the highest moral, ethical, spiritual standards of conduct expected. When they are persons of warmth, affection, sensitivity, and caring, the blow to those who depend upon them for care and help is so much the greater when they abuse. The capacity so many of these same clergy seem to have to give of themselves in ministry seems to heighten the impact of the fall, thus compounding the tragedy.

Impact on Leadership

Church polity is not a fixed entity these days. There seems to be an increase of cases of congregationally autonomous groups

[7]David Brubaker, "Secret Sins in the Church Closet," *Christianity Today* (February 10, 1992) 30–32.

electing strongly centralized elder boards, sometimes electing them to office in perpetuity. One Episcopal priest remarked to me that her Church is definitely a mix of hierarchy and congregational rule. Polity is definitely a fluctuating reality. However, when we study a particular congregation's response to clergy misconduct, we need to keep in mind that in their pain and confusion people will tend to seek out someone to blame. Careful study of how a particular congregation's polity works out in practice is absolutely vital to clear understanding of congregational dynamics.

One of the first places people focus is with the question Who's responsible for this person being in this powerful place of influence? If the polity is congregationally centered with an elected board of elders, for example, these elders usually bear the brunt of the people's wrath. Those who have served on the search committees that invited the perpetrator to serve in this church come under scrutiny. In the minds of those who identify with the victim, leadership people are often seen as negligent of duty and come under attack for that reason. Persons who identify with the clergyperson's cause will attack the leadership for bringing the case out in the open. Division of loyalties occurs around these and many other issues as people begin to take sides in the melee.

I am aware of one congregation with a more hierarchical polity, whose members are still calling for an appearance of the diocesan bishop to make an apology, even though many years have passed. People want things righted again, justice executed, and the pain taken away. As a result local leaders report becoming exhausted, harried, anxious, depressed, and irritable, depending upon their personalities and defense styles. The rumor-gossip-attack cycle seems to go on and on.

In my own denomination, with its strong emphasis upon congregational autonomy, one of the ways the issue of polity comes up is around whether to disclose the abuse to the entire ecclesial public, who might either know the perpetrating pastor or hire that person later. Since there is no centralized office that controls clergy placement, disclosure is one means of protecting unsuspecting search committees from hiring former perpetrators. Those Churches with more central control over the issue of placement or movement of clergy may have less need to use public disclosure, at least from the perspective of preventing an abuser from moving on to another congregation, since a note in a personnel file should be sufficient to guide future decisions. Hopefully, people who are charged with ensuring the safety of future congregations will read the files!

One lay leader who had been deeply involved with a church council in such a situation made this comment: "You can't win! No matter what you decide to do to lead in this kind of situation, you get criticized and maligned." But this leader also wisely stated: "People need to have their feelings validated in order to begin the process of healing." Depending on their position in the system, some people feel there should be more mercy, others that there should be more severe consequences. Still others are concerned about their own hurts so much that they don't want to be reminded of anything that feels hurtful at this point.

Nancy Hopkins warns us that people must be reminded that the pain experienced is not originally caused by the victim's coming forward nor by any subsequent drawn-out legal process involved but from the original act of sexual misconduct. This warning illustrates how people will tend to lash out in many directions with no real consciousness of how unreasonable the direction of their wrath might be at the time.[8]

Staying on top of all of this leads at worst to burnout or at least to serious levels of physical, emotional, and spiritual fatigue. One afterpastor told this author: "I'm so sick and tired of dealing with this mess, I can't stand even contemplating the subject anymore!" As a result, these leaders often can no longer interact with needy people in caring or sympathetic ways but rather come off with defensiveness and "shorter fuses."

In leading a congregation through the experience of revelation and healing, we often find that for some people letting go of a fallen leader is extremely difficult. They want to be forgiving, to read out of the situation the best interpretation they can; they get impatient with others who want to bring rapidly moving consequences down on the perpetrator. The acceptance of very bad news about a person to whom they have been loyally and even

---

[8]Nancy Myer Hopkins, "The Congregation Is Also a Victim," Special Papers and Research Reports (Washington: Alban Institute, 1992).

lovingly related for months or years is extremely difficult. Leaders who come to intervene are viewed suspiciously. These leaders may be judged as being "bad persons" rather than persons who possibly make some bad decisions under pressure. On the other side, anger from those who sympathize with the victim comes through as, This should never have happened! Where were you! Catch-22!

Leaders can benefit from thinking in terms of systems with a set of concentric circles of church members, beginning with those who are closer to the leadership and moving out farther and farther to those who are only marginally involved and much less knowledgeable about what is going on. Each successive circle has its own character and set of reactions built out of a mix of truth and error, positive or negative interaction with leadership, feelings about who has control (and their own helplessness with being away from the center of control), and their own subculture of interpretive frameworks. When a successive series of revelations occurs over a long period of time, perhaps with increasing evidence of perpetration in more than one case, the factors we've listed above become more and more complex. Each time additional data appears, the emotional impact varies according to the interpretive framework and systemic position of the person(s) who hears it. Reports and reactions mix together in ever-increasing cacophony.

At one church, for example, an associate pastor discovered the pastor acting inappropriately with a woman from the church but received an explanation from the pastor of a sort that caused him to hesitate reporting to the church board. Only a couple of local church leaders were informed of the problem. They kept their eyes open, but nothing more happened for some months. However, when it was later revealed that the pastor truly had several liaisons with women, the circle of those who knew grew to the entire board of the church and a denominational official. Through spouses the news began to spread to certain others in the congregation. The interaction between those who knew was of one level of comprehension; those who were outside the circle were picking up only bits and pieces of the story, and the information and resultant interpretive framework was not accurate. Reactions varied, therefore, somewhat on the basis of what was known and what interpretation was known or made up by each person or group. This illustrates for us how in a single congregation one can find several different "stories."

The issue of development of "parties" is also complicated by the way people more frequently see themselves as victims than as responsible agents. That is, we resist seeing ourselves as needing to be responsible holders of information in the process of being interpreted, rather than as possessors of "the truth," until everything has been clarified. It is certainly correct to say that everyone in the congregation is victimized to some degree. But people tend to focus more on the potential of being hurt by the information or circumstances and jump into defensive stances over it rather than holding the data in suspension long enough for further clarification and a chance for resolution to occur. This usually creates a need for control, a hardening of positions, and a development of factional subcultures.

Those who defend the perpetrator may do so out of a genuine belief in his or her innocence; they may insist on believing the denials and misleading statements of the perpetrator out of loyalty or friendship. As time goes on—and it usually does take awhile for all this to happen—the perpetrator confesses the truth, and people are caught powerfully in the vice of despair and shame; they have to face the way they have been betrayed. The whole principle of trusting clergy and church leadership is involved. The shame of facing the I told you so! We knew all along there was something rotten here! statements of other members is difficult to bear, and those who believed the perpetrator may likely fade away toward another congregation or entirely out of the institutional Church.

Other issues can serve as a focus for anger and frustration with leadership and can redirect or detour energies that should be focused on healing the church's leadership-membership woundedness. Examples would be the financial state of the church, the purchase of an organ, the decision to start or finish a building project, disagreements over philosophy of ministry. If some other issue was already causing upset feelings in the congregation at the time of the revelation of clergy abuse or exploitation, the simultaneous resolution of the two streams of conflict will probably be very difficult. Anxiety levels will be higher and spiritual unrest much deeper. Leadership will feel they have lost control, and people's accusations of incompetence will trouble and perhaps hurt them deeply. Afterpastors, those who follow the offender, keep running into strange dynamics that are fueled by all of this, even years later; they need special orientation to deal with it.[9] Old problems may come bubbling up from the past to rejoin this new issue and complicate the whole scene. One church pastor testified, for example, that issues from pastors' tenures back as far as twenty years were now reappearing in people's conversation.

The general orientation has changed in the last ten years from keeping everything under a blanket to being more forthcoming with the truth and eschewing secret keeping. However, when attorneys enter the picture, leadership is often hamstrung concerning giving out information to the congregation, since the adversarial bent of legal process severely limits information sharing. Unfortunately, this tends to speed up the rumor mill. Opportunity increases for more factions to form and for confusion to grow. To help stop this negative downward spiral we should always urge that as much truth be told as possible without further harming the victim or compromising the legal process.

The Perpetrator's Influence on the Process

One factor that often colors the story: perpetrating clergy often are more clear about the positive ("beautiful") aspects of their relationship with victims than about the possible negative fallout, and they resist any picture of themselves as "evil" or "criminal," attacking vociferously anyone who paints the picture that way. So when they tell their side of the story, they get sympathy from people about the good side of their personality but are not able to deal honestly with their "shadow side" and its negative fallout. When the anger at them explodes for crossing sexual boundaries or misusing power, the perpetrator may retreat into a seemingly self-righteous protective shell. One executive minister put it this way: "I've learned two things working with offenders: (1) their denial is strong; (2) their subterfuges are im-

---

[9]Nils Friberg, "A Denominational Survival Kit for Afterpastors," "Clergy Sexual Misconduct: A Systems Perspective," Nancy Myer Hopkins, ed., Special Papers and Research Reports (Washington: Alban Institute, 1993) 36–39.

pressive!" This plays havoc with the process or sorting things out, and factionalism grows around the confusion.

The issue of how the "confession" is done can be a key to how the reactions of people are shaped. If the clergyperson makes a brief but factual description of the wrongs without blaming the victim, nondefensively taking responsibility in appropriate ways, then it will probably not raise any further problems. But if the confession includes lengthy and highly manipulative statements, people will be incensed, feeling they have been further victimized by the power given to this person to further injure their sensibilities. Some confessors might even stoop to some lame attempts to exhort the congregation in some way, spiritualizing the "lessons to be learned" and receiving in return an angry condemnation for their intrepid audacity to repossess the role of spiritual teacher. Secondary and tertiary victimization through these confessional statements should be avoided at all costs. Thus it is unwise to allow the perpetrator to address the congregation directly. Letters of confession may be used, but these need to be examined carefully lest further harm be done to anyone. This is a "minefield."

It takes a long time for some people to rearrange their mental and emotional frameworks around the confessed perpetration. How the confession is done is one influential factor in this rearrangement, but each member's ability to recognize they are capable of doing similar wrongs is usually limited. There will be moments of sympathy and empathy. Then there will be repeated emotional journeys back into judgment and rejection because of the damage and difficulties caused to the congregation and to the victim(s) and family. Much of this is influenced by levels of spiritual health and maturity, as discussed above.

The Impact of Media Coverage

Media coverage can bring the congregation a great deal of anxiety, self-judgment, shame, pain, embarrassment, and defensiveness. When a case of a priest's sexual misconduct hit the press in the Twin Cities, several of his former churches were thrown into emotional chaos and turmoil. Under such circumstances the membership feels shame, guilt, fear of judgment, revulsion, or any combination of these emotions. Fear of negative fallout from the media can be a powerful emotional issue for leadership. They often fear further damage, liability, unjust charges, lies, and manipulation by reporters. The list of possibilities goes on. If there is opportunity there ought to be careful planning to decide what information to release and when, in consultation with legal advice and denominational leadership.

The media issue intensifies whenever there arises the specter of litigation, court proceedings, or attempts at settlements in the high-dollar range with its attendant endangerment of the financial viability of the church or denomination. There are then additional complications in people's feelings and reactions. Every court scene, with its adversarial stance, its haranguing, the attempts at discrediting by twisting motives and data, brings more excruciating pain and shame and anger to involved observers. The "camps" of people are usually further solidified and polarized, and woundedness increases. There will be palpable distress over the possible undoing of the church's viability as an entity. Some will run away, others will stay on the periphery, yet others will stay with the struggle of the core group. These latter may bond even more closely together. Because of this bonding, this group may have the best resources for giving good support to the victim and family as well as for providing for follow-up on the needs of the perpetrator in his or her growth and healing.

Associate Staff

Other persons on the pastoral staff can be harmed as well. They are influenced, of course, by the quality and nature of their relationships with the perpetrator and by the sense of responsibility and prevention they imagine they could have exerted on the situation. They might have been in a position to observe and modify events. If they had suspicions, now that the revelation is out their feelings are powerfully amplified, since they might be held—or hold themselves—accountable or responsible. They may express profound grief over the "fall" of their colleague. Or they may be relieved, even happy, to see things out in the open that they had not previously known how to judge or assess.

If an associate pastor was the offender the senior pastor's reputation is often on the line, and how the case is handled becomes a referendum for that senior's future ministry. If the senior pastor was the offender, associate staff will also carry the added burden of shaky job security. An associate might well ask, Where will I end up if the senior pastor gets fired or removed, and my job is up for grabs? The already shaken confidence in church authority gets mixed with this fear of losing one's job. The associate wonders, Who is watching out for me, anyway? One associate this writer knows kept notes on the senior pastor's questionable activities for several months. His attempts at confrontation were brushed aside. Since the associate only had suspicions to go on, he was caught for many weeks between his fears that the pastor was in moral failure and his anxiety about what would happen to the whole church staff if proof were to emerge.

Spouse

If the perpetrator is married, the congregation often raises questions around the state of the marriage of the perpetrator. This adds to the burden of the spouse and children of the perpetrator. Their adequacy or role-competence is often questioned, even in the same breath with statements like, I feel so sorry for them—they must be hurting terribly! One newsletter for spouses of pastors recently carried a clear message that spouses must "care well for their pastor-spouse." Victimization continues and grows through these dynamics. When there is interaction between the perpetrator's family and other members of the congregation, there can be additional emotional pain and defensive reactions involved that add to the emotional soup. The perpetrator's family might blame the people in the congregation, or the congregational members might be attacking the perpetrator's family. We observe many situations where the spouse strongly defends the perpetrator—not a surprising discovery. In terms of systemic interaction, everyone in the system hurts more as some player on the scene lashes out at another.

Grief

Another article in this volume deals fully with the issue of grief.[10] Suffice it to say here that the grieving period for those in the most pain and agony can last for many months. Every phone call that reminds us of "the mess we're in," or any business item that arises, or any inquiry about the situation from someone outside the church reemphasizes the pain and the grief, the agony and the remorse, the shame or the anger.

The closer the relationship people have had with the pastor and the more intense (whether negative or positive) their relationship, the more impact there will be on emotional life. Those people at the further reaches of the congregational circles, perhaps not very involved on a weekly basis, probably will have very different kinds of reactions from those at the core. Other factors could be brought up here, such as levels of psychosocial and spiritual development, any previous experiences of betrayal of trust, relationships with the leadership of the church, family networks, and intermarriage of families in the congregation, which all bring to bear their own complexity upon this situation.

A clergyperson's leadership style will reflect his or her personality and spirituality. Thus, laypeople will have built up either trust or mistrust around that style. Many people we've talked with had entertained long-time suspicions about the trustworthiness of a perpetrating clergyperson previous to the revelation of the misconduct. They may have noted a certain manipulativeness or emotionally controlling style. It is difficult to know if those suspicions are attributable to the features of that clergyperson that are directly related to the perpetration. It may be a hindsight shaped too forcefully by the present knowledge of the behavior. Or it may be an accurate association. Whatever the cause of the suspicion, some people may indeed be picking up on emotional dishonesty or lack of integrity long before knowledge of the more problematic behavior emerges. These persons will berate themselves later for not having acted on their suspicions by checking with leadership persons in the congregation or with external ecclesiastical authorities.

[10]See Mark Laaser, "Long-Term Healing," p. 232.

Roman Catholic Archbishop John Roach sounds a sobering caveat that we need to avoid giving the idea to congregations that complete healing is possible this side of the final resurrection, or that we can undo all harm done.[11] The damages do last a long time and are probably broader and more profound than we can grasp. However, just as with those who have lost a child or spouse to a sudden death, though the pain may endure most of a lifetime, the amount of pain felt on a daily basis can be diminished significantly thorough effective grief work and support groups. So with congregational wounds: careful and thorough work with congregations has hope written all over it.

Hypervigilance

Another effect is the hypervigilance around the question How can we prevent this from happening again? Members ask, How can we enforce accountability with future pastors and leaders? How is power to be effectively criticized? People's styles will vary greatly around how they defend themselves from further pain. Afterpastors will experience this hypervigilance as a resistance of certain members to investing themselves again in the activities and decision making of the congregation. Others will be controlling, insisting on stern, rigid structures. In other cases this hypervigilance may be directed toward only one side of the issue, that of sexuality, combined with a lack of willingness to submit to realistic, yet humble, balanced education around boundaries and power.

Pastoral Care

What does it mean to care for people in such a situation? Pastoral care is often complicated by the perception that giving care to one side or the other of the controversy is aiding and abetting, collusion, or taking sides. Prohibitions from attorneys about contact with the very persons who are the most wounded or hurting also stand in the way of pastoral care. For example,

---

[11]"Understanding Sexual Issues in Ministry," Archdiocese of Saint Paul and Minneapolis, 1992.

the family of the victim may be considering a lawsuit against the church, causing the afterpastor or the lay caregivers to avoid the family and their networks so as not to feed misperceptions or endanger their own status with the rest of the congregation. This points up the need for neutral-ground caregivers, such as hired visitors or advocates who are trained to give pastoral care in these situations.

The Apparently Unaffected

There will almost always be a large group in the church who are genuinely not as emotionally affected by events, whose defensive style is to distance themselves from emotionally loaded issues, whose rallying cry will be Let's move on! One church this writer visited had a majority of members who seemed to be distancing to cope with their feelings. They preferred not to listen to the pain, the upset feelings, the feelings of engulfment, the complaints, the accusations and counteraccusations, of the more overtly wounded in the congregation. The distancers might well be drawn into some group situations where they can hear more of what is happening with their fellow members.[12]

Sexuality

Often congregants express surprise that a minister would have problems in the sexual area. People don't expect that clergy are sexual, for some reason, or they don't expect them to struggle very much with it, since by definition, clergy are supposed to be victorious Christians. Janet Fishburn makes this important point, and our interviews confirm her perception.[13] "A pastor shouldn't have this kind of problem." Unfortunately, too many seminarians also make this assumption and don't prepare themselves adequately to deal with their personal issues around sexuality. But the whole Church must assume responsibility for educating everyone,

[12]See Chilton Knudsen, "Understanding Congregational Dynamics," p. 75; also see Harold Hopkins, "The Effects of Clergy Sexual Misconduct on the Wider Church," p. 116, both in this volume.

[13]"Male Clergy Adultery as Vocational Confusion," *Christian Century* (September 15–22, 1982) 922–25.

including seminarians, congregants, and active clergy.[14] We need not only the legal and structural prohibitions about clergy sexual malfeasance, along with clear consequences; but for better prevention we need ethical, spiritual, moral, and legal consciousness-raising at all levels of church life.

People's trust in their own ability to manage their own sexuality is often negatively affected by clergy sexual misconduct. Unfortunately this usually means that the mixed feelings about one's sexuality that are always present now get more negatively weighted. One woman reported: "We're all whispering to each other now, Watch yourself! We've become paranoid about sexual things!" They wonder about rearranging their evaluations of appropriate touch, hugs, friendliness, of certain forms of joking. A grace-filled and balanced approach by teachers and preachers can help meet this need.

Spiritual and Theological Issues

As I mentioned at the beginning of this article, serious spiritual doubts arise for many congregants around clergy sexual misconduct. These might include the role of God in providing protection from evil (why did God not stop this?); the apparent spiritual strength of a pastor one moment and the revelation of great capacity for deception and evil the next (if we can't trust such a talented leader, who can we trust?); the injustices inflicted by the situation (the suffering spouse, family members, children on both sides); the structures and spaces associated with God and the spiritual life of the community. Much like an event of untimely or cruel death or disaster, people's worldview is seriously jeopardized for a time. When we tie this theological confusion together with the personal issues of personal maturity or lack thereof, we can easily understand why the provision of quality ministry following a traumatic termination is so critical.

In interviews we have noted that there is often a spirit of challenge in the jutted jaw that accompanies comments and questions. One man put it: "How could someone who claimed to be

---

[14]Cf. Donald Clark, "Sexual Abuse in the Church: The Law Steps In," *Christian Century* (April 14, 1993) 396–98.

led by the Holy Spirit do such things?" "Is our theology all wrong?" was another's question. One person said: "It's like going through a train wreck—sometimes you just get scratched up a little, sometimes you die. People on the same train have a great variety of wounds and threats to their well-being." Metaphorically, it appears to them that the engine pulling the train, that is, God, might be at fault. More than an issue of theodicy—a vindication of divine justice in the face of evil—this requires a patient sorting out of the feeling issues from the thinking and theological values.

Sacred spaces and rites may need cleansing and rededication. Patient pastoral care through the afterpastor's preaching and visitation can bring enormous benefits. People need reassurance about the reliability of rites such as baptism, marriage, and confirmation performed by an agent who was at other times engaging in egregious abuses. However, we ought not try to hurry these doubts out the door, since the emotional burdens are often wound around the cognitive dissonance. Emotional needs take time to get worked through.

Self-doubt is one very real element for leadership people in this situation. I was duped. How can I trust my judgment now? Are my instincts good, or not to be followed? How could I be so blind, so deaf, so unaware? Can I lead again? Has God really called me to lead? How can I be sure? This issue takes time and spiritual renewal to be healed.

The Victim

There is often the blaming of the victim. Most people in our day are (or should be) aware of this well-established human tendency to blame victims. This arises as part of the long-standing view of women as seductresses, as posing an evil trap for clergy (and all other males). As true as it might be that some behave seductively, we are now being well informed by counseling and legal principles that professionals are *always* responsible for the safety of the personal boundaries of anyone who comes to them for help.

Congregational members will need educating to change their perceptions and interpretations around this. As Marie Fortune has so clearly stated, clergy sexual malfeasance cannot be classed simply as adultery—it is professional malfeasance of the most heinous sort, since the well-being of a person of lesser power has been placed in the clergyperson's hands and fiduciary trust has been violated for the clergyperson's advantage.[15] The general public is only recently becoming aware of professional ethics along these lines, and the old ideas die hard. Many will still say, She probably seduced him! Perpetrators will sometimes play on people's perceptual and emotional ambiguity about this. In several cases we are aware of, the settling of this issue remains one of the most resistant features of the healing process.

Finally, in terms of biblical material on this subject of congregational impact, we could easily examine with profit the pastoral epistles for standards for bishops, pastors, and deacons, especially in 1 and 2 Timothy and Titus. For example, a leader in the church is to be one who is self-controlled, hospitable, able to teach, not violent but gentle, not quarrelsome, not a lover of money or a recent convert, one who has a good reputation with outsiders, is not overbearing, not quick-tempered, loves what is good, is upright, holy, disciplined, above reproach, temperate, respectable, not given to drunkenness, manages his family well, sees that his children are obedient, does not pursue dishonest gain, keeps hold of the deep truths, is sincere, tested, and husband of one wife. A tall order! However, it is easy to imagine how the opposites of these qualities and actions would be devastating in varying degrees upon congregations.[16]

I wonder if the situation of sexual misconduct in Corinth would not bear some study. Though not involving a pastoral leader, the violation of proper boundaries (a man having sexual relations with his own step-mother, in violation of the prohibited degrees of marriage in Lev 18:8) might well have been infusing great complexity to the other issues the Apostle Paul was dealing

---

[15]Lewis Rambo, "Interview with Reverend Marie Fortune, August 8, 1990," *Pastoral Psychology* 39:5 (May 1991) 305–18. Cf. also Majorie R. Peterson, *At Personal Risk: Boundary Violations in Professional-Client Relationships* (Norton, 1993); see also Karen Lebacqz and Ronald G. Barton, *Sex in the Parish* (Louisville, Ky.: Westminster/John Knox, 1991).

[16]Adapted from a summary chart in *The New International Version Study Bible* (Grand Rapids: Zondervan, 1985) 1839.

with. Was Paul an afterpastor? Was that the mysterious thorn in his flesh? Knowing what we know now about the impact of sexual misconduct, the factious behaviors described in 1 Corinthians 1–3 might be partially created by the dynamics of sexual confusion and chaos represented in chapter 5. While there is no direct reference in the text to this dynamic being involved, it is worth pondering.

Even though we might, as a result of all we're learning, now recognize a much greater need for mutual accountability in the body of Christ, we are often afraid to do what we must to bring it about in a way that is grace filled, yet providing of justice. To simultaneously stand up for victims, deal with angry and confused congregations, and help clergy deal with their problems demands a great deal of us, both spiritually and psychologically. It is obvious from this survey of the effects of clergy sexual misconduct on congregations that there is much more to this than meets the eye. There are multiple issues, some subtle, some blatant, but they mix in a way that can leave the congregation and its leaders in a deeply wounded state of affairs for long months and years.

Understanding Congregational Dynamics

Chilton Knudsen

The parish telephone tree had worked well. A large group of people were coming out for the emergency congregational meeting of St. John's Church. As people got out of their cars and moved into the church building, they speculated aloud to one another about what could be so important as to require this hastily called gathering on a weekday evening. Had the building burned down? Some reported rounding the corner, seeing the building apparently unharmed, and feeling immense relief. Others wondered if there had been a tragic or sudden death of a parish leader. Still others inquired if there had been a delcaration of war somewhere. Clearly, something dramatic had happened. And what would follow did, in many ways, feel like all of these possibilities rolled into one.

Voices quieted, and an air of watchful dread settled over people as they saw grave expressions on the faces of parish leaders who directed them into the sanctuary. There, sitting at the front near the altar, was the bishop, together with a few others—a denominational staff member, a retired pastor known to many from long service in a neighboring congregation, and three strangers. Nearby stood Helen, the ranking lay leader of the congregation, whose face and manner betrayed high anxiety. As people settled into their seats and surveyed the scene, it dawned on some of them that there was a notable absence in the gathering. Where was the pastor?

Helen stepped to the lectern and introduced the bishop, noting only that an important announcement would be made. The bishop read from a prepared statement: The pastor had just resigned following a preliminary investigation. The investigation was prompted by reports that the pastor had been sexually intimate with parishioners, people who had come for pastoral care or spiritual direction. The pastor was now undertaking an intensive psychological evaluation in another city. The bishop's carefully chosen language spoke of "sexual misconduct," "substantiated allegations," "continuing investigation," "support services for the complaining parties and the pastor's family," and "commitment to a congregational healing process." Copies of the statement were distributed after the bishop read it.

The bishop introduced the group at the front. Two were described as "crisis counselors." They would be available at the meeting's end in the two offices off the main hall to listen to and support people who might want to seek them out. Another was the denomination's attorney, who had directed the investigation. The headquarters staff member was introduced as the person who would oversee the various ongoing issues in the case. The retired pastor would be taking Sunday services and providing pastoral coverage for the near future. The bishop urged that all present try to remain throughout this meeting so that information could be clarified and, after that, feelings shared.

The bishop called for questions, limited initially to the content just presented. The opportunity to express feelings would follow. After a moment of shocked silence, the questions came in a flood: "What exactly are these allegations about?" "Who brought the reports to the bishop?" "Where is the pastor? What is the address of the place?" "What makes you so sure there's any truth to these absurd accusations? Is there proof?" "Will this be in the newspapers?" The bishop carefully responded with "what can be told now." It was clear that some were not satisfied with what they called "vague or partial answers." Some vociferously demanded to be told all the details.

Throughout the gathering body language showed shock, agitation, and hostility. Some people took out tissue and dabbed at their eyes. People began to watch one another's reactions closely. In spite of the bishop's urging, several people walked out. Side comments and whispered conversations began. Some people grabbed for the hand of the person sitting next to them. A few people had rather faraway looks, appearing to have their attention elsewhere.

The bishop invited other comments: "There are doubtless many feelings right now. Let us hear from you. I would only ask that no one speak a second time until all who wish to have spoken once. And while feelings are running high, no one is to be treated discourteously." With increasing momentum, further comments came: "Let's find out who the troublemakers, these so-called reporters, are and take care of them!" "Our pastor is such a wonderful person! How could anyone make such an accusation!" "What's going to happen to our church?" "You mean our pastor is not coming back? Ever? I came to this church because of the pastor!" "This is ridiculous! I've been around the church almost every day, and I've never seen anything! Our pastor would never do anything like this." "Our pastor belongs here with us, so we can offer support in this hard time." "What about the pastor's family? Have they had anything to say about this?" "I think you, bishop, are out to get our pastor. I hear that you two had a big disagreement about our outreach ministries." "Even if something did happen, aren't we the church? What about forgiveness?"

Similar comments continued. The bishop referred again to the retired pastor's role. As the evening drew to a close, further plans were announced. The judicatory staff member would come out soon for another meeting to set up a series of opportunities for healing. People who felt that they had important information to bring forward were invited to contact the staff member or the bishop. Everyone was urged to listen to one another with care even if they disagreed. Parish matters should continue as much as possible. In closing with prayer, the bishop mentioned "all those who are affected by this," including those who came forward to make the reports. In departing that evening, one long-time member of the congregation, with a voice full of emotion, said to the bishop, "Why do we have to hear all this? Why couldn't it be taken care of quietly?"

Although the people of St. John's Church probably shared the immediate agony voiced by the long-time member, they have in fact been introduced to a healing process whose fruits will be apparent only over time. I have been personally involved in many such meetings as well as in the work leading up to and following such gatherings. Even with the variations I have observed, the story above is almost predictable. Meetings like this have taken place in small rural congregations, large urban and suburban ones, and in yoked or clustered settings. We have learned many things about congregations in the aftermath of sexual misconduct. Those who have participated in congregational disclosure-healing processes, in any of the several roles, find remarkable consistency from one circumstance to another.

In the evolving area of ministry to congregations in the aftermath of sexual misconduct, it is the congregations themselves who have been our teachers. The authors represented in this volume as well as the many others engaged in similar work in a variety of settings have brought to this previously uncharted territory a collection of relevant skills and interests. They represent family systems, congregational development, conflict resolution, pastoral theology, human-resources management, psychiatric assessment, and denominational and judicatory leadership. This article is a report on the state of our learning. Although the circumstances have been altered and merged, the stories themselves accurately convey the painful yet hopeful discoveries that have emerged from our work.

The long-time member's questions to the bishop, "Why do we have to hear all this?" is a vital consideration. What is risked when such a disclosure takes place? And what happens if some kind of disclosure process does not happen? What are the consequences of following the course that the long-term member described—taking care of it quietly without any public acknowledgment? It is our experience that the long-term health of a congregation in the aftermath of the sexual misconduct of clergy or other church leaders depends primarily on which of these two approaches is followed: (1) careful disclosure and the pursuit of an intentional healing process, or (2) taking care of it quietly, without disclosure and with no structured healing process. With careful disclosure tailored to the circumstances and a customized healing process, such congregations can recover and even thrive. If the decision is to cover up the incident and deny the congregational impact, a predictable set of symptoms is likely to develop.

The Mystery of a Troubled Congregation

The bishop shook his head as he walked to his car. It had been a long meeting with the lay council of Faith Church, where they had just lost their third pastor in five years. Clearly, there were tenacious patterns in the congregation's life. Somewhere within those patterns, the bishop thought, was a circumstance, an issue, a dynamic that would explain the rapid turnover of pastors. The bishop mentally reviewed the congregation's recent history, beginning with the first premature pastoral departure.

After the first pastor left, one of the bishop's staff did the vacancy consultation and heard a long recitation of the faults of the departed pastor. They *had* to get rid of this pastor—he was never in the office, never made house calls, preached terrible sermons, was too liberal, spent too much time on community issues, didn't return phone calls quickly enough, and had gravely offended some of the pillars of the congregation by his sympathetic posture about AIDS. The litany of complaints sounded legitimate if a bit exaggerated. Although the members of the lay council had diverse opinions as to the deficiencies of Pastor One, all agreed that a new pastor would make the difference.

A second pastor was called. Within a year, word was out that Pastor Two was too scholarly, preached too long, was not a warm person, didn't pay attention to the older members, couldn't get people to give enough money, and made too many changes in the worship. Besides, she was too young. She spent too much time with her family. In fact, there was speculation that she had serious marital troubles—the family seemed to need quite a lot of time and attention. They needed an experienced pastor, someone who knew how to work with older members, someone who was more traditional. Someone who was more the "old time" model of a pastor—always available, always generous with his time.

The bishop recalled an exit interview he had held with Pastor Two, who reported episodes of obstructionism, back stabbing, and power plays. People made decisions and did things without any communication. She had come to the church one day to find that the locks had been changed without anyone's knowledge. Inquiring about that, she was told that "there seemed to be some strangers hanging around outside the church, so we just called a locksmith to take care of it." There were secret meetings to gather criticism from the older members, open hostility to any discussion of new ideas, and veiled references to a long-ago pastor who was so warm and friendly that everyone in the community spoke of him fondly. Pastor Two lamented that people would complain about not being visited in the hospital, but their hospital admissions were never reported to the church office.

In the face of criticism about pastoral skill, Pastor Two was bewildered. These folks seemed to have no trust of clergy. Without trust, pastoral care was impossible. People withheld from the pastor any of the life issues that pastoral care addresses. The bishop remembered Pastor Two's desperate search for another post: "I have to get out of this church before I lose all sense of my own gifts and skills. I'm already feeling at the end of my rope and my family is tired of seeing me beaten up."

When Pastor Two left and Pastor Three was called, there was much enthusiasm. Here at last was the person who would get this congregation moving. The honeymoon period lasted almost two years. During the third year, the congregation quietly slipped into isolation. No one represented the parish at the Annual Missions Fair held each year. The pastor stopped going to denominational gatherings. Attendance began to fall. People would make and then break commitments to various parish projects and activities. The long-time secretary quit, complaining that people expected her to do everything. No material was turned in for a monthly newsletter except for the items written by the pastor.

An unsuccessful stewardship campaign yielded a bare-bones budget, barely enough to cover the pastor's salary and the building utilities. The only energy in the congregation came from a small group of people who clamored for a new pastor; someone who would bring in new families, get church programs running again, put out a more interesting newsletter, and bring back some of those generous donors who had drifted away.

At that point, denominational staff suggested a consultation process. But the congregation insisted that was nothing wrong with them. Those fancy high-priced consultants with their newsprint and psychobabble? Not for them! They just needed to get the right pastor in there, someone who would inspire them. They only wanted the denomination to get them some good names for their search process, not the kind of weak pastors they had seen before. Why did the denomination keep suggesting these inadequate clergy to them?

The bishop shook his head again as he eased his car out of the parking lot. This place was a "clergy-killer." They seemed like nice people. They sounded sincere. One at a time, the members were talented, gracious, and bright. But when they got together in a group, they alternated between hopelessness and a state of organizational chaos that made every decision, however small, a battle of wills. Why do some congregations seem to chew up and spit out their clergy? And why do some congregations persist in self-defeating patterns that endure over several pastorates?

There are may subtle and complex reasons why congregations are "clergy-killers" or seem to suffer from tenacious patterns of organizational chaos. The surrounding community may have experienced a significant transition (e.g., flood, fire), possibly abrupt and traumatic. It may be that the congregation itself was born in anger, a breakaway group that had left to establish itself in protest. Perhaps a powerful family's iron grip on the church has stifled its creativity. There may have been denominational upheavals that left the congregation depleted and battle weary. A too-ambitious project may have failed, leaving people embarrassed or burned out. Or patterns of conflict avoidance may have settled in, causing an accumulation of bad feelings that festered under a veneer of artificial congeniality. When these factors are part of the congregation's history, people will usually be able to point to them and discuss them without much anxiety.

But for some congregations, a pattern of organizational distress and anticlericalism is rooted in a painful, unacknowledged secret that has been hovering invisibly within the congregation. Like radioactive waste, the toxin of the secret infects the organization: sapping energy, distorting perceptions, and scrambling normal life processes. Like radioactive waste, the toxin works at an imperceptible level, showing its effects cumulatively and over the long term. And like radioactive waste, it eludes detection until someone with astute diagnostic skills (and more than a little courage) considers the possibility that is so hard to talk about—that there is a history of sexual misconduct that was never acknowledged, never resolved.

An accumulation of experience tells us that distressed, clergy-killer congregations are often the secondary victims of past sexual misconduct by a pastor or other church leader. Whether the offender mysteriously disappeared or stayed in place for a number of years, sexual misconduct became a toxic secret within the life of the congregation. And the effects of this toxicity accumulated over the years, perplexing succeeding pastors, denominational leaders, and even the congregants themselves.

Elsewhere in this volume, the range and variety of sexual misconduct is detailed. What we have seen in our work with congregations, however, makes it clear that the *fact* of sexual misconduct rather than the type of sexual misconduct is a fundamental wounding reality in a congregation's history. In much the same way as families are crippled by the skeleton in the family cupboard, congregations that carry this secret suffer predictable patterns of organizational distress. And as families sometimes do, congregations can unconsciously exert quite a bit of energy defending and protecting themselves from opening the cupboard and naming the contents.

It is important to note that a congregation may present any or all of these patterns even if no one knows anything for sure about the sexual misconduct. This is because there always is some knowledge or intuition or suspicion. It seems that there are no absolute secrets in the mysterious intimacy of congregational life; there are just degrees of knowing. The secret may be confined to a few, or there may be vague, nonspecific uneasiness about a previous pastorate, or there may be circles of gossip or speculation. In all of the suffering congregations I have known, one or more people admit (usually reluctantly and sometimes after many years) that the secret of sexual misconduct was not really a secret at all. When important information is carried but not acknowledged in a congregation's life, we see congregations that look a lot like Faith Church.

Our work with congregations that have experienced sexual misconduct in the remote or recent past has revealed remarkable similarities in the patterns that tend to develop. The term "pattern" here is used to describe a cluster of symptoms, behaviors, and attitudes that compromise congregational health, productivity, and joy. These patterns seem to serve a variety of purposes:

(1) They provide a distraction or smoke screen. (2) They keep the secret protected. (3) They provide avenues of discharge for underlying rage and anger. (4) They symbolically express, often in distorted ways, the nature of the secret. (5) They serve to compensate for a diffuse sense of violation or shame. And, of course, over time, patterns become accepted routine. Even though the patterns themselves may be counterproductive there is an investment in preserving what is familiar. These patterns endure not only because they serve these purposes but because they become hardened over time into "business as usual."

What are the specific symptoms, behaviors, and attitudes we have seen in our work with congregations who are secondary victims of sexual misconduct? The case study of Faith Church serves as a focus for exploring what these patterns look like in congregational life. Churches will differ in the expression of these various patterns; some will show the entire range of patterns, some will move through various patterns in any sequence as the years go by, some will exhibit severe patterns at times of stress, others will show patterns in stubbornly chronic consistency. The categories detailed above obviously overlap, and all organizations will show these patterns to some degree. Congregations that have experienced sexual misconduct will most often display these problem dynamics with more tenacity and intensity. And quite consistently, congregations will react defensively to having these patterns pointed out to them. To better recognize the patterns it is helpful to describe them in more detail.

Distraction and Smoke Screen Patterns

When a painful secret or suspicion dwells within an organizational system, the system will sometimes develop subtle and usually unconscious defenses against recognizing the disturbing reality. Patterns evolve that foster confusion and unclarity. These patterns may include the following:

1. Persistent confusion about responsibility, lines of authority, and roles played by various parties.
2. Focusing on the trivial and routine in a way that fosters avoidance of more significant issues.

3. Secret meetings that sidestep stated avenues of governance.
4. Sabotaging and undermining persons in the exercise of their tasks.
5. Erratic, slanted, or inadequate systems of communication, both written and verbal.
6. Weak or absent processes for evaluation and feedback, especially concerning clergy, staff members, or parish leaders.
7. Absence of any consensus as to mission, financial priorities, personnel policies, premises use, and administrative procedures.
8. A pattern of overactivity, of biting off more than can be chewed, of multiple enthusiasms without follow-through.

In the case study of Faith Church most of these symptoms are apparent. In many churches people would freely acknowledge the presence of these patterns. What is usually less readily acknowledged is the net effect of them; that is, the resulting distraction, lack of clarity, and blurry confusion that serve to obscure the underlying issue.

Often congregations will make heroic efforts to break such patterns. They will draft new bylaws, reorganize, buy new computer software, replace the newsletter editor, develop a new mission statement, and form new committees. All of these ventures may in fact yield helpful results. If, however, the old patterns have evolved to serve the purpose of screening a secret, congregations will revert to those patterns after a period of time unless the underlying issue is exposed and resolved. I have often heard congregational leaders express frustration about this tendency: "We spent all that money on a new desktop publishing program, but we still can't communicate," "We revised our organizational chart, but people still don't know who's responsible for which area." Persistent organizational chaos may be rooted in a pattern that serves to distract people from a painful chapter in the corporate history.

Protecting the Secret

Patterns that serve to protect the secret are similar to those listed above. In this category, however, the patterns tend to be more overt. An objective observer may be more likely to ask, What are they hiding? Congregational patterns that protect the secret include the following:

1. Defensiveness about the congregation's history or a particular era within that history. This might be seen when a congregation celebrates an anniversary, or when the congregation is asked to construct a timeline—a helpful exercise often undertaken during an interim period.
2. A persistent reluctance to remember past events—a kind of selective amnesia.
3. Spoken or unspoken rules or taboos against discussing certain subjects or events.
4. Circulation of inaccurate stories (which may take on mythic proportions) about the reasons for a leader's departure from a congregation.
5. Tenacious overidealization of a previous pastor or church leader.
6. The mysterious absence of files, meeting minutes, correspondence, or other records from a particular period of time. Some churches have a wall on which they display photographs of clergy who have served in prior years. An attentive observer may notice irregularities or gaps in this photographic record.
7. Subtle or overt discrediting of people who have "left the church" (it might be that they "know something"; discrediting them assures that anything they "know" will be met with skepticism if expressed).
8. Resistance to reaching out to lapsed members or inviting them to return.
9. Fear and avoidance of renewal programs that promote "story sharing" among participants.
10. The unexplained sudden disappearance of a formerly vital program, for example, the abrupt disbanding of the children's choir or of family camp programs.

Certainly, there are many possible explanations for all of the observations mentioned here. But taken together with other data, these instances may suggest conscious or unconscious efforts to protect the secret of sexual misconduct. In some churches it is possible to see a dramatic change in tone and body language when taboo subjects are raised. Where these congregational patterns are present, an observer or consultant often has the feeling of walking through a minefield. One senior warden, a lay leader in an Episcopal congregation, told me how it was to carry the taboo secret for many years:

> I knew about what happened. They came to me first, before they complained to the bishop. The bishop told me he would move Father "Smith." But he told me that I couldn't talk about it, not even with my wife. This was the *bishop*—I was raised that you trust the bishop like he was almost God. So, I had to watch out all the time. I was afraid that if the secret got out, someone would blame me. I had to cut back on going to church. It was just too hard to hear them praising Father Smith like he was a saint. I was really alone. I finally had to get away from the whole thing. I left the church completely.

Avenues of Discharge for Rage and Anger

When congregations or individuals have been injured, betrayed, or frightened, they often experience anger. If injuries accumulate with no avenue for acknowledgment and resolution, rage is the result. In a self-perpetuating cycle, rage shows itself in actions that injure others, multiplying and extending the rage. Congregants who also carry anger and rage about other life experiences are at greater risk of reacting in anger to congregational injuries, including the injury of sexual misconduct. Anger and rage are normal reactions to real or perceived injury.

To distinguish between these two states, we may describe anger as focused on particular circumstances and rage as diffuse and generalized. Congregations may experience anger or rage even when they cannot pinpoint the cause of their feelings. Or they may behave in angry ways, yet deny the feelings of anger. Especially in religious communities, anger is not an acceptable feeling. Thus anger may be acted out rather than spoken out. The following are some of the signs of anger and rage in a congregation:

1. Persistent patterns of scapegoating in which someone or some group becomes the lightning rod for the discharge of anger. Often the group targeted represents a vulnerable population within the congregation.
2. Blaming, faultfinding, excluding, and various forms of verbal abuse.
3. Voting with the pocketbook, withholding contributions.
4. The selection of anger "targets": often, a denominational executive, clergy in general (anticlericalism), parish leadership, succeeding pastors ("afterpastors" is the term we have come to use for this group). Afterpastors usually become the targets of displaced anger, and everyone involved needs to keep that possibility in mind.
5. Blaming the victim; that is, anger is directed at the person(s) who report personal experiences of abuse or exploitation. This is true whether the reporting victims have made reports about incidents within this congregation or another.
6. "Stoning the messenger"; the anger is directed at the person(s) who present specific or general information about sexual misconduct. This includes authors of articles and books, conference or workshop presenters, journalists, and often denominational spokespersons.
7. Helplessness and depression as expressions of anger and rage. Congregational depression (loss of energy; pervasive sadness; nostalgia about earlier, happier times, real or imagined; despair about the congregation's future) is a frequent result of denied or unexpressed anger.
8. Demanding dependency, in which congregations both demand and resent assistance and attention (often from the denomination or from neighboring churches).
9. An artificially "nice" attitude, especially when coupled with smothering or intrusive concern.
10. Manipulation, power struggles, competition, and "terrorism" (manipulation through angry outbursts or threats).

Succeeding pastors are especially puzzled. They can't understand the free-floating anger, distrust, and self-defeating behavior they encounter in the congregation. The material on afterpastors in this volume treats this issue of displaced anger at greater length.[1] Noteworthy, too, are the comments I have often heard from perceptive people who visit such a congregation: "There's just something wrong there. . . . I couldn't put my finger on it . . . but I'd never go back there. . . . People seem to be angry about something."

Symbolic Expressions

Because religious organizations concern themselves with ultimate issues (good and evil, life and death, sin and forgiveness) and with matters of meaning, they operate in the realm of symbol, ritual (the manipulation of symbols), and mystery. It follows, then, that religious organizations will express themselves symbolically. When sexual misconduct is a part of a congregation's story, there may arise behaviors that are laden with symbolic meaning. These symbolic expressions often tell far more of the story than any other expressive mechanism. It has been especially fascinating to collect and explore some of the symbolic avenues by which congregations try to name their experiences with sexual misconduct. Some of the symbolic avenues we have seen are the following:

1. A sudden obsession with the exterior appearance of the church building.
2. A preoccupation with veiled or overt sexual matters (e.g., the marital status or adjustment of afterpastors; denominational controversies about human sexuality, birth control, censorship of art and literature; and discussions about the participation of gay and lesbian people in the life and ministry of the church). Of course, these are important matters for all church people to consider. What is noteworthy here is the disproportionate attention given to these issues as opposed to other concerns.
3. Symbolic reenactment of sexual misconduct through the selection of future pastors (or other church leaders) who also offend sexually or otherwise violate accepted professional norms.

[1]See Darlene K. Haskin, "Afterpastors in Troubled Congregations," p. 155, and Nancy Myer Hopkins, "Further Issues for Afterpastors," p. 165.

4. Persistent sexual humor, innuendo, curiosity, or flirtation as an unusually frequent pattern of congregational behavior.
5. Extreme rigidity as to gender roles, the ordination of women or their involvement in positions of church leadership, or similar issues such as discrimination against divorced people.
6. Naiveté, denial, or pseudoinnocence as to the possibility of sexual misconduct or abnormal sexual activity (incest, for example) within Christian communities.
7. Disproportionate attention to liturgical style or issues regarding the conduct of public worship, including heated controversies about who is eligible to participate in the rites and ceremonies of the church.

We have seen an amazing variety of symbolic expressions. Whenever an unexplained issue involving sexuality, purity, image, contamination, or other such themes emerges, it may represent the symbolic avenue of expressing the congregation's experience of sexual misconduct.

Feelings of Violation or Shame

Any transgression of a boundary, any breach in accepted norms, any betrayal of trust, constitutes a violation. The corporate response to violation, whether or not the violation is actually known or acknowledged, parallels that of individuals. The sexual misconduct of clergy or other church leaders is a violation at many levels, and most offenders also breach boundaries other than sexual ones. Within the mystery of human sexuality lies much that is glorious and much that is fallen. Shame, a sensation of flawedness and contamination, is a complex human response primally rooted in the awareness of our fallen (including our sexually fallen) natures. When persons or groups experience violation, they may react to the violation directly or they may find subtle ways to express the resultant shame. They may

1. become hypervigilant, suspicious, and distrustful;
2. become passive, allowing themselves to be trespassed upon in other ways;
3. become preoccupied with displaced boundary concerns;

4. suffer poor self-esteem, a common sign of shame;
5. isolate themselves, withdrawing from denomination, community, or other relational networks;
6. subtly or overtly discourage involvement of newcomers in the life of the church or harshly measure visitors to see if they are "our kind of people";
7. show excessive concern about the reputation or image of the congregation;
8. become preoccupied with matters of doctrinal purity or demand conformance to unusual forms of piety;
9. use the tactic of guilt to pressure members into making commitments of time or money rather than affirming free choices grounded in faith;
10. seek desperately for quick-fix solutions, grasping at various popular programs of spiritual or organizational renewal;
11. lapse into a dynamic of judgmentalism, by which harsh yardsticks are used to evaluate some or all of the aspects of congregational life.

When congregations live within a history of boundary violations they experience a variety of consequences. It is helpful to remember that boundary concerns are often at the root of issues such as who gets keys to the church building, which outside groups are allowed to use the premises, and who is a "real" member of the congregation. Attentive observers will note the underlying sense of violation and the subtle shame that undergirds such congregational patterns. In this last category of congregational violation and shame, as in all of those noted above, it is useful to remember that congregations, like individuals, are always trying to express themselves. It is a matter of attentive listening and careful perception to understand congregational patterns as revelatory of possible painful secrets expressed in the cryptic language of symptomology.

What is important in assessing congregations is that the symptoms described above are persistent even when efforts have been made to erase them. All congregations show some of these patterns. But congregations that have a history of sexual misconduct are unusual in that they resist having these patterns pointed out, often deny that the obvious problems even exist, or portray themselves as simply having some idiosyncrasies rather than having patterns that thwart their mission and ministry. Further exploration of the emergence of these patterns follows.

Why Do These Symptoms Emerge?

A few key concepts need consideration. A congregation is more than a group of people who attend Sunday worship. A congregation is, in various ways, like a family. Some proudly use that terminology in describing themselves. The fact that this designation contains inherent flaws and fosters various troublesome dynamics (as noted by Marie Fortune[2] and others) has not erased the reality that this is how many congregations see themselves. Family-systems experts have described many parallels between families and congregations,[3] and their work reminds us that churches, like families, adopt patterns that serve to mitigate or to manage anxiety.

The term "family" does point to the parental image of pastors and other leaders; whether or not these people are titled with parental terminology, many congregants consciously or unconsciously see authority figures at least partially through that lens. This means that there is likely to be some unspoken, unconscious "traffic" within the congregation much as there is in families. What the "family feeling" means for congregations experiencing sexual misconduct is that the normal nurturing and protecting role of authority figures has been abdicated. The environment feels less safe; the motivations of leaders have become ambiguous. The normal tensions (felt by all parents and indeed by all professional caregivers) between self-sacrifice and self-gratification are resolved in favor of self-gratification at the expense of those whose implicit trust is quite appropriate. It also means that "family secrets" will have power long past their time if sexual misconduct has "been taken care of quietly."

[2] Marie Fortune, *Is Nothing Sacred? When Sex Invades the Pastoral Relationship* (San Francisco: Harper & Row, 1987).

[3] Edwin Friedman, *Generation to Generation: Family Process in Church and Synagogue* (New York: Guilford, 1985); Peter Steinke, "How Your Church Family Works: Understanding Congregations as Emotional Systems" (Washington: Alban Institute, 1993).

Congregations are like families, indeed, but another image is also helpful. A congregation is a community. Communities have a kind of fundamental unity, made all the more obvious by the diversity that communities are able to embrace and sustain. Communities have a shared story, a set of cultural norms, and a system of traditions and traditional roles. Information is disseminated, decisions are made, and resources are managed according to the community's own unique processes. When the community is a faith community, all of these elements are interpreted within a transcendent or spiritual context that shapes the language, defines the values, and grounds the unity within mission and vision. When faith communities experience sexual trespass, a subtle separation between sexuality and spirituality ensues. This separation compromises the important role faith communities can play in addressing sexual ethics in light of spiritual values.

The temporary or permanent departure of a church leader presents one of the most significant transitions a faith community or church family can make. When sexual misconduct is the issue and the circumstances surrounding that leader's departure are disguised or withheld, congregations experience grave jeopardy in fundamental ways. The congregation's story is no longer whole; the story loses its power to inspire and sustain unity. One parishioner (from a congregation that was kept in secrecy for over twenty years) told me, "We were like a book which had one of the main chapters torn out of the binding. We knew there was a section missing, but we didn't know what it said. Nothing made sense without that chapter."

Without at least some information regarding an experience of sexual misconduct and the opportunity to process that information together, a congregation begins to develop a false sense of itself. The congregation does not have the chance to discover its true nature as a place in which all of life, the tragic as well as the joyful aspects, is brought into the light of faith. Congregations thus become crippled, unaware of the power of religious faith to transform human experience. A faith community that has not been allowed to rise to the occasion of processing painful information is like an overprotected child who does not discover the substantial inner resources or coping mechanisms that are summoned forth in difficult times.

A serious injustice is done when sexual misconduct is "taken care of quietly." In that instance congregations are implicitly and perhaps unwittingly told that they are too weak to handle their burdens. Or they are given the subtle message that the reputation of clergy or other leaders is a more important consideration than the long-term health of the congregation. This attitude of protective paternalism, and the denominational self-protection that sometimes goes with it, furthers injustice by suggesting that clergy and church leaders get to live by their own rules.

Justice for congregations that have experienced sexual misconduct begins, as justice always does, with truth—truth about their circumstances, truth about resources available to meet their needs, truth about the responsibility that attaches to the power of the ministerial office. "We could have faced it together, if only we had known the truth," one parishioner said to me. What are the important issues in truth telling to congregations?

Considerations about Disclosure

A good checklist for those who are planning a congregational disclosure about sexual misconduct includes the following considerations: Who will do the disclosing? How will it be done? When will the disclosure happen? What risks should be weighed? What should happen after the disclosure?

There is no one set formula for disclosing. Circumstances will differ, and it is important that the disclosure process itself be seen in the full context of healing. We do not disclose in order to discredit, defame, or punish offending clergy or other church leaders. Disclosure is a prayerful decision made with concern for the welfare of all parties involved. And disclosure is never done without provision for an intentional, supported healing process. "They just came and told us what happened, and we never heard from them again," complained several people from a parish where I later consulted. "They left us worse off than we had been before they came."

Who Should Disclose?

It is usually most helpful for disclosures to come from recognized authorities such as bishops, district superintendents, senior denominational executives, or regional overseers. In nondenominational churches with congregational polity, the senior layperson in the congregation may be the right person. But in this case, it is helpful if another religious authority—a seminary faculty member, a respected minister from the local community, a recognized expert in congregational healing—participates in the disclosure. In the case of St. John's Church, described above, the bishop made the announcement but was clearly acting in concert with the others at the front of the sanctuary. Involvement of appropriate others makes it clear that the information given is not the conjecture of just one (perhaps biased) person.

How Should Disclosure Happen?

In considering how disclosure is to happen, responsible parties need to remember that shocking information is hard to absorb all at once or in only one form. In the case of St. John's Church there was a prepared statement that the bishop read. Copies were then passed out to all present at the congregational meeting. While some people have used the avenue of a letter sent to the homes of all congregation members, our experience has shown that a carefully structured congregational meeting has a number of advantages. In a meeting everyone hears the information at once in the context of the gathered community.

The opportunity to learn of and react to difficult issues in visible companionship with one another builds the sense of community at a time when fragmentation and division may loom as feared possibilities. If people are left to open a letter in the privacy of their own homes without a gathering time in which to make initial responses to the information, they miss the opportunity to turn to one another for support. The use of worship space as the site for such a meeting conveys the important message that we are, even now, in God's presence.

When Should Disclosure Be Done?

Disclosure of information about sexual misconduct ideally happens as soon as there is sufficient material to constitute a responsible disclosure. This, too, will depend on the circumstances.

It may be important, where there is a dispute or denial about the facts of the case, to wait until there has been some investigation or adjudication of the complaints. If the pastor or leader is to be placed on a leave of absence or is to spend time away from the congregation while other matters are pursued (e.g., evaluation or treatment or further investigation), then the absence itself will raise questions that must be addressed through a careful communication strategy. Our experience teaches us that it is much wiser to tell a carefully defined amount of limited truth than to tell an outright falsehood about the pastor or leader's absence. One pastor's absence was described as "away on family business." When the real truth of sexual misconduct was finally revealed, the congregation was outraged at the earlier deception, and healing that outrage was even more difficult than healing the wound of the sexual misconduct.

A frequent question we hear is Should the secret be told even long after the fact? In assessing this possibility involved parties need to (1) be as sure of the facts as possible, (2) sense that the congregation needs this disclosure if it is to heal, and (3) be as careful in planning this kind of disclosure as they would be in planning a disclosure about current matters. It often happens that persons come forward to report sexual misconduct that happened years ago. Reports like this come more often now, most likely because the wider discussion of these issues allows people to revisit their own experiences. A large number of people from diverse congregations I have worked with have told me something like this: "We all knew that he was having affairs with women he counseled. . . . It was seen as a kind of lovable quirk he had. Now I see that he was engaged in a pattern of exploiting vulnerable people and that we were all engaged in a conspiracy of silence. We even made up stories to explain why some families abruptly left the church."

When such awareness comes, the time is ripe for a process of disclosure and healing. In such instances, it is the *disclosure*, not the time of the offense, that is relevant. We have participated in disclosure-healing processes that have taken place years after the offense. If responsible parties are willing to take time to carefully plan and gently support a congregation through a disclosure process and follow-up, old wounds can be reopened and finally

healed. These are some of the most profoundly moving transformations we have seen.

What Are the Risks?

There are, of course, many risks in making the kind of disclosures described here. And these must be weighed carefully as
plans are developed. One of the first concerns often raised is the
risk of legal liability. What if the accused pastor or leader sues the
congregation or denomination for libel, slander, defamation of
character, or loss of livelihood? While such suits are often threatened, they are actually quite rare.

Good legal advice that weighs the risks of disclosure against
the real and known risks of silence or cover-up is important here.
To minimize any possible liability responsible parties need to use
care with language (allegations or reports should be described as
such until an adjudication is complete) and need to adhere carefully to denominational policies and procedures. Legal action is
also far less likely when appropriate pastoral and other resources
have been extended to all parties concerned.[4]

There are other risks to consider in addition to those of legal
liability. One risk is that the disclosure itself will reopen related
wounds in those who have experienced other sexual trauma in
their lives. This is why disclosures like the story of St. John's
Church are done with a multidisciplinary team that includes
mental-health professionals. Information about counseling and
other resources must be made readily available so that people can
access those resources easily and privately.

Another risk of congregational disclosure is that a good deal of
further information may be unleashed. Perhaps there were financial irregularities such as embezzlement of funds. It may become
clear that others not only knew of but colluded in the sexual misconduct. We have sometimes found that disclosure opens a
floodgate of other reports, including reports of sexual misconduct occurring in several other pastorates. While the emergence
of this new information opens the possibility of extensive healing

---

[4]See Margo Maris, "'. . . that which is hidden will be revealed' (Luke 12:2)," p. 3 of this volume.

and new life, the issues can get very big very quickly. The team needs to be prepared for its task to become ever more complicated as things progress.

Just as the disclosure is set within a team context, so also is the ongoing healing process most helpfully guided by the team principle. Many judicatories (dioceses, synods, presbyteries, districts) now have congregational crisis teams trained and ready for assignment. In other situations, a trained consultant guides the development of an ongoing healing process. Many of the authors in this volume have played such a role. What is vital to keep in mind is that disclosure *inaugurates* a healing process, it does not *constitute* a healing process. Our experience teaches us that the first months after a disclosure are the "window of opportunity" for healing to occur and that healing always involves certain consistent elements.

Elements of Healing

Several concepts have been helpful in discovering and understanding the elements of healing in a congregation: the practice of trauma debriefing, the grief process, the creation of safe space for ventilation of feelings, the stages of sexual-abuse recovery, and the discipline of pastoral theology (especially, the importance of Scripture and other faith resources in reflection upon experience).

All of these have played a part both in diagnosis and in healing for congregations. A good healing process for congregations would include participation from people who are skilled in each of these specialties. As healing processes for a congregation are developed, each has its part to play and its wisdom to contribute. And we have learned that a complete healing process not only involves several disciplines but usually takes a year or longer.

A congregation that has heard about sexual misconduct has experienced a trauma, in somewhat the same way as those who have lost a home to natural disaster. They need to be supported in facing the trauma and talking it through. And like other victims of trauma, congregations may try to seal over the pain with hearty assurances that it could have been worse or I'll be fine; I'm ready to look ahead. Trauma victims often react with such protective denial only to find themselves later suffering in various ways. The disclosure process itself should be an experience of trauma debriefing.[5] The process of disclosure and the provision of processing time to acknowledge the trauma are vital to minimize the premature "we're fine" reaction, which obstructs true healing. Our experience with congregations tells us that the insistent early protest, "We're fine," is a trauma reaction and not a reliable indicator of recovery. When such protests cause the healing process to be short-circuited, we see the later development of the kinds of patterns described earlier.

Disclosures of sexual misconduct are experiences of loss. The loss may center around the loss of an ideal or the loss of a dream. Many people grieve the loss of an ideal image of ministry or of the church. Or the loss may be about the removal of a pastor who was loved and appreciated. For those who experienced grace and goodness in that pastor's ministry, the sheer loss of the person leads to grief. It is always important in a healing process to affirm the good that was present in a ministry, whatever other factors may have been present. People need to know that they do not have to "give up" their good experiences with a pastor or church leader. Grieving a lost relationship involves embracing what was good in that relationship as well as what was painful or problematic for others or for oneself. Grieving may involve a desire to say goodbye. Sometimes it is not possible to say a personal goodbye to a pastor who has been removed. But people can be supported in finding the kinds of closure they need as they grieve. Transition rituals (for example, the welcoming of a new pastor or other leader) are important moments of looking back as well as looking ahead.[6]

It is often helpful to include in a healing process specific education about the stages of grief. This helps people place their own experiences and those of others in a larger context. It may also help people understand one another better; people who are in the anger stage of grief, for example, are easier to accept if their behavior can be seen in perspective. Although hurtful behavior to-

---

[5]Chilton Knudsen, "Trauma De-Briefing: A Congregational Model," *Conciliation Quarterly* 10 (Spring 1991) 12.

[6]Chilton Knudsen, "Pastoral Care for Congregations in the Aftermath of Sexual Misconduct" (unpublished paper, 1993).

ward others cannot be sanctioned simply because there is grief present, expressions of grief need to be accepted for what they are. Bonds can be deepened in a faith community if people have allowed one another the various expressions and stages of grief. This requires the provision of safe space for the ventilation of feelings, settings in which no one will be shamed or criticized for what they feel. Various models have been developed to meet this need for church groups in the aftermath of sexual misconduct.

As secondary victims of sexual misconduct, congregations are well served if their healing process includes some of the dimensions of sexual-abuse recovery. Certainly those who have been directly victimized need specialized care, and referral should be made for both mental-health and advocacy services for victims. Part 1 of this volume deals with the needs of the primary (directly affected) victims. An important dimension of sexual-abuse recovery is clarification about responsibility for the abuse, and this is an area of confusion for many church people. It is easy to jump to the quick conclusion that there has been an "affair" if the sexual misconduct involves adult victims. What congregations need to wrestle with is the unique role of a pastor or trusted church leader, the imbalance of power that can result when vulnerable people place their trust in designated caregivers,[7] and the special obligations that come with ordination or placement in other forms of church leadership (youth leader, lay pastor, outreach minister). The growing understanding of the dynamics of incestuous families also sheds helpful light on congregations that have experienced sexual misconduct. William White has given careful thought to the issue of incest dynamics within organizations, and much of what he says can be applied to churches as well.[8] Whether we think of incest or of other forms of sexual abuse, justice for victims (including secondary victims) involves clarity about who bears the responsibility for abusive behavior.

Congregational healing happens within the life of a faith community. The resources of faith can be usefully mobilized at every

---

[7]Pamela Cooper-White, "Soul Stealing: Power Relations in Pastoral Sexual Abuse," *The Christian Century* (February 20, 1991) 196; James Poling, *The Abuse of Power: A Theological Problem* (Nashville: Abingdon, 1991).

[8]See William White, *Incest in the Organizational Family: The Ecology of Burnout in Closed Systems* (Bloomington, Ill.: Lighthouse Training Institute, 1986).

stage of a congregation's healing process. But these faith resources do not serve the congregation's healing process if they are seen simply as spiritual Band-Aids. Like the people of St. John's Church, who were quick to mention forgiveness, congregants often grasp at spiritual concepts and can misappropriate them in a desperate effort to avoid the hard work of healing. Many congregations we have worked with report that they came to truly understand the gift of faith when an experience of sexual misconduct forced them to reexamine their beliefs. Forgiveness, for example, is a process involving contrition, repentance, amendment, and conversion of life. Forgiveness is a strong and holy reality, but it does not sidestep issues of accountability and restitution. Sexual misconduct can be the occasion for discovering profound spiritual meaning under the terms that so often roll readily off our tongues.

Members of one congregation told me that their healing process involved an awareness of the identity of the real pastor in their midst. "I think we began to see Pastor 'Smith' as head of the congregation rather than Jesus Christ. When we heard about sexual misconduct, it was as if Jesus had failed us. Slowly, we realized that ministers are human. Only Jesus is Jesus." Other congregations find in their healing process that the Scripture "The truth shall make you free"(John 8:32) has new meaning and does, in fact, transform other areas of life. One congregant told me that the experience of a congregational healing process inspired his family to finally "get honest" about the terminal illness of an elderly parent, a secret everyone had been conspiring to hide from everyone else. And one congregant who had strenuously resisted a congregational healing process finally came to report, "I never really knew why justice was a religious issue. I didn't like those liberals who were always talking about God's justice. Now I see that justice means protecting the vulnerable and not letting them be exploited. Especially by my own minister."

Congregations that have been supported in facing disclosures of sexual misconduct and have been assisted in an intentional healing process become places of joy and health. We have been about this work of congregational healing for enough time now that we can see the long-term effects of such healing processes. What we see are congregations that do not cover up or deny their history but integrate that history into their ongoing life and ministry. Their experience of pain, integrated in the light of faith, has made them compassionate. They have more energy, and they have first-hand experience with the journey from slavery to freedom, from death to new life.

Healed congregations have healthier relationships with their clergy and church leaders in seeking clarity regarding roles, systems of accountability, and pastoral practices. They understand and embrace shared responsibility for their community life. They report to us, often some distance down the road, that the disclosure and healing they initially feared and resisted has brought renewal and strength. They know they are stewards of the profound trust placed in them as God's agents in the world. And they are still teaching us.

The Effects of the Misconduct Crisis on Non-offending Clergy

Kevin McDonough

For nearly a decade it has been impossible to attend a gathering of clergy without hearing conversation about the sexual misconduct scandal in the churches. Sometimes, especially in the last three or four years, this is so because clergy sexual abuse and exploitation have become frequent formal topics on the agenda at official meetings. More often, however, it is simply because the specter of this painful issue is seldom far from the minds of clergy "whenever two or three are gathered" for any sort of business.

Many of these discussions reflect a feeling of stigmatization, of being singled out unfairly for scrutiny and criticism. Increasingly, though, I have seen clergy groups drawing on their resources of professional competence and, especially, on their faith to address with openness and creativity the challenges posed by clergy sexual misconduct. Contrary to both public perception and the fears of clergy leaders, therefore, this issue is far less debilitating to the general body of clergy than anticipated. For example, a recent survey of morale among Catholic priests[1] in a state particularly hard hit with very public cases of clergy abuse shows that clergy members' satisfaction with their job continues to be very high. Drawing on the fundamental Christian story of

---

[1]Victor Klimoski, "The Relationship Between Participation in Continuing Professional Education for Clergy and Perceived Role Stress and Role Satisfaction" (Ph.D. diss., Univ. of Minnesota, 1988).

the passion and resurrection of Christ, we will look at the reactions of non-offending clergy to the sexual-abuse crisis in two parts. First we will look at signs of death—the senses of shame, guilt, and loss that afflict many clergy. The second part will look at signs of life, at the creative engagement of clergy in addressing the abuse and exploitation challenge.

Signs of Death

Since the mid-1980s clergy members have been confronted more and more frequently by the reality of clergy sexual misconduct. In their offices they hear the stories of people abused by clergy when they were children or exploited by a previous pastor to whom they had gone for help. Returning home at night, they see television news shots of personal friends being led handcuffed into courthouses or read newspaper reports of how their own denominational superiors mishandled complaints. Congregational members confront them in anger at what they perceive as the dysfunctionality of all clergy, and they catch the subtle and sometimes not-so-subtle signs that they themselves are caught up in the broad web of suspicion. The continuing scandal, therefore, has caused signs of death to appear in the perceptions that clergy have of themselves, of the particular ministry in which they engage, and of the broader Church. Let us examine each in turn.

Clergy Self-Image

Many clergy members grew up in families and communities in which the profession of ordained ministry was held in exceptionally high regard. While some pastors and priests trace their vocation to an extraordinary conversion that changed profoundly the path of life they had lived in childhood, recruitment studies show that for young candidates the single largest factor in choosing the ministry is parental and familial support. Across denominational lines, therefore, clergy have perceived their profession as uniquely trustworthy and valuable to society. In turn, congregational members and society as a whole have reinforced such a perception.

The misconduct scandal of the past decade has caused many clergy members to question the trustworthiness of their vocational field. Clergy speak of a sense of shame at their own ordination and a hesitancy to wear distinctive dress and other signs of office in public. Such a reluctance to wear clerical dress a decade ago was more often tied to a desire to avoid the pressure of the immediate trust and self-confession that strangers on the street and in airplanes might place in "one of the cloth." Several clergy have told me about their reluctance to wear clerical dress today in order to avoid having to explain that they were not child molesters. Having been able to count on public good will for so long, it is discouraging and confusing to face a precipitous decline in trust.

A second sign of death affecting clergy self-image is a sense of guilty knowledge about the past. Several pastors have spoken of a profound regret at what they now understand to be a mishandling of concerns raised to them over a decade ago by people who had come to seek help from abuse or exploitation. One pastor has spoken of a dramatic confrontation with a woman who had come to him twenty-five years previously to ask for his spiritual counsel in dealing with the sexual advances being made by a neighboring clergyman. She told him that she respected his good intentions but that his "forgive and forget" advice of a quarter century ago had left her with a profound sense of guilt on her part and unresolved justice in regard to the offender. This particular confrontation had a happy ending, since the exploitation victim had in the meantime worked through these issues from her past, and her pastor, a man remarkable for his openness to new insights even in his late sixties, was ready to see a new perspective and ask her forgiveness for the inadequate help he had provided. For many others, however, there are vague memories of painful situations poorly handled and now apparently irredeemably lost.

Another form of guilty knowledge is present in those who blame themselves now for not having acted on their sense in the past that a colleague, subsequently discovered to be an abuser or exploiter, was "not doing well." They blame themselves for not having intervened more strongly when they saw a colleague abusing alcohol, struggling with depression, isolating him- or herself from peers, or being consumed with rage. They wonder whether some timely action on their part might not have saved pain for victims, the Church, and their colleague.

In addition to a sense of guilt at their own knowledge or suspicion of abuse by others, many clergy struggle with embarrassment at their own previous boundary violations. For some few clergy, this takes the form of a recollection of explicit exploitation or abuse on their part. For the great majority it is something far more subtle. Some speak of their mishandling of the transference reactions of persons who came to see them years before. Others regret their participation in conversations filled with inappropriate humor and double entendres. Still others remember their participation in encounter sessions or T-groups in the 1970s. One bishop recalls that "just as I had finally convinced myself that I had to hug people in order to show that I was open and warm, they made it a crime to touch your parishioners."

Recollection of their own previous boundary violations generates fear among many clergy that they will be the subject of a lawsuit and of public embarrassment. Such fear is compounded by discussions about false-memory syndrome and copycat suits. This makes for a potent mixture of righteous indignation, a sense of victimhood, and a self-doubt bred by the nagging question Did I do something I have now forgotten that offended or harmed another?

A final sign of death in regard to their own personal choices and lives is the way the misconduct scandal focuses and deepens the vocational dissatisfaction felt by some clergy. The dissatisfaction may actually have its roots in other areas—in the clergy member's own personal life or in the broader Church. The shame, guilt, and fear, however, become an icon of the clergy member's unhappiness. I have not spoken to any clergy who have abandoned the ministry in direct response to the misconduct crisis (unless they were themselves perpetrators). But more than a few have spoken of the misconduct issue as a catalyst for facing other sources of unhappiness and pain.

The Ministerial Setting

Signs of death are present not only in the reflections that clergy have about their own vocation, but they also manifest themselves in the particular ministerial setting in which they find themselves. Here again we can see several manifestations of the destructiveness of clergy sexual misconduct. The simplest and most direct question facing many ministers is what they should say to their congregants, students, or other recipients of their ministry about clergy misconduct. Ambivalent themselves about the causes and meanings of misconduct, they recognize that something should be said, but what? Several clergy have referred to the lack of an appropriate opening for such a discussion. When specific crises appear in the press, local clergy often have too little information to respond intelligently to detailed questions. They are afraid to sound overly defensive. Some fear that they might merely be drawing attention to something that people find unimportant, while others fear making their people uncomfortable by addressing difficult topics.

There is a deeper confusion in the particular place of ordained ministry that is generated by the misconduct crisis. Clergy wonder what sorts of boundaries are appropriate in their own setting. Pastors who are new to their placement may discover that their predecessors freely hugged parishioners, exchanged large gifts with co-workers or congregants, dined frequently in the homes of community members, or offered extended spiritual counseling sessions to troubled parishioners. Since these practices have created expectations on the part of some people in the particular setting and disagreement or even fear on the part of others, the new minister inherits an emotionally charged atmosphere.

Perhaps even more difficult is the situation of those who have been in a particular setting for an extended period of time but have grown increasingly uncomfortable with the pastoral patterns they have created. Having acquiesced to invitations from some, they now feel trapped by the unclear boundaries they have previously tolerated or even encouraged. Not wanting to give offense to obviously needy people, they wish to begin setting clearer boundaries but have no idea how to do so. Particularly when a clergyperson has been in place for an extended period, those uncomfortable with his or her ministerial style have disappeared into the ranks of inactive or absent congregants, while those most likely to reinforce older patterns have become co-workers, church council leaders, and regular social connections.

A third sign of death in the ministerial setting is an increased suspiciousness about particular individuals or groups of individuals who seek the help of a pastor. People once thought of as especially needy are sometimes relabeled as dangerous. Many clergy recognize that simply belonging to a church community is an essential lifeline for chronically depressed people, some mentally ill people, or even for those whose unique spiritualities or familial situations make a certain congregation feel like "home." In different ways such people are usually satisfied simply to be associated with worship or other community activities. In times of acute crisis, however, they may expect and even demand attention, help, and intensive emotional interaction from the community's clerical leadership. The resulting late-night phone calls, intrusive conversations at the beginning or end of worship, and frequent requests for meetings take on a threatening tone for clergy who feel that their inevitable inability to satisfy seemingly overwhelming needs will result in a lawsuit. In many cases it is precisely this tension that motivates clergy members to learn better and more professional disciplines. But in all too many overreactive situations, clergy members attempt to prevent the problem by driving away the potential problem-source. People who would otherwise find sanctuary in the church find themselves unwelcome because of their threatening "abnormality."

A special and especially painful case of this last sign of death is the involvement of youth in the parish or other ministerial setting. Many clergy already consider ministry to youth to be too great a challenge. The emotional volatility and alternating religious indifference and intensity of teens make a successful youth ministry an extraordinary achievement even under the best of circumstances. Add to this current suspiciousness about any adult who spends signifi-cant time with children and the result is the definitive statement of one clergyman: "I minister only to parents. Their kids are their own responsibility." While such distress sometimes is the motivating force for a creative rethinking of approaches the Church might take with youth, too often, the fear generated by the misconduct crisis is enough to paralyze the efforts of a local congregation and its leadership to care for its young members.

The Broader Church

Extending beyond both the personal vocation of the clergy and their particular ministerial placements, the signs of death associated with the misconduct crisis include the broader Church. Many misconduct complaints often seem to involve either inadequate screening or insufficient response by denominational leaders once the offense becomes known. For many clergy it is in regard to the implications in the broader Church of misconduct that the greatest pain is felt.

There is a double bind operating. On the one hand, many clergy express anger at the past refusals of their superiors to provide either adequate training or timely intervention. They blame their denominational leadership structures for permitting the problem to flourish when it might have been preventable or at least containable, thereby reducing their own anguish and preoccupation.

On the other hand, clergy see current responses of denominational leadership, including background checks and swift intervention procedures, as a threat to their rights. Many clergy believe that judicatory leaders are now willing to make an example of an innocent but accused clergy, either from the naive belief in the trustworthiness of all complainants or from a sinister conclusion that "it is better that one man should die for the country." The synodal official charged with responding to complaints in one Protestant statewide office has been the subject of a concerted attack by members of that state's clergy. Believing that one of their peers was the subject of an ideologically motivated kangaroo-court procedure, they have used both the formal complaint procedures of their denomination and an informal talking campaign to press for the removal of the official.

Catholic priests from dioceses around the United States have commented to me that they believed that their bishops were completely uninterested in protecting their rights. They say that past inaction on the part of bishops was not the result of the protectiveness of religious superiors but institutional blindness and laziness. These same qualities, they say, characterize the star-chamber proceedings in which clergy are guilty until proven innocent. As a result, denominational officials find themselves in a curious "damned if you didn't, damned if you did" position, while local clergy judge themselves to be abandoned.

Furthermore, for many clergy the misconduct scandal is linked in one way or another to other sex and gender issues in the

Churches. Conservative clergy frequently cite the breakdown of traditional sexual morality and the diminishing of clear public boundaries around clergy work as causative factors. They see the sexual politics of the last generation in the Christian Churches, including expanded leadership roles and ordination for women, shifts in teaching on homosexuality, and the breakdown of Church support for permanent marriage as factors that create a sexualized Church environment.

Progressives look to an entirely different, even opposite set of factors as the cause. Sexual abuse and exploitation are, they say, the product of institutionalized sexism and a paternalistic power structure in the Church. They argue that repressive sexual morality, particularly as taught to ministry candidates in the seminary, interferes with the normal maturation processes of future pastors. The discussion around sex and gender issues in particular denominations has taken on a harder edge in the light of the misconduct scandal. Ordination of "out" and active homosexual candidates in the mainline Protestant Churches, the relaxation of the celibacy requirement for some Catholic priests, ministerial placements for women in all denominations: these issues are cited alternately as cause or cure for clerical misconduct.

Finally, clergy are giving a painful look to other issues in the broader Church through the lens of the misconduct crisis. The relative place of psychological counseling and spiritual assistance is undergoing a sometimes caustic reexamination. The adequacy of seminary training for the practical challenges of pastoral ministry is again under attack. For heirarchical Churches the role of the bishop is strongly disputed, particularly when a bishop has responded inadequately to complaints. At the same time, congregationally organized Churches find themselves establishing more centralized procedures for clearing ministerial candidates, especially when local congregations prove inadequate to the task of screening or placing qualified ministers.

Signs of death though all these things are, they are also demanding creative multidimensional and multiprofessional responses from the Churches and their clergy. I have noted a sort of "middle passage" for clergy groups in several denominations, a time when the challenges of the misconduct crisis seem insurmountable. When clergy members find cherished and comforting beliefs about themselves, their place of ministry, and their ecclesial communion falling apart, the temptation to abandon the ministry and sometimes even faith itself is quite strong. This dark night of the clergys' collective soul does not seem to be permanent in our experience, however. In fact, clergy around the country are drawing on a whole wealth of resources to convert signs of death into signs of life. Let us take a look at some of those developments.

Signs of Life

In reviewing the pain and loss experienced by clergy as a result of the misconduct crisis, we looked first at its impact on their own personal sense of ministerial vocation, then at the impact in the particular ministerial placement, and finally at their relationship to the broader Church. We can detect signs of life in regard to each of these areas.

The Ministerial Vocation

Clergy in recent years have shown an increasing interest in the self-care issues being raised in the larger culture. Many clergy initially resisted this discussion, motivated as they are by an ethic of self-denial and sacrifice. As many clergy have looked at their offending peers, however, and thought, "There but for the grace of God go I," they are reexamining the personal-health movement with a different urgency. Whereas clergy service organizations a decade ago spoke of the life-enhancing benefits of sabbaticals, appropriate vacations and days off, proper medical care, and so on, there has been a subtle shift in recent years to emphasize the preventative dimension of self-care. Focused a decade ago on avoiding burnout, many clergy today only half-humorously say they are seeking to avoid arrest. Clergy retreats and efforts at renewing the marriages of clergy members have a new significance to clergy who have learned something more about the fragility of their vocation.

There also seems to be a renewed attention to peer support issues. Many have noted that a significant number, though not all, of offending clergy were loners, isolated from their peers even before offending. As a result, clergy support groups and mentoring networks seem to have an attraction for many today that was not true a decade or more ago.

Many clergy members report a new interest in addressing the professionalism of their approach to ministry. The word "boundary" had only a geographical meaning in the vocabulary of many clergy as late as the mid-1980s. Today pastors are asking about their own personal limitations and ministerial gifts. There seems to be a greater openness to ongoing education and formation. Even clerical dress, which two decades ago was abandoned by many as an offensive barrier to closeness with the people, is being reevaluated by some because of its assistance in marking when the pastor is "at work," distinguishing those times from when he or she is "just like everyone else."

Finally at this personal level, some clergy have spoken about the misconduct crisis as a motivator for their own renewal in prayer, confession, and conversion. Intercessory prayer for those harmed by clergy and for the clergy who have done the harm characterizes many church gatherings. Some speak of the scandal of abuse and exploitation as having forced them to reconsider their own sinfulness in the presence of evil, even in the Church. Whether the metaphor is "sin and redemption" or "twelve-step recovery," an easy optimism about human perfectibility is ceding to a renewed reliance on grace.

The Ministerial Setting

In local ministerial settings life is also showing itself in several ways. Courageous efforts are being made in congregations of many different denominations to speak openly about the misconduct crisis. This author has watched and worked with several congregations while they faced the pain of misconduct in their own particular history. Local clergy leadership did not shy away from their responsibility in that effort. Victims of abuse or exploitation report that they have found a greater willingness on the part of some clergy, although sadly not all, to hear them out and support them in their healing. Some clergy are resisting the temptation to defensiveness on the part of themselves and their congregational members, refusing to label misconduct reports as nothing more than press sensationalism or Christian bashing or "attempts to make an easy buck." Several clergy have indicated that they did not know how preoccupying this question was for their people until they decided on their own to address it, often in response to some local crisis. They report consistently that the reaction they receive is, Thank you, pastor, for speaking to us so honestly. We have been hoping someone would say something for a long time.

A particular dimension of addressing the crisis locally is the creative involvement of co-workers in the congregational or chaplaincy setting. Some clergy have invited lay staff members or lay congregational leadership to help them in reflecting on the history and needs of the particular congregation. They have searched out resources for staff and leadership formation, and they have set the expectation that all of the ministries in the local congregation would reflect a renewed understanding of pastoral power and its limitations. They have associated lay leaders with themselves in addressing the problem to the congregation as a whole, thereby breaking down a good deal of suspicion about clerical secrecy.

Moreover, clergy are leading their local congregations in the development of referral networks as part of an honest acknowledgment that most congregations simply do not have the resources to address all the problems that come to them. A pastor in a small town in a rural part of a midwestern state asked his co-workers and lay leaders to make an inventory of the kinds of problems they had seen in the last year. They developed a list of professional resources, some of them local and some of them available only in a large city seventy miles away, from which truly competent service could be obtained. The pastor helped other congregational leaders address the fear that somehow they were failing if they could not take care of everything locally. Finally, he spoke with the whole congregation, creating a background against which specific referrals would be understood as a respectful assistance with healing rather than as off-putting abandonment.

A final sign of life at the local level is the current reevaluation of the importance of supervision and accountability in local ministry. Few positions enjoy greater autonomy than that of the pastor of a congregation, especially after he or she has had a few years in which to consolidate that position. Denominational offices are generally far too small to provide regular review. Local lay leadership committees may at first be suspicious of a new pastor, but over time they become dependent on his or her ministry and are far less likely to challenge questionable practices. Local clergy are showing greater interest today than a decade and more ago in formal, objective, and regular procedures for evaluating the effectiveness of their work.

The Broader Church

Even in the broader Church clergy are finding signs of life as they address the scandal of the misconduct perpetrated by their peers and friends. Although some denominational efforts are met with suspicion and fear, many clergy are relieved that their leadership is finally responding. In my experience a particularly important step in winning clergy cooperation is that the denomination should involve clergy in the development of policy and procedures as early as possible. When confronted with a *fait accompli* by their superiors, clergy almost reflexively resist. When invited into the process, however, clergy offer valuable insights and even defer to synodal expertise, especially if its sources are lay professionals such as psychologists and attorneys.

A second sign of life may be ambivalent in its theological meaning but is absolutely necessary for ministerial integrity. It is a greater sophistication on the part of clergy about the kind of business standards that must characterize even a small not-for-profit organization like a local congregation in the 1990s. The misconduct crisis has motivated many local clergy to seek the advice of professionals outside their own communities before making major decisions, especially those with potential legal implications. The ambiguity in all of this is, of course, the danger of a Church run by its lawyers. The willingness of many clergy to face a changing environment and to acquire the sophistication necessary to operate in it, however, should be viewed as a sign of life.

The misconduct crisis is also prompting many clergy and other ministers to engage in a kind of ethical reflection that otherwise might not have taken place. They are concerned not only about personal boundaries but also about professional standards. They look at accountability not only at the congregational but also at the denominational level. In many places clergy are sitting down with health-care and mental-health-care professionals, with social workers, and with other community human-service providers to examine common issues of training and standards. Publications such as the present volume have emerged as a direct response to the misconduct crisis.

Finally, clergy in some places are attempting to address the broader social implications of the Church's own particular crisis. They see that child abuse is not only or even in large percentage the peculiar province of priests, youth workers, and other clergy. Some pastors are finding ways to encourage their congregations in addressing child-protection issues in the broader community. Others see that the exploitation of professional position is not confined to the Church but also touches academia, the professions, and the political establishment. Working to clean their own house, some clergy also find a powerful motivation to address similar concerns in related fields.

Conclusion

Public attention to the misconduct of a small but significant number of clergy has had a powerful impact on nearly all members of that profession. As pastors and others see the sacred trust to which they have devoted their own lives being violated by others, they experience genuine grief and anger in regard to their own vocation. They find themselves estranged from the particular ministry entrusted to them, wondering if their own instincts are correct and fearing that their people no longer respect them. They eye their religious superiors with suspicion, doubting their competence and questioning their good will.

Such understandable reactions in many cases are being transformed today, by the grace of God, into a new creativity for the Church and synagogue. Clergy have learned more about their own fragility from the offenses committed by their brothers and sisters. In many cases they are addressing their congregations forthrightly and leading them into healthier patterns of ministerial service. They are engaging in the challenges of the broader Church with concern and intelligence. These developments, of course, are uneven. Local cultures and even the personality of a particular denominational leader can advance or hold back these transformations. Some areas of the country have known repeated and very public scandals. Among these some have used such pain as a motivator for change, while others are paralyzed and stunned into inaction. Other parts of the country have to date escaped public scandal. In those areas as well, clergy have had to decide whether to mount a preventive effort before scandal arises or to count on their luck holding out. Change is nothing new for clergy, but it is safe to predict that clerical ministry will look significantly different a decade from now, and in large part that change will have been motivated by the current crisis. It is my own confidence that, while death may seem to prevail for a time, the result for people of faith will be new manifestations of life.

The Effects of Clergy Sexual Misconduct on the Wider Church

Harold Hopkins

In this article I will summarize some experiences and reflect on some learnings, personal and institutional, about the impact of clergy sexual-boundary violations on the wider Church. By "wider Church" I mean persons and communities other than primary offenders and their immediate families, victims and their immediate families, friends and local congregations in which the abuse has taken place. I will focus on church executives, other clergy in the system shared with offending clergy, clergy and laity in general, and to some degree the public beyond the Church.

My particular perspective and experience is that of an older male who has been working for nearly six years at the national level of the Episcopal Church, U.S.A., after more than thirty-nine years of varied ordained ministry in the same Church, including nine years as a diocesan bishop.

Though the Episcopal system like all denominational systems has its own unique approach to these issues, my experience indicates that Roman Catholic, mainline Protestant, and other denominations have much in common in the ways they are impacted by clergy boundary violations of a serious nature. This seems to be true whether they are from the conservative, liberal, or middle of the larger ecclesial systems, both Jewish and Christian.

Individual denominational polity, to a large extent, determines the way Churches respond, however. The more congregationally structured denominations that do not have a clear administrative center and/or "bishop type" figure will respond to the issues largely according to the needs and perspectives of the local church leadership. This may mean that there is a greater variety of response to clergy sexual-boundary violations from different congregations among, say, the so-called free Churches and less overall coordination of response from judicatory officials, if any. However, even in the more centrally organized and administered Churches such as the Episcopal, Lutheran, Roman Catholic, Methodist, and Presbyterian, there are still likely to be significant differences in response between regions, dioceses, synods, and so forth. Not everyone is up to the same speed or at the same place even in a single, more centrally governed denomination. Thus developing and administering a consistent, unified response to these problems is a distant goal even within a given denomination, to say nothing about the response of "all the Churches" as a whole.

Many of the procedures for response that various denominations are developing, whether from some regional or national center or not, tend to have much in common, however. The ecumenical movement is, fortunately in my opinion, alive and well in this field at least. Many denominations that would ordinarily have little substantive interaction are sharing and learning from each other directly. This crisis has the effect of setting aside differences that might normally impede significant cooperation and of drawing Churches together in united efforts in spite of themselves. I remember clearly one national meeting of judicatory heads from several different denominations in which virtual unanimity was reached regarding the authority and accountability of ordained persons in the exercise of the pastoral ministry even though there were wide divergences on other aspects of theology and ecclesiology.

Most denominations are still on a rapid learning curve regarding these matters. Someone has aptly said that helping the Church address this particular area of concern is like building a plane while you're flying it. That is certainly the way it felt five years ago, and it still does.

For example, when I started my work with the national Episcopal Church in 1988 I did not really expect to be spending much, if any, time on matters of clergy sexual abuse. I had had some experience with the problem as a diocesan bishop but not a lot. Today it is a problem that is almost overwhelming in general impact, consuming increasingly greater chunks of personal time and energy. Conversation with other church leaders indicates that my experience is far from unique.

In the past six years or so, many excellent resources—books, tapes, study guides, conferences, and the like—have been produced both by religious and by secular agencies. But not much more than six years ago we barely had the vocabulary to talk about—let alone apply—the concept of clergy "abuse of power." Today this principle is at the heart of most conceptual models of response to clergy misbehavioral crises. A paragraph from the report to the Episcopal bishop of New York states:

> "Clergy" must also guard against confusing the personal qualities they bring to their ministry with the true source of their power, which is God's grace. Personal qualities such as attractiveness, intelligence, ability to communicate, age (especially when dealing with children), gender (viewed against the backdrop of a traditionally male-dominated society) and force of personality or "charisma" are often sources of priestly power and may be used and useful in the work of the ministry. But relying on these qualities, rather than on grace, in exercising authority and jurisdiction will inevitably plant the seeds of destruction in what may appear to be a successful ministry.
>
> It is important to understand that the abuse of power is a larger issue than sexual exploitation. Power is abused whenever a priest takes advantage of other human beings in any way, or uses institutional or personal gifts for selfish ends.[1]

Much of the helpful work on boundaries in professional-client, pastor-congregant relationships was just being developed and in the early stages of coming into some general acceptance five years ago.[2] In a not much longer time frame than that the behavioral sciences and related disciplines have clarified and made much more

---

[1] "Report to the Bishop of the Task Force on Clergy and Sexual Misconduct of the Episcopal Diocese of New York" (New York, November 1993) 12.

[2] Marilyn Peterson, *At Personal Risk: Boundary Violations in Professional Relationship* (Minneapolis: Norton, 1991).

available to the interested public new ways of understanding human psychosexual dynamics from both health and sickness perspectives. There have been many instructive developments in the psycho-therapeutic field as well. The relatively new concept of sexual addiction is now widely (though not universally) accepted and often helpful in diagnosis, treatment, and recovery of offenders.[3]

Both popular and formal academic writings from feminist and womanist perspectives have aided in but sometimes complicated the Church's understanding of and response to issues of male patriarchal assumption and use of power of many different kinds and degrees in both Church and society.

The legal profession is sometimes accused of cynically capitalizing on and exploiting this crisis to its own benefit. Though this may be occasionally true, in my experience most attorneys bring their resources and expertise helpfully to bear in assisting church leaders with careful, just, and compassionate response to out-of-bounds clergy behavior. I know many lawyers who serve the church pro bono or on a greatly reduced fee basis from a deep commitment to helping bring about truth, justice, and healing for all. It is also a widely accepted fact that many of the more damaging effects of litigation enter the picture only after the Church has botched up a response to substantive accusations of clergy misbehavior.

Even the media, in spite of the practice of focusing primarily on the sensational elements of clergy misbehavior and an uncanny tendency to distort or misinterpret facts, has had an important role. Calling the attention of the public to the problem has at least helped to break through a deep systemic denial in both Church and society. One doubts if the Churches would have made the sort of responses they are making today without the media's support of a complainant's desire to go public and tell the truth, thus holding the Church's "feet to the fire."

Not so long ago the Church's stunned and defensive reaction to increasing evidence of pathology and/or sinful behavior on the part of a small but significant number of its clergy was largely one of denial, self-protectiveness, and blaming of the accusers. The

---

[3]Patrick Carnes, *Don't Call It Love: Recovering from Sexual Addiction* (New York: Bantam, 1991).

shift that is under way today, though by no means everywhere complete, clearly is toward compassion, justice, and a desire to face the pain of individuals and communities; and there is a growing willingness to both wait upon and work toward the gifts of forgiveness, renewal, and recovery that God alone can give.

Though I think the Churches and all who care about justice can and should take some encouragement from this progress, there is still long-term damage being experienced, especially by primary victims of clergy sexual abuse and their families. This situation sometimes exists, tragically, even when sensitive attempts at solutions have been made by the Church. In particularly egregious cases real restitution and complete healing seem distant if not impossible goals to reach. A fair number of people will be carrying scars with them for the rest of their lives. The Church will be living in and with its responsibility for this pain and damage for a long time to come.

It is also common experience that the older the case of abuse, the more difficult effective response and resolution often is. Many cases currently causing the greatest pain to institutions and individuals are ten years old or considerably more. Most church laws and disciplinary procedures simply have not anticipated the kind of ethical crisis we are now facing. Civil, criminal, and ecclesiastical statutes of limitations have run out in most old cases, further hampering action against a number of unquestionable perpetrators. Victims understandably may see this inability to act—or to act in any decisive way—as a further example of ecclesiastical stonewalling. The fact that the events took place in the long past does not lessen the pain that victims may feel currently.

However, our figurative plane is indeed airborne, though still under construction and remodeling; there is fuel in the tank and helpful but not complete navigational aids to steer by. Both expected and unexpected head winds and down drafts are regularly met, which require small and large course corrections. Nevertheless, the plane is flying on, and it will not turn back.

Impact on Clergy Other Than the Offender

An Episcopal priest at a recent conference related his experience while traveling by air. He noted an older couple beside him reading and discussing a news story about a Roman Catholic priest having been sentenced to prison for a number of incidents of child sexual abuse. The man turned to the clergyman and said, "If I were you I would be ashamed to show my face in public with that collar on!"

The priest said that he was furious, defensive, and mortified at the blanket of guilt by association that was thrown over him by the comment and was unable to make anything but a stammering response. He also admitted that he does not wear his collar while traveling as regularly as he once did.

This experience and its impact, while perhaps more dramatic than many, seems typical of a public attitude that is contributing to the discomfort of many clergy. It also represents the confusion, ignorance, and powerful sense of betrayal that many laypeople feel when they read about clergy sexual offenses. It is, after all, true that most clergy do not commit sexual offenses against their congregants. It is just another aspect of the far-reaching power of clergy sexual misbehavior that the majority of clergy may feel they bear some shame and responsibility for the behavior of the few.

Clergy sexual abuse is like an old boot thrown into a calm pond. The ripple effect from the initial splash extends far from the spot where the boot hits the water, agitating the whole surface of the pond and more subtly but measurably eroding any shore it touches. However, clergy sexual exploitation not only touches the "shores" of the Church, it also reaches and damages its very soul and center, almost as if the whole pond has become poisoned. The old boot sits on the bottom; in certain light you can see its vague outline; now and then a fisherman hooks onto it and momentarily hauls it to the surface; if the pond level drops it may reappear. It never seems to go away but lurks there waiting to be rediscovered again and again.

Reasonable trust and confidence on the part of the laity toward ordained leadership is a touchstone of a healthy congregation and even of a denomination. When that trust is seriously undermined many people are negatively impacted, often in profound and subtle ways.

In coming into contact with many clergy as I am privileged to do, I detect a correspondingly subtle but clearly evident siege mentality, a kind of drawing around of the wagons in defense against both actual and perceived threats to the clerical person and profession. This reaction is undoubtedly engendered from a number of complex sources in these times when all leadership seems to be suspect and open to ridicule. But the effects of clergy misbehavior is certainly one of them and has its own unique dimensions and impact. A fairly recent survey in *Newsweek* indicates that general public confidence in priesthood and ministry as a profession has taken a considerable plunge in recent years.

One comment making the rounds in clerical circles is indicative of many feelings: "The ministry used to be a low-stress, high-prestige vocation with guaranteed employment. Now it's a high-stress, low-prestige profession with absolutely no job protection."

In a given district, diocese, or synod a publicized case of clergy sexual abuse is likely to raise anxiety among many clergy and may even divide clergy from one another and from their judicatory head. There is often a strong undercurrent of support and sympathy for the accused clergyperson (less so if child abuse is involved), a kind of "there but for the grace of God go I" sentiment. If the bishop is perceived to be less than totally supportive and caring of the accused clergy, the relationships between the bishop and some clergy may be negatively affected.

And of course if an accusation is made—whether false or justified—the whole world of the clergyperson does indeed crumble. Job, vocation, and even marriage and family are put at risk, and all sorts of related crises are precipitated. Some clergy may worry about incidents long past and settled in their lives coming to light and creating havoc. Others may fear that past or present innocent and inadvertent words or actions might be misread by vulnerable or hostile people and a false accusation consequently be made against them. Though this is not beyond the realm of possibility, there is more fear among clergy in this regard than is actually warranted, in my opinion and experience. But it is the nature of fear that it is often irrational and exaggerated, especially when so much is likely to be at stake.

A more significant problem is that guilty offenders are sometimes "getting off" due to technicalities of law or circumstance that prevent appropriate disciplinary action. There is also a tendency among many clergy, especially before exposure to and general education on the whole range of subjects related to this issue, to automatically side with the accused and to disbelieve or minimize the charges of the complainant. Even though the climate is changing, this pervasive societal attitude is one that many clergy continue to share in. It may even prove to be a factor in impeding decisive action by the bishop, who usually needs the support of the clergy in order to take action against an often-popular but offending clergyperson.

Impact on Laity

The impact of this crisis on congregations, though usually seriously damaging, can sometimes be redeemed at least in part by careful and knowledgeable church response. It is the nature of clergy sexual exploitation that it involves a betrayal of some very basic elements of the exercise of ministry. Since clergy, whether they recognize it or not, bear much symbolic power and authority, much of it associated in people's minds and hearts with the power and authority of God in very deep and personal ways, when boundaries with parishioners are crossed, spiritual damage results.[4] Many have noted that clergy sexual exploitation in the Church is similar to incest in the family, so deep are the wounds.

Not only do primary victims often lose faith in God and in the Church, so may other church members. Lay leaders in congregations where offending clergy have ministered often "burn out" as they try to manage the crisis—they themselves may become the targets of deflected anger and mistrust. It has been observed that many church-council (vestry) members leave a congregation during and after being involved in such crisis management. Some even leave the Church altogether, as may a number of other discouraged or disillusioned members.

Screening and Health Maintenance

Helping clergy understand the complex dynamics of transference and countertransference and enabling them to recognize and own the symbolic power they carry with them in the exercise

---

[4]Marie Fortune, *Is Nothing Sacred? When Sex Invades the Pastoral Relationship* (San Francisco: Harper & Row, 1987).

of ministry can often get at the heart of what the responsible exercise of good professional ministry looks like. Examination of clergy power and authority, where it comes from, and to whom clergy are accountable as they exercise it are issues that are at the heart of ordained leadership.

Many dioceses and other clergy organizations, in their examination of issues of clergy dysfunction, are becoming clearer about what good functioning consists of and how clergy can be assisted in the maintenance of a balance in their lives between work and recreation, between Church and family, and in the important connection between spiritual and psychological health. Facing into illness, in other words, is helping clergy understand what ministerial health consists of and how illness may be prevented. The maintenance of clergy health and well-being is an increasing concern in virtually all denominations.

Thus not all Church and clerical response to the challenge of clergy misbehavior has been defensive by any means. There are creative support systems for clergy and clergy families being developed in many denominations. It is being recognized that the job of religious leader is indeed a particularly demanding one fraught with risk and danger as well as joy and fulfillment. That many clergy may need more help and support from the church system in which they serve is an important learning.

Likewise, issues of more careful evaluation and screening of those presenting themselves for ordination or seminary are arising in many denominations. While many recognize the important and obvious truth that perfection not only is not required but impossible of attainment for clergy or anyone else for that matter, a number of people who are drawn to professional ministry may bring with them significant character deficits, which if not addressed can make them vulnerable to boundary violations of all sorts. Mark Laaser has said that he feels a number of people are drawn to ordained ministry seeking some sort of deep ontological healing for past behavior, or arising from early childhood experiences (especially of sexual or physical abuse) or other personality deficits.[5] Ordination obviously does not automatically

---

[5]Mark Laaser, *The Secret Sin: Healing the Wounds of Sexual Addiction* (Grand Rapids: Zondervan, 1991).

bring about that healing and in fact may exacerbate such feelings. The Church in general and those who train clergy in particular are not as naive about many "calls" to ordained ministry as once was the case; however, the general lack of truly effective screening instruments remains a serious problem.

Financial Impact on Churches

It is extremely difficult to put any sort of dollar figure on the cost to Churches for this crisis. The obvious and most notorious cost is related to various civil suits in which judges and/or juries have been willing to award substantial amounts to aggrieved church members. At any given time most denominations stand exposed to millions of dollars in claims, some said to be approaching billions over a period of ten years or so. Not all of these claims are found justified in court, of course, and if so found may be settled for less than initially claimed in the suit. In addition, a substantial number of cases are settled out of court and never reach public attention. It is important to note here that the primary cause of these expenses is not the suits themselves and the subsequent damages awarded but the offending behavior of some clergy, to which the suits are often a response of last resort.

However, there are many less obvious economic factors that must be taken into account. If one adds up the actual time spent on a given case by those managing the crisis, costs for travel, for psychological and medical evaluation and counseling of the accused clergy and families, incidental attorney's fees, phone calls, the cost to congregations for supply clergy, for terminal-leave settlements for clergy and for appropriate pastoral care of accusers, various meeting expenses, consultant's fees and education and training programs, the costs of case management are seen to be very high indeed. In addition, some officials note that total income to a church in the throes of one of these crises frequently drops markedly.

It can safely be assumed that the larger denominations have several (more likely, many) of these situations running simultaneously or sequentially. Especially in these times of decreasing financial support and generally rising expenses, which most denominations are experiencing, the financial impact of clergy abuse can be a significant negative factor in overall denominational functioning. But the costs to church leaders involve much more than finances.

Effect on Church Leaders

It is difficult to obtain any concrete data on the direct effect of having to manage these crises on the souls and psyches of those people who are responsible for the management of them. Those usually responsible beyond the local level are likely to be the denominational judicatory head and senior support staff. Sometimes there are staff persons with special portfolios designated to assist with a response, as for example, persons with pastoral or clinical counseling training. Often there is a response team to which different dimensions of a crisis are delegated and divided among specially trained individuals.

But the ultimate management of the whole case falls almost invariably to the "bishop," the person who is overseer and chief pastor of the whole denominational or regional system. Such leaders are immeasurably helped by having a good understanding of the needs of laity who may have been injured by clergy as well as of clergy who may be justly (or unjustly) accused of sexual misbehavior. Such knowledge does not come about automatically but must be obtained through special education and experience. The bishop and senior staff are essentially accountable for helping the church to become, as James Poling puts it in his helpful theological treatment of this subject, "a loving community that is both inclusive and just."[6]

Thus pastoral care includes more than helping and defending clergy. It may also mean holding clergy accountable to their vows, to God, and to the Church and society as well as providing comfort, support, and care in time of trouble. Sometimes the most pastoral thing a bishop can do is to help—to force, if necessary—clergy to face up to their transgressions, personal problems, and aberrant behavior.

Not only does individual church polity affect the way this pastoral ministry is exercised, but each individual church leader manages and interprets the issues according to his or her own

[6]James Poling, *The Abuse of Power: A Theological Problem* (Nashville: Abingdon, 1991).

personal understanding and experience. We all bring our own unique baggage to this subject, which each of us must try to be as cognizant of as possible so that we don't negatively impact others with our own unresolved issues. It is by no means unheard of that bishops and other church officials, as either perpetrators or victims, have their own present or past experiences of exploitation, harassment, or abuse to come to grips with. That this may affect their responding to such behavior in others is obvious. At the very time of this writing I have the task of trying to convince a bishop that a tearful "confession" of a serial pedophile should not be taken solely at face value and that he must do more than simply absolve the clergyman and allow him to continue his work in the church with young people. One wonders if the bishop has read any newspapers at all in the last five years.

Thus there are many issues that a church leader may need to consider and deal with personally before (or while) trying creatively and sensitively to manage a specific crisis. The situation is not so much one of "physician, heal thyself" as it is of "pastor, work on understanding your own personal issues," one of which may be a very serious lack of knowledge.

Common Issues Judicatory Officials Experience

One of the many double binds for bishops and most senior judicatory personnel is that they are at once both pastor and judge to accused or troubled clergy. In addition they are appropriately seen (and see themselves) as pastor not only to clergy but to the whole community of faith, including the complainant. This gives rise to deeply conflicted and unclear expectations that are often difficult to sort out, let alone to respond to effectively.

I vividly remember one occasion on which I had to confront a clergyman with allegations of having sexual relations with a parishioner. It was particularly difficult for us both, since we had enjoyed a close friendship. When he admitted the charge, I asked him, "Why didn't you come to me sooner; I, your friend and your bishop?" He answered, sobbing, "I wanted to come to you as my friend, but I was afraid to because you're my bishop." Clearly the role of bishop was, for him anyway, an impediment to receiving the pastoral care he needed and, at some level, desired.

Furthermore, speaking for the Episcopal Church at least, there is a notable lack of clarity in the minds of many clergy about what it means for the bishop to be pastor—a term most clergy value highly for themselves and have many personal meanings and behaviors around. For many it seems to mean flatly that "the bishop should be there for me whenever I need him/her, no matter what I have done, for he/she is my helper and defender."

This issue of pastoral role, image, and function is central to effective management of clergy sexual misconduct. It is not unusual for the accused clergyperson to be a personal friend of the bishop and/or in charge of a prominent and influential congregation. Out-of-bounds clergy are by no means always the ineffective and most needy ones. Sometimes the most serious offenses are committed by those who are very competent and much loved and admired by their congregants and the community at large. The actual and symbolic authority of the judicatory head may pale with respect to that held by the accused clergyperson.

Common Sources of Personal Stress

Confused Expectations

As I have indicated, the bishop or other leader is a focal point for conflicting expectations: by accused clergy, their families, or their supporters, but also by the complainant and his or her supporters, by the congregations in which the offenses or alleged offenses took place, by the whole diocese (synod, district), and even by the larger secular community.

The accuser wants just complaints heard and matters set right; the accused wants to be protected from harm; the Church wants the matter solved quickly and set to rest. All expect to see justice done. But justice (and love) may mean different things according to one's own personal perspective.

This means that from the start judicatory leaders are bound to handle some things inadequately or wrongly in several people's eyes. They are second-guessed with great intensity, even by those who have reasonably accurate information about what the facts of a given situation are. They are open to criticism, often vicious, by those who have incomplete or erroneous information about the case, which is usually most people. Sometimes bishops themselves do not have reliable information or access to good advice and counsel, or they do not appropriately seek it out. And few people who have not been in the bishop's shoes understand that at every turn there are soul-searing Catch-22s to be faced by those managing the crisis.

Psychological profiles of many clergy indicate that they tend toward perfectionism, that most have a pretty high need to be liked, and that most don't like conflict at all and will try to avoid it at all cost. We are thus describing a situation many leaders experience as one of high personal stress.

Truth Telling

A primary ingredient in responding well to these problems is open communication and truth telling. Many authorities make the case that telling what truth can responsibly be told and breaking the power of the secret is a primary path toward individual and systemic healing.

In many church systems the norm until quite recently has been just the opposite. We have covered up, protected the clergy and their professional status, blamed the complainant, and not taken him or her seriously. We have tried to protect the institution from scandal and harm by keeping our members in the dark and treating them, some have said, like children.

New norms are taking the place of the old ones: take the complainant seriously and try to meet his or her valid requests; act on reasonable *prima facie* evidence; seek the truth and tell the truth that can be told; hold clergy accountable when they injure those who have trusted them; focus on trying to understand and change the institution through broad education on the issues.

Even though there is evidence that a cover-up makes everything worse for everyone, truth telling is usually a hard item to sell to some people. Resistance to truth telling often goes with denial: it didn't happen; he didn't do it; it was her fault; it wasn't so bad; telling will only make matters worse; our church will be destroyed if people find out. While these are well-meaning responses, they arise largely from ignorance and irrational fear.

But when one tells the truth that can be told, the crisis manager appears to lose even more control over what is usually felt to be an already chaotic situation. "The truth will set you free" is an accurate enough aphorism in the long run. "But first it will give you fits," could well be added.

Pilate's cynical question of Jesus is also relevant here: "What is truth?" Or, whose truth is it that you are hearing and telling, the offender's or the complainant's? Truth in these situations is often an elusive commodity and, if eventually found, is sometimes found not to be simple. And often the truth is painful even to talk about. Also, the bishop may feel that he or she knows the truth but for any number of reasons cannot get it to the point where it can be revealed, as when an innocent person would be revictimized or when an obvious (but popular) offender denies credible charges outright and stonewalls to the end. Clergy usually have a high commitment to truth and like to believe they can know what it is, especially if it is religious or moral truth. To be forced into a situation where they may have to make decisions without having "the whole truth and nothing but the truth" is not a comfortable spot to be in. All of which adds up to more personal stress for the manager.

Control Issues

For clergy who expend considerable effort trying to keep their lives and jobs under reasonable control, there is also troubling news. Few of us like unpleasant surprises, and these crises are guaranteed to be seedbeds for surprises. Bishops may need—here and elsewhere in their lives—to learn to let go of the need to feel in control—wise advice indeed from the AA community. Rabbi Edwin Friedman in his book *Generation to Generation* speaks about a leader's "nonanxious presence" in crises.[7] The leader tries to stay connected to people and their needs but also tries not to be internally panicked, triangulated, or captured by them. And some people do try aggressively to capture and triangulate leaders.

But Friedman's term "nonanxious" can be misleading. Of course we may feel anxious when things get out of control. One can't do away with anxiety by denying its presence. The point is

[7]Edwin Friedman, *Generation to Generation: Family Process in Church and Synagogue* (New York: Guilford, 1985).

not to let our anxiety control or manage us to the extent we become either overinvolved or inappropriately distanced from the crisis. (Most of us have an innate tendency to react one way or the other to crises and conflicts.) But this kind of mature behavior is a tough order that calls for good emotional and spiritual resources, clear personal boundaries, and an understanding of one's own personal style. It also means being in touch with one's own deficits and valid needs.

No matter how we handle it, another guaranteed stress point is that if the bishop does things right and appropriately reveals the facts of the case, he or she may lose even more control of an already chaotic situation. And people will expect the church leader to control the damage being done to individuals and to the Church at large.

Timing Issues

A common expectation held by most persons involved in these crises is that they should not only be dealt with quietly but also quickly. I've touched on the "quietly," now let me address the "quickly."

The longer these matters drag on, the more opportunity there is for the unexpected to happen; the more letters or demands for appointments from angry and injured people for the bishop to respond to, the more complicated everything gets. One issue seems to merge with another. These crises have a way of developing their own momentum, sometimes even spinning secondary crises off from the primary situation. People on all sides become frustrated and the process itself becomes a target. Positions for and against the clergy and complainant harden into armed camps. And the longer things last, the more likelihood there is that errors in judgment will be made.

But time also has a way of allowing the real issues to surface; people may begin to become a bit clearer about what they need and want and about what is possible of achievement. This is especially true of complainants who have access to good counseling and advice, of congregations that have good help, and of some offending clergy who honestly face the implications of their behaviors.

So, a rapid resolution, sought after by most, can actually be an enemy, though its opposite, a careful and deliberate process, is not always an early ally. The truth is that these issues can rarely be settled quickly, no matter what one does. And often, when one thinks matters are settled, they arise again in new form. I find bringing closure to many situations of serious clergy exploitation a very elusive goal. Thus there is more stress for those managing the process, namely the executive and his or her helpers.

Deflected Anger

It is a common experience that church leaders become the focal point for a great deal of free-floating rage when they enter these situations. Most people involved feel powerless, victimized, used, betrayed, injured, by one or more persons they have trusted or by the Church in general. These powerful internal feelings often take the form of generalized anger. And it is frequently directed at bishops and their staff people as well as at the congregational staff and at lay leaders and others who are "just trying to help."

This same anger may also be directed at complainants and sometimes, in inappropriate ways, at the perpetrator. It is not pleasant to feel the brunt of it, whether by letter or phone call, in interpersonal situations, or in larger congregational groups. It is often devastating, especially when one has been trying hard to understand and be of help. One particularly difficult circumstance arises when the spouse, usually the wife of a clergyman who has clearly offended, tries to protect him out of her own personal fear, denial, and co-dependance. Then the bishop may well be seen as the enemy of the priest and the family and be treated as such. This may even happen when the clergyman admits to charges.

Sometimes, of course, church leaders do make bad mistakes, and people are appropriately angry. It may, more than occasionally, happen that the bishop also feels that the anger of the victim at the Church (and at him or her) is valid, that he or she ought indeed to take more or different action but is prevented from doing so for legal or technical reasons. This is another particularly difficult bind. But stressful though it is, if one can listen to, feel, and stand with the person expressing the anger, a door toward eventual healing may open. I have in my memory a letter from one particularly intuitive and articulate victim who, it felt to me, blamed me for everything bad that had ever happened to her in her life, and for making matters much worse by what she experienced as my grossly inadequate response to her demands and needs. I felt, and still feel, that I and those with whom I worked had done a good job for her under difficult circumstances. In a personal meeting she raged and cursed and cried out in violent anguish—at me even more than at her primary offender.

My initial response was to feel personally wounded and badly misunderstood, but either by grace or total confusion or both I said nothing defensive to her; I tried to keep appropriate eye contact with her and to make it clear that I was listening; that was all I could do. She left the meeting a shaking, emptied shell. Months later a letter came from her telling me about her beginning recovery and the pivotal role my reception of her anguish had played. Of course it was not so much I who was the target of it, but the Church, which she rightly associated with my person and her own pain. As far as I know, however, she still has not returned to the Church.

I hope my point is being made that managing cases of clergy misbehavior is often a very stressful activity for bishops and other church leaders and those who assist them. In their little scale that helps individuals "quantify" personal stress, the Alban Institute lists dealing with cases of clergy sexual exploitation as secondary in degree of stress only to the death of a spouse. Many bishops are dealing with several of these problems at a time, and over a long period of time.

One Methodist bishop said to me at a meeting, with a strong note of frustration in his voice, "I did not become a bishop just to spend major portions of my most productive years picking up the pieces after clergy sexual abuse!" Another leader remarked, "I am spending far too much of my time on the results of clergy sexual problems, and most of them took place long before I came into this [leadership] position." Still another bishop commented: "I consider myself a good, experienced pastor, but I often find myself unable to respond or responding only barely adequately to what are justified pastoral needs of victims. I am damned if I do, and damned if I don't."

Comments like these obviously raise all sorts of issues regarding leadership stress management, self-care, self-knowledge, and other practices that can lead not only to personal health maintenance but also to effective job performance. Let me say again that it is crucial for church leaders who deal with these issues to do so in close contact with others not only for more effective crisis management but also for the interpersonal support that such a team approach alone can give.

An Important Emerging Concern

There is a fairly widespread assumption that all instances of serious sexual misbehavior by clergy are essentially similar and must therefore be resolved in the same way: invariably by dismissal upon determination of guilt from ministerial functioning. Such an automatic assumption is a mistake. It is also a mistake to assume that the offender will ordinarily be restored to full ministerial functioning after the fulfillment of certain minimal or vague conditions, such as a six-month period of therapy.

It can safely be stated that no two cases of clergy sexual offense are identical. Unless we are to conclude that this type of offense is an "unforgivable sin," we must give careful consideration to each situation as we try to be faithful to God's call to the Churches to be forgiving communities living in hope of transformation and in the knowledge of redemption and resurrection.

Such hope for renewal can only be sustained by moving into— and eventually by grace, through—much of the pain that inevitably resuls from incidents of clergy boundary violations. The temptation toward an easy abdication of responsibility for dealing with extremely complex matters must be resisted. The natural urge toward compassion for offending clergy must be carefully balanced with compassion for those who have been injured and concern for the administration of justice for all parties, so far as that is possible.

The question can then be phrased this way: Is it ever possible for a member of the clergy who is truly recovering from sexual offenses to be restored to ministerial functioning, and if so, under what conditions? The key phrase, of course, is "truly recovering." How can one provide reasonable assurance that a convicted and/or confessed offender's efforts in recovery are having a truly positive impact that will prevent further offenses from taking place? It is not always easy to tell!

One further general point: a number of authorities make a broad distinction between offending sexual behavior that is predatory (and usually repetitive with more than one victim) and situational behavior, which is occasioned by unusual stress or other particular circumstances. There is substantial agreement that predatory and/or repetitive offenses are very serious in nature and are likely to result in a much less hopeful outlook for eventual restoration to exercise of ministry. It is an easy and dangerous mistake to confuse predatory and situational offenses. Careful investigation into all the circumstances, including in-depth medical evaluation of the accused, is virtually always advised when credible accusations are made.

Below is a list of ten conditions necessary for favorable consideration of restoration to active ministry by a recovering clergy sexual offender. The list is not exhaustive; there are likely to be additional issues that arise in specific cases. And even if all are conscientiously fulfilled they do not guarantee an absolutely risk-free result.

1. The recovering offender admits wrongdoing.

   Not infrequently deeper understanding of responsibility for the wrongdoing and the full nature of its impact on self and others, as opposed to a mere superficial admission of guilt, is a process that evolves over time with expert therapeutic assistance.

2. The recovering offender cooperates willingly with any imposed discipline.

   "Willing cooperation" may also grow over time. It is important that therapy not be confused or equated with discipline and that there are no unresolved, pending, or anticipated criminal, civil, or ecclesiastical actions involving the clergyperson.

3. The offender participates willingly in individual, family, and/or group therapy, as deemed appropriate. Formal spiritual direction may also be appropriate.

Participation in therapy is often a difficult and painful process. It is normal for participation to be resisted at some points and more willingly sought at others.

4. The recovering offender willingly attempts to make amends to any injured individuals or communities.

Often amends can only be made partially, sometimes not at all or not until some future date. Making amends may always remain a potential action, depending primarily on the timing and needs of any victims(s) and on other circumstances outside the direct control of the offender.

5. The recovering offender gives strong evidence of having learned about his or her own psychological issues and personal psychosexual dynamics.

The actual offending behavior is always connected to other life issues and must be examined and understood in the larger context.

6. The recovering offender understands and cooperates with any safeguards and/or conditions connected with return to the exercise of ministry.

Rarely is a recovering offender restored without some continuing conditions and/or controls for his or her protection as well as for the protection of the community at large.

7. The recovering offender receives an evaluation from an appropriately accredited institution and/or therapist indicating that he or she is not at risk to repeat the offending behavior.

Sometimes this conclusion is reached upon initial evaluation and treatment, sometimes afterwards. Sometimes such an institution or therapist cannot or will not make a clear statement about risk of repeat offense.

This evaluation may include but never be exclusively limited to the evaluation of the cleric's personal therapist.

A statement that the risk of repeat offense is high must be considered a major negative factor in coming to any favorable decision about eventual return to ministry.

Not infrequently more than one formal evaluation may be indicated. Some church insurers have underwriting guidelines in this as well as in other areas.

8. The "community" in which the recovering offender intends to exercise ministry is informed as fully as possible about the circumstances of the offense(s) and comes to substantive agreement about the offender's return to ministry.

People who may receive a recovering offender's ministry have a right to know as much about the situation as possible; however, protection of innocent persons must always be kept in mind. Presumably, opinions about the recovering offender's return to ministry will not be unanimous.

Though any primary victim(s) of the offender's ministry will presumably not continue to be recipients of the recovering cleric's ministry, it is important that such persons be informed and consulted in advance about any intended return to ministry.

9. The recovering offender personally desires to return to the exercise of ministry and understands the issues and problems likely to be connected to that return.

This means that the recovering offender has seriously considered other vocational options and still feels a call to public ordained ministry. The cleric fully recognizes that such a continuing call needs to be affirmed by the Church through appropriate channels for it to be exercised.

10. The recovering cleric has ready access to ongoing support systems and gives evidence of willingness to make regular use of them.

Ongoing support systems are not intended to be merely passive. Support persons will seek out ways to give support and care to recovering persons.

Finally, most of these factors require careful use of informed pastoral judgment by the supervisor at many points. It is important that such judgment be exercised in consultation with other appropriate and experienced persons.

A Systems Approach

One of the valuable contributions the present volume makes to this complex field of concern is that it implies and encourages an overall systems response to incidents of clergy sexual malfeasance. This is crucially important not only because there are many inter-related issues in such crises but also because each party to a particular incident has his or her own "truth" and natural biases. Injured persons see things one way, the accused clergyperson has a very different perspective, as do the families involved, the congregation, the public, and so on.

The judicatory head and staff are the primary persons who should have a good concept of the ways the various parties in an incident of sexual exploitation are likely to view an abusive event and an understanding of the particular issues and needs of each: what the common dimensions are of the damage to victims, what they need to receive from the Church, and what their goals are likely to be in a given case.

Likewise, accused clergy and their families, whether finally found guilty or innocent, have their own set of common perspectives, needs, issues, and vulnerabilities. The same things can be said of the congregation, other clergy in the system, the public in general, and so forth.

It is the church judicatory head whose goal it must be to develop a systemic perspective of the crisis in which the various elements can be conceptualized in relation to one another and to the whole. An instance of clergy sexual exploitation is itself a systems problem, and piecemeal attempts to respond to it will not be very successful. It is also obvious that human sexuality is a central ingredient in all human thinking, feeling, and acting. Broad educational efforts are essential for effective crisis response, as well as for long-term prevention. Having a broad conceptual model and a systems approach will also help an institution discover the holes and deficits in its own system and can indicate where particular assistance from outside may be advisable.

Furthermore, as a person who is primarily involved at the initial intervention and crisis level of the Church's response, I find it easy for feelings of discouragement and cynicism to arise in me. I usually see the incidents in their early discovery and hence at the furthest point from resolution. It is personally helpful to me, therefore, to stay in good communication with those who are in the long-term healing side of our Church's response. In this way I can experience through their somewhat different perspectives that people and communities do indeed from time to time move beyond pain and pathology into recovery and health. It is also important to me to be personally involved in efforts toward furthering education for prevention and not solely in crisis management.

A systems problem requires a systems analysis and a systemic response. That generally important principle is nowhere so relevant as in this field of trying to understand and minister effectively in occasions of clergy sexual misconduct.

The Offender's Family

Ann Legg
Derek Legg

"And so there is no division in the body, but all its different parts have the same concern for one another. If one part of the body suffers, all the other parts suffer with it" (1 Cor 12:25-26).

Introduction

The family of the clergyperson who has been a sexual offender is truly a primary victim of his or her betrayal. The spouse has suffered a betrayal of the marriage vows, a betrayal of trust in an intimate partner, loss of reputation, loss of role in their church and community, and sometimes even loss of faith in God. If there are children, they suffer the loss of a secure family and faithful parents, loss of reputation, and possible loss of their school and friends. Parents and siblings of the offending person may suffer humiliation, grief, loss of reputation and friends.

Chris, a musician and the divorced wife of a former Protestant minister, still suffers from depression and the loss of her marriage six years after her husband was banned from the ministry.

Mary Lou, wife of a Lutheran pastor, died of breast cancer four years after her husband was dismissed from his church and removed from the clergy roster.

Sarah, twenty-year-old daughter of a terminated Baptist minister, had to drop out of college because there was no longer enough money, even with her financial aid.

Andy, fifteen-year-old son of a Methodist minister, was arrested for a drug-related burglary two years after his dad was charged with sexual abuse of three teenage boys. He never told his parents that his best friend's parents forbade their son to ever see him again when the news of his father's misconduct became public.

Catherine, age sixty-two, died of cancer two years after her oldest son was forced out of the Catholic priesthood. She did not speak to him from the time of his removal until her death.

All of the individuals above are real people[1] whose husband, son, or father was removed from the church he was serving because he crossed a sexual boundary. It is this group, the family of the offending clergy, that, over and over again, is paid least attention to. They are fairly dramatic examples of family members of clergy removed from parishes because of sexual misconduct, but they are by no means unique. We have seen countless people with similar stories in our psychotherapy practice with ministerial families. We have come to believe that these painful events are directly related to the trauma of this betrayal of trust by the pastor.

We must point out that in our practice every offender except one was male. The exception was a clergy wife who directed the music program of a large church and had an affair with a choir member. This resulted in such an upheaval in the church that even her divorcing husband was forced to resign. In another case the object of the pastor's sexual misconduct was a fellow female pastor (who was not our client), but her identity was never revealed and she remained in her parish as the sole pastor. Therefore, when we talk about clergy and spouse, we will refer to them as "he" and "she" respectively.

Under normal circumstances when a pastor is relieved of his parish, the pain suffered by his wife and family is severe.[2] When the dismissal is due to sexual malfeasance, the emotional upheaval is compounded. The emotional ripple effect is felt hardest

---

[1]All names of clients are changed, and in some cases their stories are composites.

[2]For a discussion of forced termination see Edward Bratcher, *The Walk on Water Syndrome* (Waco: Word, 1984); Rodney Crowell, *Musical Pulpits: Clergy and Laypersons Face the Issues of Forced Exit* (Baker, 1992); Brooks Faulkner, *Forced Termination* (Nashville: Broadman, 1986); Myra Marshall, Dan McGee, and Jennifer Owen, *Beyond Termination: A Spouse's Story of Pain and Healing* (Nashville: Broadman, 1990).

by those who are closest. When these families do get attention, it is usually negative and very hurtful. Several common themes stand out when we review the case notes of the pastoral families we have worked with or have interviewed for this volume.

Common Themes

Betrayal

The first and most obvious theme, of course, is the marital betrayal of the spouse by the pastor. There are countless books, articles, plays, operas, and country western songs analyzing, theorizing, apologizing, and agonizing about infidelity and the betrayal of intimacy.[3] As far as the marriage is concerned, it really doesn't matter who the object of the violation is—another woman, a man, or a child of either sex. Infidelity is "breach of the trust, a betrayal of a relationship, a breaking of an agrement," and "the primary disrupter of families, the most dreaded and devastating experience in a marriage."[4]

Marital therapy is important whether the couple divorces or remains together. Of the ministerial families we have followed for up to ten years, the majority of marriages remained intact. A few ended therapy with separation and divorce, but in these cases the husband secretly had made up his mind to leave the marriage because the marriage had been bad for a long time, and the "other woman" simply rescued him from depression and unhappiness. These men, for the most part, married the "other woman." In a few cases, such as Chris', the wives remained faithful to their vows for religious reasons and for the sake of the children. They tried to make the marriage last but in the end were unable to recover a healthy relationship. As far as we know, none of those couples removed from their parishes because of adult homosex-

---

[3]For example, Tolstoy's *Anna Karenina*, Albee's *Who's Afraid of Virginia Woolf*, Mozart's *Abduction from the Seraglio*, Shakespeare's *Hamlet*, Verdi's *Otello*; songs such as "Guess Who I Saw Today," "I Was Married by the Bible and Divorced by the Law," "Your Cheating Heart," "It's a Sin to Tell a Lie"; Pittman's *Private Lies*, Schneider's *Back from Betrayal*.

[4]Frank Pittman, "What Price Camelot," *The Family Therapy Networker* (May/June 1989) 22. This issue has a special section, "Infidelity: A Loss of Innocence."

ual contacts, pedophilia, or ephebophilia divorced immediately. Pedophilia is sexual attraction to preadolescent children; ephebophilia is sexual attraction to adolescent children. There are far more cases of opposite-sex attraction to any age child than of same-sex attraction. We can only speculate that the relatively few cases of divorce in these instances are because the marriage may represent the only place of support in this very painful crisis. We cannot speak to how healthy or happy these relationships have been over time. Except for giving initial support or providing individual or marital therapy, the health of the marital relationship is not an ongoing concern of the church they have left.

Loss of Status and Role

A second theme, and one that demands a long period of grieving and healing, is the loss of status and role and the concomitant shame and humiliation. When the betrayal occurs in a clergy family, the damage is quite likely to be devastating because of the unique position of that family. This is a family in a fishbowl, carefully watched and often owned by the congregation. When the clergyperson is called by the parish, the family often comes along as a package, with all the expectations and demands that paradoxically might be placed both on a servant and on a leader of unquestionable virtue. Roy Oswald has said, "The clergy wife tends to be seen as the resident 'holy woman'; after all she lives with the resident 'holy man.' She's a walking target for everyone's unconscious expectations of what holy women ought to be like."[5] Barbara Gilbert concurs with Oswald's description of the clergy wife as being expected to take an active role but given no power. She writes, "She's never expected to take a stand on controversial issues—never run for public office in church—to dress properly and be silent—to be a 'holy noodlehead.'"[6]

The clergy wife may frequently see her calling as that of a servant. In extreme cases her entire identity is wrapped up in her role as the pastor's wife. She may play it as the handmaiden who

[5]Roy Oswald, "Why Do Clergy Wives Burn Out?" (Washington: Alban Institute, 1984) 11.

[6]Barbara Gilbert, "Who Ministers to the Ministers?" (Washington: Alban Institute, 1987) 12.

does the bidding of every member of the congregation as well as of her husband, or she may see her role as "mother" of the congregation—to teach, discipline, and nurture them. In some cases she may have a titled role such as music director and organist or Sunday school superintendent. Or she may simply have lived her life in the parish through her husband with no position, role, or identity of her own. Whichever the case, when her husband has to leave the church she also has to leave and loses her identity and often her reason for being.

Chris is a pretty typical pastor's ex-wife who is still struggling to recover after six years. She said, "I loved what was expected of the pastor's wife. I was already married to the church through my music. Marrying Jonathon when he was in seminary was my perfect dream." When they were asked to leave their church, she said, "I lost my personhood—who I am." She felt she had her own ministry in the church, her music, through which she was "serving, loving, caring for people." It was her greatest loss. In her case, as in many, the severance was abrupt. She had been preparing the choirs for the annual gala spring concert for several months when she was told her husband had been fired and they were to leave the church immediately. She didn't even know why at that point. She didn't get to finish the preparation or see the choirs perform.

As is often the case, the wife's only real friend and spiritual leader is her husband. Loyalty to the marriage and limitations on sharing with friends because of her husband's position gives her fewer outlets or sources of support. Because he has been disgraced in the eyes of God, the church hierarchy, and members of the congregation and because he is probably in spiritual, moral, and emotional turmoil, she has no place to turn for support and sustenance. She is left twisting in the storm, full of humiliation, anger, hurt, and fear. She has lost face and status. Sometimes, without her spiritual guide, her husband, she loses the way in her faith and may even give up on God. She certainly has periods of anger at God.

Economic Issues

A third theme causing great stress for the pastor's wife and family is the issue of economics. In most denominations severance packages are negotiated but are minimal. Crowell,[7] in writing about forced terminations in general, says that ninety days is the severance norm and only 33 percent receive emergency pay from the denomination. Some churches express their anger through money, and since sexual sin is very anger provoking, the minister's family suffers from the withholding of money. This is an obvious example of the family being punished even though it has committed no wrongdoing.

Regular income has ended for this family unless the wife is employed outside the church. Since her husband, whose career is now on hold, cannot go on to a new call and in extreme cases may be in jail, it falls to her to find gainful employment to support the family. She may or may not be prepared to do this, and even if she is, given the pay inequalities for women, she will be in the well-known position of the single parent with a lowered standard of living.

An exacerbating factor is that many clergy live in church-provided parsonages. When the job is over, the home is gone. Besides this sudden loss is the anxiety and additional expense of finding a new place to live. More and more pastors, particularly in urban areas, are buying their own homes, but they depend on the housing stipend for mortgage payments. One suburban family we know not only lost their income but their home too. The down payment for their house had been advanced by the congregation. In its anger, the congregation called the loan immediately.

Chris reported that at first neighbors and friends in the church brought groceries and sometimes meals to her house. She was very grateful, because there were times when they literally were hungry. But with every gift and every visitor she had to swallow her pride and face the shame and humiliation of her predicament. Before long all of the visits and gifts ended, and she was alone in her grief. "I became invisible," she said. "One time I was talking to a friend at the grocery store when the senior pastor of our church came by. He greeted my friend, asked how she was doing and completely ignored me as if I wasn't there."

---

[7]Crowell, *Musical Pulpits.*

Illness

When one's life is totally in the church (in rural and small-town parishes there is little other life), the wife loses her friends and her support group. She may lose her recreation and hobby partners. Mary Lou, in therapy with us before she died, said she had lost intimacy with old friends because she could no longer share her soul, her inside person, with anybody—it was too risky. With-out the resources of her normal support community, the wife becomes isolated and is a good candidate for depression and illness. This is true for other members of the pastor's family as well. Illness, then is the fourth theme in the list of damages suffered by the offender's family.

Catherine was a devout Catholic, very active in her parish and very proud of her firstborn son, David, who had been a favorite priest in the diocese. He was charged with sexually abusing three teenage girls in his parish and was subsequently laicized. Catherine was shamed. Her only defense was to deny her son's very existence, but the pain and grief continued. Priests she had become close to, through David, shunned her. Right after David was ex-posed in the media, Catherine developed cancer. The discs in her spine kept collapsing. Her doctor worked to get her to process her grief. She refused and died without forgiving or forgiveness.

We would like to say more about stress-induced illness because we think it is too often overlooked when considering the impact on the offender's family. According to Cramer and Keitel,[8] involuntary job loss is ranked among the most stressful of stressors. They go on to say that the stages of job loss are very similar to the stages of grief and that the person who is rendered unemployed, as well as his family, suffers serious threat to health, both physical and mental. Cramer and Keitel's long list of effects of dislocation and unemployment include high blood pressure, debilitating anxiety, displaced anger and aggression toward others, devalued self-esteem, irrational thinking, overexaggerated self-aggrandizement, depression and withdrawal leading to work in-

[8]Stanley Cramer and Merle Keitel, "Family Effects of Dislocation, Unemployment, and Discouragement," *Perspectives on Work and the Family,* ed. Stanley Cramer (Rockville, Md.: Aspen, 1984).

hibition, helplessness and emotional vulnerability, excessive dependency, and occupational rigidity or inability to role-change.

The effects of stress have been studied by many, including Borysenko[9] and Rossi.[10] They show the relationship between stressful life events and mind-body reactions, examples of which we mentioned at the beginning of this essay. David and Vera Mace[11] discuss several studies indicating that ministers and their spouses often have difficulty confronting their anger and are therefore more likely to repress their anger and hurt than to express it. This very act may create a metabolic shift, elevating heart rate, blood pressure, and body temperature.[12] The body, then, is acting as if it were chronically fighting a disease. In 1984 another study[13] reported that the cells critical to the immune system for warding off disease—the lymphocytes—were considerably decreased in number, for example, in men enduring the stress of being married to women dying of cancer. Gilbert[14] points out in her study that pastors' wives are the "primary absorbers of their husbands' problems," 75 percent reporting they suffered from depression.[15] Because they tend to be more isolated than other wives, they have few if any outlets for the stress they absorb; in turn, they are likely to suffer from more illnesses and to pass the anxiety to their children and other family members. For a poignant account of a clergy wife's story of termination, see Marshall.[16]

Blame

Another difficulty talked about by all of the wives was the reaction of the families of origin. Shame, of course, extended to

[9]Joan Borysenko, *Minding the Body, Mending the Mind* (Reading, Pa.: Addison-Wesley, 1987).

[10]Ernest Rossi, *The Psychobiology of Mind-Body Healing: New Concepts of Therapeutic Hypnosis* (New York: Norton, 1986).

[11]David Mace and Vera Mace, *What's Happening to Clergy Marriages?* (Nashville: Broadman, 1980).

[12]"Resolving of Emotional Pain May Trigger Physical Growth in Adults," *Brain/Mind Bulletin*, vol. 5 (May 19, 1980).

[13]"New Story of Science Including Mind in the World," *Brain/Mind Bulletin*, vol. 10 (December 10, 1984).

[14]Gilbert, "Who Ministers to the Ministers?" 31.

[15]Ibid., 11.

[16]Marshall, *Beyond Termination.*

many of these families, especially if they were active and devout members of their churches. Wives most often felt blamed by both their own parents and their spouse's parents. They either were not adequate as wives or they shouldn't have married these men in the first place. They got very little support for staying in the marriage. If they divorced, they were often shamed for their lack of moral fiber. If they became emotionally or financially dependent on their parents, they were treated like incompetent children. Several reported losing relationships with their siblings and extended families.

When male clergy acted out sexually, all of the wives reported that church gossip labeled them as frigid, inadequate women or as spoiled, self-centered children. This occurs, we believe, because some simply cannot blame their minister; therefore his wife must be at fault. The wife, who has already been a victim of her husband's betrayal, now becomes the victim of a second betrayal by members of the congregation. Mary Lou said, when this happened to her, "It would be easier to just be dead!"

Repercussions for Family

A final issue often spoken of by these clergy wives was their anxiety about their children. They felt totally responsible for the health and well-being of the children. They feared the treatment their children might receive at the hands of classmates, parents of friends, teachers, and others, and they were concerned about their children's ability to handle repercussions. They worried about their children's feelings about their father. Would they hate him, love him, lose respect for him, feel abandoned and betrayed by him? How should they handle all of these questions?

Chris reported that her three children never blamed their dad. In fact, she became "the bad guy" because, in an attempt to bring some balance, she tried to counter Jonathon's "using his children to be his best friend" after his dismissal, when his self-esteem was at its lowest. He confided in them, excused any misbehavior, gave them anything they wanted, and in general blurred any boundary between himself and them—much as he had with his victims.

The children themselves suffer most of the same losses as their parents: loss of security, home, financial support, friends and classmates, school, special situations such as achievements in scholastics, sports, music, and other extracurricular activities, and their church. They also might lose respect for their father. They often become parentified in their families, much as Chris and Jonathon's children were. They may become surrogate spouses for their parents. The children may come to believe that they are somehow responsible for their parents' feelings and well-being. It is not unusual for children to create crises in their families in order to pull the focus away from their parents' pain. One older teenage daughter said to us in a therapy session, "I had to be mom to the younger kids and even to mom and dad because they were both falling apart." In extreme cases children have become ill or depressed, have committed suicide, or have acted out antisocially, as Andy did. One perspicacious eight-year-old upon learning of her father's dismissal said, "Well, I guess we're not going to walk with the Lord anymore; he'll just have to carry us for awhile."

Parents' fears of their children suffering rejection are not unfounded. One high school youth was asked to move to a different English class by his teacher, who was a parishioner in his dad's church. Kids have been taunted, called obscene names, threatened with beatings and other punishments. The children's shame and humiliation is just as real as that of their parents. Lee Cameron discusses what happens to pastors' kids (PKs) when their father is terminated.[17] He says PKs feel victimized, bitter, and betrayed. They may not understand the reasons for their father's dismissal. The very people they may have trusted most become instrumental in their removal.

Finally, all the members of the offender's family are left with a legacy of anger and grief to live with, to process, to resolve well or badly. "It is not stress as such," LaBarre says, "but the psychic style of reaction to it that is important."[18] Unfortunately, clergy-people are often indoctrinated with the idea that anger is wrong and with the need to forgive and forget, which sometimes precludes owning the anger and being able to process it. Families of offending clergy may or may not be initially angry at the offender,

---

[17]Lee Cameron, *Helping Pastors' Kids Through Their Identity Crisis* (Grand Rapids: Zondervan, 1992) 169.

[18]Weston LaBarre, *The Ghost Dance: The Origins of Religion* (New York: Dell, 1972) 282.

depending on their ability to absorb the fact of his betrayal. But they will most assuredly be angry at his victims either for not telling right away or for telling at all, at the congregation, at the church hierarchy, and finally at God. Denial keeps them stuck in the anger and prevents them from going through the process of grieving for their losses.

Recovery

We believe that full recovery by the family requires the acceptance of all feelings surrounding their losses. For family members this recovery takes a lot of energy and a lot of time because the pain is so deep. One family member said that notwithstanding ten years of time and three years of therapy since she learned of the misconduct and had to leave her church, she still struggled with guilt feelings. She failed to come forward when she first suspected her husband because she feared being exposed and rejected. She longed to be able to talk to co-workers and new friends but couldn't risk it. Besides, she felt it would be disloyal to her husband. Chris said, "Sometimes I want to scream 'I didn't do it' because I've always felt punished for what I didn't do. I don't think we should have been told to leave our church, the kids and me. It wasn't fair." This is a major dilemma for the congregation and the church leaders. It may be that there can be no good solution for the offender's family because the congregation often splits in its position on removal of the pastor. In order to accommodate the healing of the congregation it is usually necessary that the family leave. It is hard to imagine that the continued presence of the family would not be a constant reminder of the pastor's behavior, thus causing the people to relive the shame over and over again.

If the wife remains with her husband and yet tries to stay in the congregation, the ability of the congregation to hear the details of his behavior and process their own grief in her presence probably will be greatly compromised. It is important to be clear with everyone that this painful reality for the cleric's family is just another result of the abusive behavior of the offending cleric and not the result of any subsequent decisions made by congregational or denominational officials. The only cases we are aware of in which the wife and family were not so dramatically affected when the pastor overstepped sexual boundaries were those in which the wife and family belonged to a congregation other than her husband's.

There are practical needs that must be supported. These include, for example, housing, groceries, possibly transportation, employment for the spouse, financial assistance. Once again, it is important to remember that family members are not guilty, but because of the nature of their position they are frequently totally dependent on the church, which may or must now deny them access to their spiritual home.

We learned during our follow-up phone survey for the purposes of this essay that reconciliation for Chris and Mary Lou—and countless other clergy wives—would have been provided by an opportunity to sit down at some point with willing members of the congregation to talk about the experience together. The wives wanted to be asked how they were doing. They wanted to be able to make amends for whatever they had done to hurt anybody. They wanted to be told that they were not the sinners. They wanted to be "somebody"—not the invisible nonentities they felt like in the church community.

Many immediate problems face the church congregation and the denomination hierarchy, if there is one in their polity. We would like to make a plea that they do not lose sight of and neglect the serious pain suffered by the family of the offending minister. We must remember that the family members are not the offenders; they are not guilty of the malfeasance.

There have been reports of officials calling the family together, including the children, to state the charges made and to excoriate the wife and children as well as the pastor for his behavior. This is cruel and inexcusable treatment. Children should never be included in this meeting for obvious reasons. They should be told what is happening by their parents, in detail appropriate to their age and understanding, with help if the parents feel they need it. The spouse definitely should be included because the problems are now hers to deal with in terms of the marriage, the children, and the congregation.

Depending on the charges, the pastor may have to be relieved of his duties until an investigation occurs. At a first meeting the ground rules for the behavior of the clergy couple—interaction with the congregation, participation in already scheduled activities for the wife and children, attendance at services, and so on—should be clearly delineated, with an opportunity for the couple to express their feelings and ask questions. In some denominations policy would preclude a conjoint meeting with the husband and wife. In that case the wife should meet with another church official at the same time as the meeting with the pastor, preferably an official who can be empathetically understanding and supportive.

The Wife's Need to Know

The pastor's wife may well be in shock at this point and need caring support. It is not unusual for a wife to be in denial about her husband's behavior. In one instance, even after the criminal trial of her bisexual offending husband, the wife moved away from the town still insisting he was not bisexual. In another instance the wife told everybody she could reach in the congregation that her husband was "no sexual addict" and would never betray her. He already had admitted to officials that he had crossed the sexual boundaries in his present and past congregations. He had not told his wife, nor had the officials. Not until she was confronted with details and her husband's admission six months after the offenses came to light did she stop contacting parishioners. In addition to the betrayal she now had to deal with the humiliation of her denial and of her telephone calls. We believe it is important for the spouse to not only be told of the charges immediately but to be constantly informed of the evidence as it becomes known and to be helped in accepting the truth.

One way to approach this matter of the wife's need to know is to call the couple in and ask the offender to tell his wife what the charges are in the presence of a church official. The wife needs to know the truth in at least as much detail as the congregation will be told. Immediate follow-up emotional support for both clergyman and wife will be of utmost importance.

Grief

We believe that grieving and reconciliation are one and the same process. Grief is a natural process we experience throughout our lives, for we all suffer losses—large and small—from the time we are born. Problems arise when the process is blocked by denial of feelings: "I should not be feeling this way." In the beginning the grief may be felt as hopelessness: "My life is over. I'll never be accepted in church again. God will punish me. My friends hate me." Anger at parishioners, church leaders, the Church with a capital C, and even God is likely to be present and appropriate at this time. Unexpressed anger can bring about catastrophic illness.

In the conclusion of her chapter "Unfinished Business," Elisabeth Kübler-Ross says, "Life is very simple and beautiful. Any human being who holds onto a bad mood does so only for the purpose of punishing God, destiny, the boss, the husband, the wife, the children, the mother-in-law, anything, including himself or herself. It is a waste of energy."[19] It is this unfinished business that creates the problems for clergy families, victims, and congregations.

Closure

The other groups discussed in this volume are given the opportunity to talk about their feelings. Unfortunately, the offender's family often does not get the chance. That is why we stress that the offender's family also needs the opportunity granted to the other victims. The family needs to be able to say goodbye to the congregation. Like a funeral, although nobody likes the reason for the funeral, the ritual is very important. We have found that this helps the spouse and family feel less like victims, which in turn helps them take control of their lives.

As Chris said, "I would like to have been able to return to the church in maybe six to twelve months and talked with those members who would have been willing to meet with my family and me." We agree with Chris. This is an essential part of reconciliation and healing and also would have provided some sense of justice for the clergy family. The meeting would allow explanations to be made, a sharing of sad, hurt, and angry feelings and regrets—finally bringing closure to a relationship significant for

---

[19]Elisabeth Kübler-Ross, "Unfinished Business," *Death and Grief in the Family,* ed. Thomas Frantz (Rockville, Md.: Aspen, 1984).

both family and congregation. The timing for such a meeting would depend on the recovery process for both parties.

One clergy wife poignantly summed up the feelings and experience of the offender's wife and family when she said, "The congregation lost one; I lost hundreds. Not one person from the church hierarchy ever called me and asked how I was getting along, how the children were doing. You were the first from the church to ask me to tell my story. I know we had to leave, but we still were human. Law without gospel is dead. For us, the church was without heart and soul."

The important thing to remember is that the family is not guilty and should not have to suffer the punishment of the guilty. The inevitable pain of shame, humiliation, loss, and grief is quite enough for these forgotten members of God's Church.

Afterpastors in Troubled Congregations

Darlene K. Haskin

In 1989 Parish Consultation Service began a research project, which had as its goal the development of interventions that could assist the healing of individuals and groups within a congregation where a betrayal of pastoral trust had occurred. During the course of this research Parish Consultation Service discovered the existence of a group of pastors who provided some re-markable insights into the effects of pastoral sexual misconduct. Nancy Hopkins, the member of Parish Consultation Service who first became aware of the group states, "It was an unexpected dividend that the existence of an afterpastor's group was drawn to our attention; in fact, their testimony to the pain they encounter and the apparent universality of their experience powerfully clarifies the consequences of not intervening in congregations impacted by the clerical betrayal of trust."[1]

"Afterpastor" is the term a group of pastors in Minnesota coined to describe themselves. All the pastors succeeded pastors who had engaged in sexual misconduct with members of their congregations. In some cases the misconduct involved minors; in others, adults. The afterpastors gathered to give each other support and to develop a strategy to deal with the needs of the congregation.

---

[1]Nancy Myer Hopkins, "The Congregation Is Also a Victim: Sexual Abuse and the Violation of Pastoral Trust" (Washington: Alban Institute, 1992) 2.

155

Parish Consultation Service invited these pastors and others in similar circumstances to meet and discuss their experience of ministering to congregations whose trust had been betrayed. The meeting brought together a denominationally diverse group with representation in almost equal numbers of Lutheran, Roman Catholic, Episcopal, and Evangelical Churches. The participants ranged in age from thirty-three to fifty-four, the median age being forty-seven. Both men and women were present. Participants had previously served from one to six congregations. Rural, suburban, and urban areas were represented. A survey tool was developed for this meeting, and those who attended responded to the questions, offering their insights on the effects of misconduct on the congregation and themselves.[2] It was a privilege to listen to the remarkable stories of the afterpastors and to study their responses to the questions, especially those that concentrated on the pastors' insights on how the betrayal of the congregation's trust affected them. In this essay I will focus on their stories.

As a member of Parish Consultation Service I have had the opportunity to assist in the healing process of a congregation that was in the early stages of dealing with a revelation of sexual misconduct. I have also assisted and consulted on methods for healing in several congregations in various stages of the healing process. Each of these experiences has deepened my understanding of the potential hazards faced by the afterpastor.

A final source for my reflections is a series of interviews I conducted with pastors currently serving in affected congregations. I am most grateful for the forthright, reflective, and compelling stories, information, and insights shared by all my sources.

The Experience of the Afterpastor

One of the pastors described his experience this way: "I remember struggling with being so mistrusted and wondered what I had done to earn such suspicion." He expanded on this state-

---

[2]Survey responses were taken at the Parish Consultation Service forum, October 11, 1991.

ment saying that he felt if he stayed he would go crazy. There were violent reactions to efforts at honest communication. He was constantly misheard or unheard. When he asked what had happened before he came as pastor, the leadership of the congregation suddenly had amnesia. The senior pastor had left surrounded by a whirl of rumor. "I learned that time is no healer of betrayals of pastoral trust."

Here is another story with similar themes: "I was apprised of the history of the congregation before I was chosen to be their next pastor. The first six months went fine, but the old-timers were reluctant to let me in. Then there was a financial crisis and I was blamed for it. I had no support, no one to talk to. The place was full of mixed messages. One recurring theme was, the congregation wanted to grow but didn't want to change. Fights were breaking out among and between church members, and people tried to triangulate me in those fights."

Another pastor described the life cycle of his experience. He was hailed as "our savior" when he was called to the congregation. It was a great but short honeymoon. Then it was, "you aren't doing anything." Finally it settled into a realistic level of expectation of what he was able to do. When there is public knowledge of the wounds in the congregation but no process to help the congregation heal, the pressure on the afterpastor to "fix" the congregation can be enormous. Even with the best of processes some of this pressure is still observed.

In other, more difficult cases the congregation is in denial that it needs any help. In such cases the afterpastor is often the target of the anger or rage that the members of the congregation are unwilling to admit exists. The afterpastor becomes a sort of magnet. One pastor describes his experience this way:

> Many people make career mistakes, and I clearly made a costly ministry career mistake and ended up being the scapegoat/identified patient for a very sick church, which depth of sickness had been hidden from me. It was a church with severe "secrets," only some of which were discussed when I had interviewed with their search committee, but I suppose I had "convinced" myself into believing the congregation's leaders when they said, "We have worked through all our problems." Foolish me, I believed them and accepted the call.

The pastor left this congregation after about two and a half years. He had become the target of the congregation's anger and was no longer seen able to minister effectively.

Further examples of the frustrations and even dangers of the afterpastor experience surfaced in the interviews. "I was so mistrusted, and I felt manipulated and coerced." Said another, "I was immediately the lightning rod for the conflict and dysfunctional dynamics of the congregation." An afterpastor from a small rural church realized early on that "there was great anger at me for not taking a firmer and quicker stand. Someone even threatened to burn the church down." An afterpastor, called to serve a large suburban congregation, was told by its leadership to "let sleeping dogs lie." When the congregation learned of the betrayal, hundreds of people left, and the afterpastor was blamed.

Pastoral skills are often called into question. One afterpastor who had taught homiletics said, "I felt I was preaching to a Plexiglas wall" because there was so little response to what was offered. Another described visiting a sick parishoner at her home faithfully every month for a year. Then the person had a hospitalization, which was not reported to the pastor. As soon as he heard of it he went to visit the woman. Her husband reacted with rage and asked, "What kind of a pastor are you?"

My perception is that the life cycle of an afterpastor is relatively short, usually no more than three to five years. Afterpastors who last longer are probably in situations in which one or more of the following are true: the level of betrayal was relatively slight, the congregation recognized its need for healing, good assistance was made available to the congregation, and the denomination was supportive to the afterpastor. More on these conditions later.

The Effects of Ministering to a Wounded Congregation

Afterpastors were asked to describe how ministering to a wounded congregation had affected them in three distinct areas of their lives: health, family, and vocational calling.

On Health

In the area of health there were some remarkable outcomes, both positive and negative. For some the wounds of the congregation forced them to confront their own woundedness. They could not begin the healing process with the congregation until they had begun their own journey toward wholeness. A number of afterpastors entered chemical dependency treatment. Others sought therapy or counseling. One began a better regimen to control his diabetes. Another began a regular exercise program to help manage stress. They learned to ask for what they needed in order to take care of themselves. Only then could they begin to help the congregation focus on its need to be healed.

Other afterpastors experienced adverse effects on their health. Physical symptoms such as headaches, rashes, sleeplessness, chronic fatigue, and high blood pressure were reported. Psychological issues, especially depression and anxiety, required attention. Isolation and loneliness began when the pastors were cut out and set aside by congregations who demanded their total attention. Some felt shame in becoming the congregation's scapegoat. There was also guilt over the ineffectiveness of their pastorate. One afterpastor went to the hospital in an ambulance to be diagnosed with severe stress. Another gained over thirty pounds. One of the interviewees remarked, "I had not realized the kind of stress that the pastorate caused until I had moved out of it."

On Family

"We were competent parents, but parents on the edge and just grinding it out. There was little energy or patience for a pre-schooler's disruptions or a two-year-old's tantrums." So began a litany of stories from afterpastors looking back on their experiences. "As a family we were excruciatingly lonely and isolated," remarked a clergy couple from the Southwest. "Our kids made no friends. There was no energy left for them and we had very short fuses." Upon leaving the pastorate the eldest child in the family said bluntly, "You're not so crabby now that we're out of that place." For one couple in particular the marriage was jeopardized. The afterpastor and her husband became antagonistic and verbally violent toward each other. The children asked them often if they would make it as a family. It was an abusive, crazy, lonely time.

Remarkably, some afterpastors saw their family situations as stable, intact, and moving ahead in spite of what was happening at the church, although they acknowledged they had to spend more time away from home.

How do we make sense of such divergent outcomes? Those afterpastors reporting positive family outcomes seemed to be surrounded by a strong support system that included one or more of the following: peers, mental-health professionals, and judicatory officials. Those reporting negative outcomes were more likely. alone and on their own, feeling vulnerable and insecure. It is isolation that is most responsible for undermining the family and demoralizing the afterpastor.

On Vocational Calling

Did the afterpastor experience affect the vocation to ordained ministry? The answer is yes and no. For some it strengthened their vocational call: they felt closer to God and renewed in their faith from the experience. One spoke of maturing in his spiritual life. He has become "more real," learning that there are no quick or easy answers. He was forced to go beyond "Sunday school" spirituality to deal with the complex difficulties raised by the pastoral misconduct. He noted a new appreciation for the divine call to be merciful toward the individual who was sexually inappropriate while being faithful to the demands of justice for the victims and the congregation. Another mentioned that it was a rich spiritual time even though it was very difficult.

For a few the vocational call had become a concern. The experience of afterpastoring had left a nagging question: Is it possible to minister in such a congregation and stay healthy? One afterpastor said he would not take a call unless he could be assured of his safety. Many afterpastors felt inadequate because they left without resolving the issues that faced the congregation. Had they compromised themselves and their calling to serve God? Was there life in the church for them after all this trauma? Pastoral counseling and spiritual direction helped many of the afterpastors explore these questions and many others. For some this meant a return to congregational ministry. For others it meant leaving church work altogether.

The afterpastor has a critical role to play in helping the congregation heal. A congregation that has been traumatized requires a sense of safety and stability. The afterpastor's ability to provide what the congregation needs is dependent on his or her personal well-being. If the physical, emotional, and spiritual needs of the afterpastor are not attended to, the church will not be helped or served. Openness, self-knowledge, and self-awareness are key to carrying out a healing ministry while remaining healthy. One afterpastor explained that his appropriate level of revelation of his own issue with alcoholism and the support he received outside the congregation in dealing with that issue has helped the congregation to heal. The afterpastor need not be harmed by this challenging ministry. It can, in fact, lead him or her to growth that otherwise might not take place.

Elements of Recovery for the Afterpastor

Adequate Information

No recovery can begin without adequate information about the situation in which the new pastor finds him- or herself. Knowledge of preexisting conditions is necessary in order to be prepared. Nils Friberg identifies the information needed:

> What actually happened? What is not yet known? What are the feelings and attitudes present on the scene? What types of grief over the loss of the perpetrating pastor are present? What grief over possible loss of victim's presence? How did the congregation learn of the events? How much do they know? Who knows what? What reactions to both the perpetrator and the victim are evident? What theological formulations are being brought up by the congregational members? What issues can be sensed around worship, liturgy, and sacred spaces as well as issues around the symbolism of clergy persons' roles? Is there a need for "recertifying" those sacred places, roles, and symbols? Are people attempting to deal with the issues or push them away? Are there victims and families who still need attention? Are factions forming themselves? What past attempts to heal have succeeded or failed? Reasons? What past problems in the church lie under the surface or mixed with the dynamics of this event?[3]

---

[3]Nils Friberg, "A Denominational Survival Kit for Afterpastors," in "Clergy Sexual Misconduct: A Systems Perspective," ed. Nancy Myer Hopkins (Washington: Alban Institute, 1993) 37.

As Friberg's questions suggest, the afterpastor needs to be aware of a broad array of concerns if he or she is to be successful in assisting the congregation to heal. Without full information the afterpastor is placed at a dangerous disadvantage and is limited in his or her ability to help. Whenever possible the whole congregation should be given the same information as the afterpastor. The power of the secret needs to be broken. If the afterpastor is put in the position of being the keeper of secrets, he or she will be compromised as a healer.

Support

A second element of the afterpastor's recovery is support from denominational heads and peers. It would be tremendously helpful to form a support team that could meet regularly with the afterpastor, helping to sift through congregational issues as they arise and to develop strategy responses to the issues. The composition of this team might include a seasoned mentor-pastor, a counseling psychologist or pastoral counselor, an attorney, and a denominational official. Variations in the nature of the polity would affect decisions about who would be involved and how they would function, but Friberg's message is clear and strong. Don't leave the afterpastor out there alone! The afterpastor needs strong public support from denominational officials.

One afterpastor mentioned how very important it was for him to have a chance to reflect on his experiences in a peer supervision group. The availability of some kind of peer support group, preferably of persons who are also ministering to wounded congregations, gives afterpastors a chance to discover that they are not alone in dealing with difficult circumstances and that negative events are not necessarily due to any fault of theirs but may be a predictable outcome of the congregation's woundedness.

Personal Healing

A third element in recovery is personal healing. The healing process may include individual and/or marital counseling, spiritual direction, and attention to physical well-being (exercise, physical exams, etc.). Friberg suggests that judicatory officials should provide a list of resources for personal care and guidance concerning how to finance the use of these resources. There needs to be a structure for follow-through and regular checkups with a process of aftercare that stays in place until it is no longer needed. The wounds of the congregation will take their toll on the afterpastor and can easily open old hurts or unresolved issues. Careful attention to personal healing helps ensure that the person called to be the congregation's healer will be able to carry out that mission effectively.

Education

A final element in the recovery process is training and education. Courses in conflict resolution are a must. The Alban Institute is an important resource in providing such courses. Courses are held often and in strategic geographic locations across the country. Identification and understanding of dysfunctional systems can be valuable. Friedman's book *Generation to Generation* is a good beginning.[4] Finally, classes in communication, group dynamics, creative problem solving, and decision theory are all helpful. Local colleges, universities, and community learning centers are likely sources for these classes.

Conclusion

First, it has become clear to me that congregations or denominations charged with selecting an individual to serve as an afterpastor must be very thoughtful in their choice. The afterpastor of a wounded congregation faces extraordinary difficulties. The traits that a selection committee should look for include extensive practical experience in conflict resolution and the theoretical knowledge to interpret that experience, tremendous personal maturity and stability, a very clear sense of personal limitations, and a good sense of professional boundaries.

Second, an afterpastor probably won't be able to serve a congregation for more than five years. Two factors lead to this conclusion. The position is so stressful that it is difficult to remain in it for any great length of time. Also, the afterpastor is often blamed for the difficulties the congregation suffers as the result

[4]Edwin Friedman, *Generation to Generation: Family Process in Church and Synagogue* (New York: Guilford, 1985).

of the betrayal of their trust. This scapegoating can make it nearly impossible for the afterpastor to remain as the congregation's leader for any length of time.

Third, the afterpastor cannot do this job alone. He or she will require a great deal of support from denominational officials. The support is not likely to come from the congregation because the members are struggling to deal with the betrayal of their trust. It is critical that sufficient mechanisms for support and reflection be made available to the afterpastor.

Fourth, the role of the afterpastor is to provide the congregation with a sense of safety by providing high-quality pastoral and administrative ministry. The congregation also requires professional help such as grief therapy, anger workshops, and education on the nature of sexual misconduct and the uses of power. Additionally, individual members of the congregation may find themselves in need of counseling because the pastoral misconduct has opened old wounds or brought to the surface unresolved issues. The afterpastor cannot be expected to be the healer of the congregation and also its pastor. These are two separate roles and too much for any one person to handle.

Finally, the denomination and the congregation need to have a clear sense of what they expect of the afterpastor. This will require that some outside facilitator help both of these bodies identify the issues the wounded congregation is facing and the role the afterpastor can play in helping to restore the health of the congregation. The ultimate responsibility for intervening in the congregation's sickness belongs to the larger Church.

The role of the afterpastor is very difficult. It makes enormous demands on the individual who chooses to accept it. But there are many congregations who need the care and attention of clergy who can help them recover from the trauma of sexual misconduct. If these pastors can be trained and properly supported, they can help these congregations recover while remaining healthy themselves. The reward to the minister is not likely to be immediate or direct, but those who accept the call to pastor these congregations provide a very great service to the people of God.

Further Issues for Afterpastors

Nancy Myer Hopkins

The dynamics in congregations where trust has been betrayed are so complex that the afterpastor frequently has difficulty distinguishing useful and legitimate feedback from that which originates as a result of displaced anger at the former pastor. There is a danger of viewing every difficult relationship with congregants as a result of past betrayals of trust and therefore of oversimplifying the situation and engaging in reciprocal blaming. In extreme cases the afterpastor may take no personal responsibility for her or his own defensive reactions, which can contribute to the downward spiraling of all relationships.

One way of determining the presence of displaced anger coming from some congregants is to ask, How does this congregation compare to others I have served in? If former congregational pastorates have been much easier, that is a good indication that what is now being experienced is due to the malaise in the congregation and not largely due to the actions of the afterpastor. This is a helpful reality check for those who have served former parishes; it is not for those who are new to ordained parish ministry. There seem to be a surprising number of first-time pastoral appointments in troubled congregations.

It is very hard for afterpastors who are being attacked to avoid getting defensive. Unfortunately, the experience of being an afterpastor often brings out the worst in people, and any weakness is likely to come to the surface. Therefore, self-knowledge and understanding of the dynamics will be invaluable. Adding to the strain is that while one may be able to talk in general terms about what is going on if the former betrayal of trust is public knowledge, it is probably not helpful to confront directly an individual who seems to be projecting displaced anger. Because such displacement is a largely unconscious process, the best defense for the afterpastor may be to develop a thick skin but to simultaneously work in other ways on self-differentiation.

Self-differentiation for congregational leaders is a concept that has been developed by Friedman.[1] In a systems approach to leadership the leader must define his or her own self while staying connected to others in the system. The leader will take nonreactive and clearly defined positions on issues, sticking to defining the self and not others in the system. Well-differentiated followers will then feel they have permission to take their own nonreactive positions, which does not necessarily mean agreement. The more dependent, poorly differentiated members of a congregation, however, will attempt to sabotage this process. Friedman describes it thus:

> The more poorly differentiated members of the family will be quickest to feel the pull-out when the head of the family tries to emerge from the undifferentiated state of the organism. What they feel will be at the deepest cellular level, because they have fused with their leader. It is almost as if they experience part of their own self being ripped away. Their response is unthinking, automatic, and always serious. It bypasses the "conscious" and is more biological than the "unconscious." It is like a "twitch." It is instantaneous, and . . . the nature of the response tends to be that which succeeded in triangling the leader in the past.

Bear in mind that Friedman is talking about *normal* congregational dynamics. When these insights are applied to troubled congregations, one must consider the probability that all those undifferentiated people would probably have been fused to the pastor who betrayed their trust and are now transferring that fusion to the afterpastor in a tremendously reactive setting. It is a wonder anyone emerges from many of these situations with their sanity intact. This points up an essential need for personal sup-

---

[1] Edwin Friedman, *Generation to Generation: Family Process in Church and Synagogue* (New York: Guilford, 1985) 228–30.

port such as that given by friends, family, denominational leaders, afterpastor support groups, and a therapist.

Another, simpler way of expressing Friedman's theoretical approach is to say that afterpastors must recognize that not everyone in a congregation will be scapegoating the pastor who follows. If one can find the healthy ones and look to them for support and honest feedback, this will help. However, the healthy ones are not necessarily those people who think the afterpastor is just wonderful, who will never challenge him or her on anything. In fact, unthinking, excessive admiration of the pastor is the flip side of negative projections, and both are equally suspect. Also, if there are some laypeople who seem to be behaving very destructively, it may be necessary to work with the lay leadership to figure out ways to reduce the expanded power they have gained in the congregation because of its troubled past.

It will be important to work through mutual expectations clearly, with job descriptions for all paid staff and volunteer leaders developed together. Boundaries for everyone are crucial to understand and follow, as boundaries are often poorly observed in congregations where there has been a betrayal of trust, and lack of clear boundaries often contributes to the climate in a congregation that allows a betrayal to happen in the first place. Even such things as living in church-owned housing adjacent to the church and the twenty-four-hour availability of the pastor are boundary issues, the parameters of which may have to be negotiated. In addition, trust must be rebuilt. This is frequently a slow and difficult process. The simple act of following through on promises made is a trust-building activity.

In troubled congregations poor communication is frequently a problem. Pastors will need to make it clear that they will respond to direct communication from the person who has an issue or concern and who can be clear about what the problem is in behavioral terms. Messages that begin, "A lot of people are concerned . . ." do not deserve a response, unless those people are willing to come forward themselves. As mentioned in Friedman's quote above, triangulation is a favorite ploy in unhealthy systems. When two people have gotten into an uneasy relationship, the response is to pull in a third person to relieve the pressure. When these patterns get stuck, they can become destructive. The afterpastor and also his or her spouse will benefit if they understand the function of triangulation and do not fall into that trap. While triangulation in the short run may temporarily make the participants feel better, it is a no-win solution to interpersonal problems, allowing people to avoid doing the direct work of staying connected.

Afterpastor support groups will do well to have regular facilitation by someone who will validate the difficulties but not let sessions continuously deteriorate into playing "Ain't it awful." It is important for afterpastors not to think of themselves as victims, yet it must be said that sometimes the only way to avoid that outcome is to leave the congregation sooner than was originally intended.

Some afterpastors who have trouble being gentle but firm might benefit from assertiveness training courses. Continuous niceness just doesn't seem to work in these settings, with the result that afterpastors often swallow resentment and have health problems or problems in family relationships. If one is prone to blowups after prolonged niceness, people in the congregation will be traumatized all over again, and this must be avoided at all costs.

The Reappearance of Old Cases

Two particularly difficult situations are the following:

1. Denominational leaders know about a former pastor's behavior but do not share the information with the afterpastor when the call to ministry is made. When the afterpastor finds out what happened, as is inevitable, she or he feels enormous and justifiable anger. To enter such a congregation without knowing why the inner dynamics are so dysfunctional is extremely difficult, and one can be blindsided at every turn. If this happens the afterpastor will do well to be direct with the leadership in asking for full knowledge and then assessing with them if the case can be opened up with the congregation.

2. Occasionally the denominational leadership will have no knowledge of a former pastor's behavior, but many people in a congregation will know and will spend a lot of energy maintaining the secret. Typically information emerges when congregants are traumatized by a new event involving sexual abuse, either in the congregation or in the wider community. New and publicized cases will often bring to the surface half-repressed memo-

ries and result in people coming to see the afterpastor with stories of a former pastor's abusive behavior. In this case the afterpastor will immediately need to document the information and
bring it to denominational leaders and ask for an investigation
and help in assessing if the case can be opened. In both of the
above scenarios it then becomes the judicatory leader's task to
aggressively pursue such cases; the afterpastor must not be left to
do an investigation. Afterpastors can listen to anyone who voluntarily comes to them, but conducting investigations or leading
any subsequent healing process is not appropriate. This is because the afterpastor is already inducted into the system. If he or
she is perceived to be the one who is going to change the rules
of how this congregation operates as a system, then he or she is
in great danger of being further scapegoated well beyond what
seems to be "normal" scapegoating in these circumstances.

How to Assess if an Old Case Can Be Opened

Unfortunately not all cases can become public knowledge. It
is difficult to open cases without a charge from a victim. Furthermore, if a person is known to be a victim, she or he can be supported but must not be pressured to bring forward a complaint.
Pressing charges is a profoundly painful and risky undertaking,
and a victim must want to do so and be well prepared for such
an event.[2] Unless the victim wishes it, his or her identity is never
revealed during the truth-telling process. In some instances,
however, even if the name is not given out, people will know
who that person is. This presents those who are managing such
a case with a major dilemma. The general rule we follow is that
the needs of the victim take precedence over the needs of the
congregation. In one case an afterpastor waited (mostly) patiently for two years for the victim to arrive at the point where
she was ready to come forward, and then it was possible to begin
the congregation's healing.

Other difficulties are presented if the accused cleric has died
and can therefore not speak in his own defense, or if the cleric

[2]See Margo Maris, "' . . . that which is hidden will be revealed' (Luke 12:2),"
p. 3 of this volume.

plea-bargained with judicatory officials, offering to resign if he could do so quietly. Yet another situation involves a cleric who was mildly disciplined for one abusive episode but has moved on to pastor another congregation in another district. If he or she is subsequently found to have other victims, it is sometimes hard to get his current judicatory official to impose any further discipline, even though, in our view, such discipline is well justified.

Another all-too-common occurrence is when the pastor divorces his wife and later marries a woman from the parish. The congregation is the primary victim under such circumstances, because most people will assume, rightly or wrongly, that the relationship with the second wife developed before the divorce, thus constituting a boundary violation.

The statute of limitations can be a problem in many of these cases. This law varies from state to state and among denominations and judicatory districts, creating a lot of confusion. Just because the statute has run out, however, does not mean that something cannot be done to provide both a measure of justice for the victim and an open process for the congregation.

When an afterpastor is feeling the squeeze of life in a very troubled congregation, the urgency felt to deal with the past can seem overwhelming. There is often a temptation to move too quickly and without carefully thinking through all the ramifications of opening a case. We do not advise that old cases be opened without the support of lay leadership and judicatory officials. Outside assistance is vital for assessing readiness and designing and conducting congregational meetings. In the latter phases of healing the congregation will do much of its own work; but at the beginning, all members, including the afterpastor, will simply be a part of the congregation and not in a visible leadership role.

Here again, the complexity of these cases is obvious. Each one must be judged on its merits with an eye to pastoral concern for all parties involved. Certainly whenever discipline is meted out to a clergyperson, the congregation has a right to know, and if that clergyperson is eventually restored to congregational ministry, his or her future congregations are entitled to know the story as well. Until we reach the point when this is automatically done, we are destined to have many hurting congregations who will often in turn hurt the pastors who follow.

Sometimes we are asked if the congregation can do its own healing without openly talking about the truth of events. Each case must be judged on its merits, but in general our approach is to say that it is the secret that many people may know about but do not have permission to talk about that is the central cause of the congregation's difficulty. Once the secret is exposed, then all the other elements of a healthy system can be developed, up to and including spiritual renewal as the ultimate outcome. Using the metaphor of the elephant in the living room that everyone is trying to ignore usually gets the point across.

The Role of the Afterpastor When Healing Has Begun

It is easier to pastor a congregation after the case of abuse has been openly dealt with and strategies are in place for continued healing. However, there will still be many fragile and vulnerable people to keep reactivity levels high, and there may be more than the normal quotient of troubled people present, some of whom may behave destructively. This is the point at which the afterpastor and lay leaders might make good use of the list of characteristics of open and closed systems.[3] The congregation will have been blasted open by the truth-telling process; the trick is to keep it from closing up again.

Whenever significant changes are desired in an organization, there are ways that have been developed to make them with the least amount of disarray. Organizational development consultants can assist with exploring core values, updating mission statements, and doing both short-range and long-range planning. Any of the strictly organizational tasks will be pointless, however, if that elephant is still stomping around in the living room.

As an example of how using the open-closed continuum might work, we can look at just one of the indicators, how welcome are newcomers? Most church people give lip service to the idea of welcoming new people but then either ignore the work needed to accomplish that end or actively work against it. For one thing, growth means change, and many people are so comfortable that the last thing they really want is change. A group of lay leaders,

---

[3]See Nancy Myer Hopkins, "Living Through the Crisis," p. 201 of this volume.

or even better, the whole congregation, could profitably spend a weekend retreat on this question alone. This would involve taking a long look at what people really want *before* developing strategies to accomplish the goals. A good opening question is How easy was it for you to join this congregation?

It must be said in conclusion that not all afterpastors have such a difficult time. The variables that may affect this are listed elsewhere in this volume.[4] And there are probably other variables we haven't even thought of. We still have a lot to learn about the dynamics in congregations where trust has been betrayed. It is because afterpastors and other key lay leaders have shared their experiences with us that we know this much. The experience of being in a troubled but gradually healing congregation seems to be by turns discouraging, then exhilarating.

It may help if we remind ourselves that we are as an institution for the first time honestly facing one of humankind's most painful realities. Sexual abuse and power abuse in general have been around for centuries, with few to confront it. Until now confrontation has been courageously carried out by individuals and small groups of survivors. Now that we are beginning to do so within the context of the religious community, we must expect progress to be slow, with many setbacks. But the vision of a safe world for all of those who are vulnerable will not go away. The Church truly has an opportunity to lead in healing that is entirely consistent with the biblical story.

---

[4]See Darlene K. Haskin, "Afterpastors in Troubled Congregations," p. 155.

Communicating with the Wider Community

Mary Lou Lavallee

We call ourselves people of the good news and we enthusiastically sing the old familiar hymn that begins, "I love to tell the story." We call this "evangelism." In recent years, however, we have belatedly come to understand that one of the biggest tragedies of the Church's response to handling misconduct and abuse has been our tendency to keep secrets. Telling the story of broken vows and violated boundaries is not a good way to win friends. Much of the message of this volume is an attempt to teach us about truth telling and how that truth telling leads to individual and institutional health and healing.

The Church has been especially loathe to jeopardize the reputation of the institution by publicizing the misconduct of some of its most trusted individuals. Just as faith depends on trust, so telling the story of betrayal of trust—the public acknowledgment of broken vows—is bad for evangelism and may come perilously close to revictimizing both primary and secondary victims of abusive clergy or lay leaders. In addition, this kind of publicity tends to compound the difficulty of screening and selecting new parish leadership, and many clergy describe a ripple effect of feeling embarrassment, awkwardness, or guilt by association generated by publicity of miscreant colleagues.

These quandaries are not unique to the Church. Literature abounds with examples of "keeping secrets" in all areas of abuse, and it is a breakthrough in late twentieth-century mental health for us to come to a better understanding of the importance of truth telling, both for the health of the organization and the healing of victims. So, although the idea of publicly telling the story of clergy sexual misconduct beyond the church family strikes terror in the hearts of many church officials, it has been interesting to observe the intuitive wisdom of some parish leaders who instinctively feel a responsibility to the larger community to objectively communicate incidents of misconduct as well as the institution's response to that kind of behavior.

We could cite examples on both sides. The legal adviser in one diocese has counseled suppression of publicity in a case of misconduct in a parish where the admitted perpetrator continues to live in that same small community, in spite of parishioners' desires to alert their fellow citizens to possible repetition of inappropriate behavior. While some church hierarchy may be reluctant about publicity, however, parishioners in another case we know of felt no such qualms. Whatever their motivation may have been, they seemed intuitively to understand that the public had a right to know of admitted sexual abuse by their former clergy leader, lest another unsuspecting person be victimized. At their insistence a relatively brief factual report was prepared by the diocese and accepted by local papers.

Does the media impose unrealistic expectations upon clergy behavior? Perhaps we have led them to expect it. Virtually every religious tradition has some form of public standard for its ordained leadership. In the tradition of the Episcopal Church, for instance, the ordination rite calls upon the priest to "proclaim by word and deed the Gospel of Jesus Christ and to fashion [your] life in accordance with its precepts"; and after pledging faithfulness to Christ and the people the new priest will serve, to "pattern [your] life in accordance with the teachings of Christ so that [you] may be a wholesome example to [your] people." These are public vows made by public people who are called to serve as models to the communities they serve. Sadly, however, we have bitterly learned that some public models are subject to breaking their vows, to violating the boundaries of trust placed in them, and to abdicating the fiduciary trust that both Church and society have placed in ordained leadership throughout history.

Other articles in this volume address causes, intervention, healing, education, and prevention of sexual misconduct. Here, we specifically turn to the Church's role and responsibility in telling the story when allegations are made or proven and to suggest ways to fulfill those responsibilities while diminishing further harm or embarrassment to victims and/or the institution.

Many of us in local church communications are journalism amateurs and view the secular media with some degree of fear or suspicion—not always without cause. Let me suggest some guidelines that have served well over the years—some gleaned from personal experience, others from the advice of colleagues and conversations with local reporters. In almost in all cases I am referring to small-town publications, not the Associated Press or national moguls or the electronic media. Fortunately, most of us don't have to play in those "big leagues," where some rules may be different.

I believe that some basic guidelines for life serve well in this case: be prepared, be truthful, and keep it simple.

Be prepared. In the several instances when the institution I work for has had (or has wanted) to produce newspaper publicity about cases of clergy misconduct that we have confronted over the last few years, the dictum "Be prepared" has served us well. I have found, when trying to deal with the secular media, that providing background material and basic information about the vocabulary, structure, politics, and policies of the Church has set a context most secular reporters have found helpful in describing or commenting upon particular incidents. I have, for instance, a basic "press kit" that includes a bit of history of our national Church as well as our local jurisdiction, brief biographies of national and local leaders, a glossary of terms of address, and descriptions of titles and hierarchical structure, as well as basic membership statistics. Whether I am seeking publicity for a happy event such as the consecration of a bishop or responding to press inquiries about troubling events, this kind of information in an organized format enables reporters to achieve more accuracy in their stories. Likewise, with the assistance of the diocesan Communications Commission, we provide such a "press kit" to local church communicators with some of the same information, as well as simple guidelines for contacting and writing for the local secular press, gleaned from our experience and the suggestions of local reporters.

When an alleged or proven episode of misconduct has occurred, we try to anticipate media interest and prepare a press release, containing what we believe to be the essential facts and chronology of the event in question, to have available if contacted by the press. We know that reporters will want follow-up interviews with various participants and will not only want but be required by their editors to do a certain amount of interpretative description. Many of us in church communications would like to just stick to the wonderful old Joe Friday line from *Dragnet,* "The facts, ma'am, just the facts." But frequently when we see our "facts" in print a day or two after submitting a press release, we feel chagrined if not embarrassed or angry with how our statement was construed by professional writers. Some of that is unavoidable, but good solid homework and preparation has frequently spared us from what seems to be totally subjective or adversarial reporting.

Let me mention a couple of other learnings, which come not from research or scholarly books but from experience in the school of hard knocks. Newspaper reporters do not write their own headlines. And when a story passes from the hands of the reporter to the editorial desk amazing things can happen. Frequently, as with the *National Enquirer,* a provocative headline sets a much more inflammatory context for a story than the facts support. Likewise, the choice of placement in a publication is beyond the control of the reporter or of those who provide the story. Obviously, while we would covet front-page coverage for the bishop's consecration, we sometimes cringe to see stories of misconduct emblazoned across page one.

An interesting dialogue on CNN's "Reliable Sources," aired on December 5, 1993, would seem to substantiate the importance of church communicators being prepared for and aware of secular press treatment of religious news. In the dialogue of that program, well-known religion reporters for secular outlets debated the media's ignorance of the inner workings of most Churches. One panelist opined that many editors might themselves be coming from negative experience with the institutional Church, while another questioned whether it is cynicism in the press or ignorance. Generally speaking, they said, the media deals with facts and religion deals with faith, and they questioned if the two could ever meet. In this arena where the power of the press meets the power of the Church, it has been my experience that being prepared and providing an educational component in additon to the facts of an event can result in more balanced and equitable coverage.

In a news story by Gustav Niebuhr published early this year in the *Washington Post* and picked up in other local papers, Niebuhr refers to the report "Bridging the Gap: Religion and the News Media" published by Vanderbilt University's Freedom Forum First Amendment Center, which says that the nation's newspapers and broadcasters "largely refuse to take religion seriously," that there are "too few full time religion reporters" and that "an unhealthy mistrust" has grown between religious leaders and journalists.

Citing another report by Rev. Jimmy Allen, former president of the Southern Baptist Convention, and John Dart, a *Los Angeles Times* reporter and past president of the Religion Newswriter's Association, the same article calls upon the secular press to train more religion specialists, invokes members of the clergy to be accessible, and urges them to "learn what journalists consider newsworthy and communicate religious actions and events that fit that definition." The problem in many newsrooms, say Allen and Dart, is "ignorance rather than bias"—and that many reporters assigned to cover religion stories are too often "intellectually lazy about getting their facts straight." While some of these comments reinforce the qualms church communicators have about dealing with the secular press, they also strengthen my suggestion to provide background material that not only makes the reporter's job easier but also more accurate.

I would also encourage communicators, whenever timing permits, to notify the congregation(s) involved prior to issuing a secular press release. Just as clergy tell of feeling the effects of the present spate of publicity about unfaithful colleagues, so, too, parish members may feel personally tainted by published stories of misconduct in their worshiping community. Inform those in charge if publicity is likely to occur. Provide a copy of the official press release to let them know what their leadership is saying, regardless of how the media reports it. If trust in leadership is shaky, candor and truth may help instill confidence.

Finally, in the context of being prepared, I might suggest that I have found it helpful, especially in sexual misconduct stories, where the possibility of litigation arising from such reporting exists, to check the initial, basic press release with church legal advisers. (My bishop calls the diocesan lawyer his "best friend" in situations like this.) The tension between the need to know and pastoral sensitivity is aggravated by the possibility of misinterpretation when publicity goes beyond church walls.

Be truthful. The second part of the trinity of suggestions that I make for church communicators is "Be truthful." Of course, the observations made under "preparation" assume truthfulness, but I repeat this suggestion because of its importance and because of my own experience as a church journalist to sometimes gloss over the more painful facts and be overly protective of the individuals and institution involved. I believe we do have a moral re-sponsibility to protect both primary and secondary victims of abuse from being revictimized by sensationalism in the press, but I am additionally convinced that true health and healing require truth telling.

Newsroom reporters work under a great deal of pressure of daily deadlines as well as personal ambition and competition among papers for "what sells." We sometimes feel that the press is an enemy to be held at bay. While I have, indeed, both personal and secondhand experience of painful media treatment, I have also found that developing rapport and professional relationships with local reporters has resulted in greater success in the mutual responsibility of both Church and press to inform rather than judge.

When rapport and respect have been developed with the media, the attempt to be evasive or euphemistic is not only contradictory to the theology of truth telling but also an open sesame for the press to invent even more sensational or judgmental views of events. I was intrigued to hear a TV publicist describing the press' appetite for scandal and saying that when trying to effect damage control, the best defense is an offense; in other words, in a scandal or crisis, get your side out fast!

How might we faithfully address the tension and cynicism that exists? In addition to training ourselves as church people to be more accessible and relevant in our press relationships, we still have unanswered questions to struggle with, especially when the news to be published is bad news.

What information, for example is "on the record," and what conversations can we have with reporters "off the record"? Probably the Church's and professional reporter's views on this will be different. The important caveat is to make sure you have established what the reporter assumes and what the ground rules are. Included in the area of candor and confidentiality is the crucial and controversial question of naming the victim. Helen Benedict comprehensively discusses this question and offers rationale on both sides of the controversy.[1] I think this is not the place to discuss that dilemma but rather to vigorously wave a red flag to church communicators to reflect and consult and, yes, pray about their responsibility and the effect of providing identifying information about either perpetrators or victims in preparing press releases.

Keep it simple. Stick to the facts—the good old journalistic basics of who, when what, where, why. The "keep it simple" principle serves us well in many areas of life, but I find it especially helpful and relevant in my communications ministry. If we are, in fact, people of the good news and if we are people who function in faith, then I think the acceptance of responsibility to tell the whole story without fear or cynicism is crucial. Few are unaware of the troubling legacy of John F. Kennedy's assassination and the perception of cover-up that has for over thirty years given rise to suspicion and mistrust. However, my experience with clergy misconduct issues and my growing conviction of the importance of truth telling and freedom of information—not only as hallmarks of our Judeo-Christian tradition and our individual civil rights but also as critical aspects of individual and institutional healing—lead me to encourage the Church to replace its mistrust of the secular press with informed and professionally wise contact with them. When we are devious or ineffective in our methods of telling the story, we can hardly cry foul if the newspapers show equal irresponsibility. Church communicators walk the excruciatingly thin line of responsibility to the rights and needs of both

---

[1] Helen Benedict, *Virgin or Vamp: How the Press Covers Sex Crimes* (New York: Oxford Univ. Press, 1992).

victims and the larger church community, at the same time accepting the ethical responsibility to tell the truth and live in the light.

Let me share an experience with you. This pattern of careful preparation and availability to the press was effective in a situation that might well have become more highly sensationalized and certainly awkward for the Church as well as the individuals involved. I think we handled it well, though unavoidably with some anguish to those directly involved. I know of no way to avoid all pain when a hurtful episode has taken place.

Almost fifteen years ago in the little corner of the kingdom where I serve the Church, there transpired a very ugly episode of boundary violaton and abuse of fiduciary trust by an ordained leader.

Officials of the Church took what, at that time, were believed to be correct procedures for responding to allegations, collecting factual information, and coming to resolution. The cleric was subsequently removed from ordained minstry. Surely not everyone was pleased with the results, but it seemed to be a closed book. The story never appeared in public.

Over a decade later, when stories of clergy sexual abuse and perceived mishandling by church hierarchy spread dramatically across the pages of newspapers nationwide as well as on national TV news and panel shows, our office was contacted by an observer of that long-ago episode. This individual was morally troubled by what now seemed to him to be an institutional cover-up. Apparently his concern was shared by others, and shortly thereafter the bishop's office was contacted by a local newspaper, which had been alerted to a possible story by an anonymous caller.

Following our own advice, we immediately swung into action. We prepared a factual release of the essential details of the events and the Church's response as they had unfolded years earlier and alerted parishes involved that publicity might be forthcoming. And come forth it did! Several stories in two different publications appeared in print. Interviews were requested, and we did our best to be responsive. However, memories of details were clouded by the passage of time and the fact that not only was the bishop who had been in charge of the original problem long-since retired, but the sitting bishop was in the final months of his incumbency.

As it happened, we had not only to tell the story to the press but also to church members, many of whom had joined these parish communities long after the violations had occurred. This required not only truth telling, but exquisitely careful pastoral care. Thanks to the expertise and experience of Nancy Myer Hopkins and her ministry of congregational healing through the Parish Consultation Service,[2] several congregational meetings were held, which ultimately led to a dramatic encounter between reporters and a forty-eight-hour-old bishop!

As the brand-new bishop and this communicator drove into the parking lot of the church where yet another group session was to take place, we were confronted by an agitated rector warning, "The press is here." Reporters from two papers with whom I had been working for the past several months had learned of this private meeting and were almost literally blocking the door, demanding access to the gathering. Thus we were presented with a conflict between our pledge to participants to provide a safe arena for discussion and our commitment to honesty and cooperation with the press.

For almost fifteen minutes we (bishop, consultants, reporters, and this author) engaged in a fervent dialogue of rights. The press was determined, but so were we, and we were also a bit nervous. The consultants reiterated our responsibility to the waiting parishioners; diocesan officials agreed to later conversation; and the reporters ultimately responded like the professionals they were, thus permitting the planned meeting to proceed.

I believe our earlier preparation and the professional trust that had been established helped solve the dilemma. The reporters were not allowed to attend the session, but the bishop promised to be available to reporters when the meeting adjourned—and he was, for an hour of candid conversation. Those in attendance were informed of the press' interest and told they were also free to talk with reporters if they wished.

Our goal was to serve both constituencies with integrity, and apparently we did, for within days the following editorial appeared in one of the newspapers involved:

[2]See introduction.

The Ghosts of the Past

There's hope that church leadership is recognizing that it must openly confront the spectre of sexual abuse, in the wake of recent harsh lessons.

In an unusual meeting at St. _____ Church, in _____ Monday, Episcopal church officials discussed the troublesome topic of _____. [He] is a former Episcopal priest who once served at _____ Church, in _____. He is alleged to have sexually abused young men and misappropriated church funds throughout the 1970s.

[He] was forced to step down from his post in 1981, and the reasons for his dismissal were kept secret.

But times have changed for the Episcopal Church.

Officials called Monday's meeting for a convincing reason: They wanted to give [his] alleged victims the chance to tell their stories. In the words of Episcopal Church Bishop Robert Denig, these people were all treated with a "we believe you" attitude. They were given the chance to talk publicly about embarrassing things that had eaten away at them for 12 years.

The meeting was not a public one. Church representatives correctly met with people behind closed doors to protect their privacy.

But those officials also talked with the press after the meeting, and that made all the difference in the world.

Victims were still protected. But church officials were candid with reporters. They explained why they were meeting and what they were trying to accomplish.

The Episcopal Church seems to have learned a lesson here—that when a church leader abuses a member of his flock, the church benefits no one by burying the issue. It must confront it, do what it can to help the victims, and be as open as possible with the public.

In the end, it may not right all the wrongs that were done. But by making the issue public, the church can possibly prevent further incidents. Possibly tomorrow's culprits will think twice before they attempt to hurt someone.

They will know that the public is watching.[3]

For a church communicator this is high affirmation and a measure of confirmation that with preparation and candor we *can* "tell

[3]"The Ghosts of the Past," *Sentinel and Enterprise,* Fitchburg, Mass., February 26, 1993.

our story" without obscuring the Good News we have to share with the world. It is also good news that the Church is confronting sexual abuse when it occurs in our community and, perhaps even more significantly, is studying, teaching, telling, and trying to recall itself to standards and expectations to prevent further abuse.

I have been surprised, dismayed, and encouraged at how much I have heard and read in the press about the influence and motivation of reporting since I have been reflecting about this article. Surely the Church is not its only target. One needs only to cite Admiral Bobby Inman's anguished perception of media judgment when withdrawing from presidential appointment, as one example. However, I have been heartened to hear esteemed media personalities ponder the need for a stronger code of ethics, for healthy skepticism versus cynicism, for strong editors and humane reporters, so that the lowest common denominator of journalism will not prevail.

In the end, however, the function of reporters is simply to report. My hope is that we will prepare ourselves to act with honesty and candor so that our stories, and theirs, will be shared with the community for the building up of the kingdom.

One Reporter's Story

Roxanne Moore Saucier

The Fall of a Maine Pastor

The date was Ocober 15, 1985. The pastor of a conservative, independent church in Maine announced that he would resign the following month. The reason? "Adultery." This was not just any pastor of any independent church. This was a prominent man who had made a name for himself nationally. His congregation was huge by Maine standards, and he had been willing to take on the state bureaucracy over how much control government should have over church-owned schools. He had even run for governor.

This news was not covered by religion reporters—no secular newspaper in Maine had one, and most still don't. Besides, a story such as this was hard news, and didn't belong on the "church page" anyway.

Over the next six months a variety of staffers at the *Bangor Daily News* covered the story. Letters to the editor came fast and furiously, either urging forgiveness or condemning the one who had made a name for himself by casting human behavior in absolutes. Letter writers offered comparisons to Elmer Gantry, Richard Nixon, Jim Jones, King David.

Two weeks after the pastor's announcement several parishioners split from the church and announced the formation of a new congregation with its own church school. The schism didn't end the division within the original congregation, however. A

184

few weeks later, as the pastor stood in the pulpit for a prayer meeting, half of those attending walked out.

Finally, some eleven weeks after the news had broken, the pastor officially resigned, having recruited nationally known Baptist preacher Jerry Falwell to come to Maine as interim pastor. Falwell was candid about his hopes for the various factions to reunite as healing proceeded. Members of his staff came to Maine, while Falwell himself commuted from his Thomas Road Baptist Church in Virginia. Two months later the Maine congregation voted to call a permanent pastor, an associate of Falwell's from the Virginia ministry.

Not much was heard from the fallen pastor for a while. He pursued a different line of work, and about a year later, he turned up as a guest speaker at a church in another part of the state. Shortly afterward he told a *Bangor Daily News* reporter that he expected to become a pastor again eventually. His mistake, he told the reporter, was so common that it would not be an obstacle to his returning.

And so it happened that little more than three years after the first scandal erupted, this same pastor announced he was starting a new church—in the same city that was the home of both his former church and the congregation that had split from it. This new church would begin meeting in a conference room of a motel.

One Congregation Heals, Another Begins

By the time the new church was started in early 1989, I was on the staff of the *News*, with about half of my time devoted to writing and editing the religion pages. While I did contribute background and other small bits of the coverage, the stories of the return of this controversial figure were led by the bylines of others. One morning, in answering a colleague's phone, I talked with Jerry Falwell, who criticized the pastor for starting a new and competing church in the same town. Eventually the formation of this new congregation changed my involvement in the continued reporting of this case. Even though I was only too glad to be needed elsewhere on the day services began, I sensed that my time would come.

I had steered clear of the church where the controversy had exploded because I thought its parishioners had had plenty of attention from reporters and surely didn't need one more on their backs. But the new congregation was still considered news—again, publicity was driven by the magnet of a still-controversial preacher. It seemed time also to give the original church the opportunity to talk about its progress. The congregants were now being led by a new pastor, who had succeeded Falwell's associate. The new spiritual leader had been a church member in the 1970s before going away to study for the ministry.

The original congregation had indeed made progress, it turned out. The increased membership wasn't back up to the much-published figure of three thousand the new pastor told me, but the church would only hold half that number anyway. Since dropping its bus ministry years earlier, he said, the church had seen its numbers dwindle some time before the resignation. Even in its heyday I doubt that it was the largest church in the city, much less one of the largest in New England, as had been implied.

One year after the former pastor's return, his new congregation bought a local church building that had been in the community for a number of years. Our religion pages run items for both churches when asked, and I have covered events at both churches. They are regular, church-page, noncontroversial events. But over the years this controversial figure, his departure, and his return have been covered not only by local media but by other publications, even *The New York Times* and *People* weekly magazine. *People* magazine, interestingly, was the only place where I saw the woman involved referred to by name.

From the beginning the minister himself termed the misconduct "adultery." The media went along with that characterization. If the woman agreed to participate, didn't that make it a consenting relationship? Not necessarily, most reporters now realize. Today reporters are increasingly considering the balance of power, even when the other person is an adult. They are asking, Is she or he also a parishioner? Possibly a staffer or volunteer? Receiving counseling from the minister?

These questions of power came into clearer focus for me in May 1993 when I heard the sermon of a Unitarian-Universalist minister who had attended a denominational conference on clergy sexual ethics. For the first time, I heard about the concept of predators and wanderers. Predators go looking for involvement. Wanderers encompass the many—both clergy and laypeople—who don't realize that their expressions of "affection" cross boundaries and can get them into just as much trouble, regardless of intent. I also heard about how difficult, if not impossible, it is for two people to go from being pastor and parishioner to being consenting adults in a sexual relationship.

A few months later, an editor asked for a localized sidebar to an Associated Press story on an organization for women who had been involved with priests. The premise was that, even if these women were or had been parishioners, these were relationships between consenting adults. It was a premise I did not buy. My sidebar quoted the Roman Catholic chancellor and also the minister who had enlightened me about the balance of power.

Most Visible: The Catholics

Over the years, I have written about or heard about clergy misconduct in connection with a variety of denominations and independent churches. In Maine as in the rest of the country, the Catholic Church has the greatest visibility. In this state between one-fifth and one-fourth of the population attend Catholic services. That does not include lapsed Catholics. Nationwide the misconduct problems of the Catholic Church, usually allegations involving children or teenagers, became public in the mid-1980s in Louisiana because the survivors decided to speak out. The case of former priest James Porter, who wound up in the courts as a layman, brought the issue to Minnesota and Massachusetts, and now it seems to be everywhere.

And yet accusers of Catholic priests did not go public in Maine until early 1993. In a space of eight months cases involving six named priests and one unnamed were covered in the media. The seven cases, spanning some thirty-five years, included one retired priest and several active priests. Three were active priests the diocese had known about earlier. A spokesman said the Church had handled those appropriately and promptly with evaluation at a treatment facility and whatever else may have been required. After two of the active priests were named in civil suits, they were removed from public service, as were the two named in criminal proceedings.

I am still not sure who broke the first story regarding the retired priest. It may well have been a television station that is broadcast only in the southern part of the state. The next day newspapers went with the story. One large newspaper used the name of the priest; my initial story did not.

What Do We Print? And When?

With just about any kind of allegations the media generally likes to see some evidence of charges having been filed before publicizing names. If a person calls a newspaper with a complaint of some grievous wrong, he or she is usually met with questions about whether an official complaint has been made to law enforcement or whether a civil suit has been filed. "I'm going to file suit" (or press charges) usually doesn't cut it.

In allegations of clergy abuse the statute of limitations often comes into play, as it did in this first public case in Maine. According to Maine law, the statute of limitations is six years in civil actions. There was before the Maine legislature in 1994 a bill that would have eliminated the statute in cases in which the accuser was under sixteen at the time of the alleged abuse, but despite heavy lobbying by those who work with abuse victims, senate and house committees gave it an "ought not to pass" recommendation.

That the priest in this first case was retired may also have been a factor in my not using his name right away. I had not been in on the decision-making process prior to breaking such news previously, and perhaps subconsciously I made the judgment that there was less potential risk to the public because he was retired. And yet I am very aware that clergy from many denominations who have offended have continued to serve as interim pastors or to fill in for fellow preachers who are sick or on vacation.

I knew the name of the priest in this case, but the name had not been released by the diocese, which cited the fact that charges had not been filed legally. The diocese released that information within the next twenty-four hours, and thereafter we used the name also. One thing the diocese did do at the outset, however, was give the media its Statement on Sexual Abuse of Minors by Clergy, promising removal and evaluation of the priest immediately and declaring its intention to treat everyone involved with compassion and justice.

By this time the cases were coming with astounding regularity. Little more than a week later a court announced the indictment of a priest from a religious order who was serving at a Maine parish. When the indictment came down, the diocese released information about how it had responded to the complaint months earlier but would have no comment while the situation was in the court system. The priest, who had gone back to his order in another state at the time of the complaint, returned only for the trial, then left the state again. He was eventually acquitted.

But not all the accused clergy were retired or from another state. The next was an active priest, much beloved, accused of having abused a teenager many years earlier in another parish. The diocese followed its policy, and he was sent away to a denominational center for treatment and evaluation of clergy and religious with a variety of problems. The bishop went to the priest's former parish the next weekend to speak to the parish. He did not say anything about whether the allegations might be true, but he acknowledged the people's pain and talked about how they might find their healing in Jesus. We asked for a copy of the bishop's sermon, and the diocese provided it to my newspaper. The chancellor also granted an interview about the subject of clergy abuse and how the diocese was handling it. The chancellor and the diocese's communications director have been accessible to the press continually throughout this year of allegations.

Personal Dilemmas of a Reporter

As a religion writer for eight years, it has been my usual lot to be the only secular reporter present at church meetings. If I sit through a denominational convention for two days, I can assume that most of the time I will constitute most or all of the press in attendance. Perhaps a TV station will come in for a "sound bite" between sessions but not when anything is actually happening.

To be now covering religion stories that get coverage by other media is quite another kind of experience. It has been disturbing to hear of reporters who gained access to a church official under false pretenses or of journalists who attempted to enter a school yard to talk with or photograph children who had known a particular cleric.

These behaviors made me wonder whether denominations would at some point begin to expect such behavior of me and respond accordingly. The reputation I have tried to build is of a journalist who will write the tough stories but will also try to be fair.

Without a doubt, writing stories about clergy who may have abused youngsters is one of the most difficult tasks I have had as a reporter. How often I have said to myself, "Tell me the ending, and I'll write the middle right." In other words, tell me how to discern the good guys from the bad guys. Give me something that is black and white. Unfortunately, there's a lot of gray to be covered. In many cases we may never know whether abuse happened or not. Even when abuse is acknowledged or proved, it is difficult to measure the misconduct against the good the pastor may have done over the years.

That so many of the recent cases have involved Catholic clergy has been particularly painful to me, a convert to Catholicism since my college days. Although I have not even met most of those accused, each new accusation hits me in the pit of the stomach. And though I am sure that some abuse has occurred, I have the fear that someday someone with an ax to grind will make false claims against someone who may have been important to my own faith journey. I'm not alone in that. It hurts me to hear priests say that they don't dare hug people anymore or be alone with children. Some are uncomfortable wearing their black "clericals" in public now, and because I have been one of those who has written about clergy abuse, I have been a part of that outcome. I've put my byline on eighty to one hundred thousand newspapers—too many painful times—and those stories of priests who have abused their power have also hurt priests who never touched anyone inappropriately.

That's not to say that the effects on me of doing this work have been all negative. I've also grown personally as I've learned, along the way, that priests are human beings. They may be part of the chain that involves other priests, bishops, cardinals—and in my denomination, the pope. But I do them and myself no favors when I expect them to be only slightly less perfect than God. God made them fully human for a reason.

In addition, my work as a reporter has been one part of my learning about boundaries. Listening to that Unitarian minister in the spring of 1993, I quickly calculated that neither I nor my personal clergy and clergy friends were predators. Wanderers, however, sounded like a continuum broad enough to include millions of people. My education continues.

Complications and Questions

An added complication to some of these situations is the presence of lawyers—people I don't usually have to deal with in writing about religion. Even when I am not interviewing lawyers, they may be the ones writing or editing press releases or statements. I once wrote an article with something that was very misleading because lawyers would not let the public-relations person have the last say on how a statement should read.

Another time, I was about to get some needed material for a situation that had pretty much escaped the media—a non-Catholic one, at that—and a lawyer managed to tie some knots in important tongues. I told the lawyer that I respected the decisions that had been made but I thought he ought to be aware that they could backfire. Down the road, I said, some of those affected could find their voice and decide that this particular church had interfered with their healing because of the effort to preserve silence. I've seen it happen.

Still another lawyer, despite the fact that the priest in question had never been accused of molesting anyone other than his own relatives, stated his intent in court documents to acquire the name and address of every altar server that had ever been under the priest's direction in any parish. He had asked me in a telephone call some months earlier how I as a reporter thought the diocese would respond. I don't live in any of the parishes in question, but I told him that I, as the parent of two altar servers, would object to my parish ever giving out such names to a lawyer.

In many states there is activity of local or national support-advocacy groups for people who say they have been abused by clergy. One couple told me they had started a chapter of such an organization before they ever heard the details of their offspring's story—something that finally happened in the presence of both broadcast and print media. I didn't know what to make of that. Nor do I know what to do with claims that such groups can, by their instincts, weed out those who may make false accusations.

Some of the incidents that wind up in the media leave reporters and editors scratching their heads. One cleric was accused of having a sexual relationship with one woman for a few weeks. To be sure, this may not be a relationship between "consenting adults" per se, but is it in the same category—and worthy of the same attention—as allegations concerning children or teenagers? What about a case filed by family members of a person who happens to be a member of the clergy, who say they were abused from their teen years into their thirties? If the accusers and their counsel call this "abuse by clergy" rather than "incest," how is the media to react?

One year of covering this issue in one state is nowhere near long enough for a reporter to begin to think she has a clue. I read all the books I can find, I attend workshops on the topic, and I talk to "experts." There are stil more questions than answers.

The term "cover-up" has been applied to Catholic officials, but other denominations as well seem eager to keep their problems out of sight. Many Protestant Churches also will not respond unless the accuser has gone public. Most also have not offered their policies on misconduct, although one denomination did provide what it had published in its own newspaper—when asked.

Over the years newspapers may be approached by a variety of accusers or their representatives. Sometimes the reporter is the first person they tell. The callers may then go on to establish contact with church or legal authorities, or they may not. So far, my experience has been that both the accusers and the media are more likely to follow through if the complaint involves the Catho-lic Church. There may be more "reward" for complainants in filing complaints against the largest single denomination in the United States, especially when you consider the media response. A newspaper may run a front-page story on a Catholic parish priest, while allotting a Protestant bishop only a two-inch blurb buried inside. Most newspapers I have seen allot their ink in the same proportions—unless the offending Protestant minister is also a highly visible television evangelist.

When it comes to writing a story of abuse by clergy, one difficulty is that the task involves a lot of third parties. Those accused may be totally unavailable or may speak only when there is a trial. Furthermore, it is always uncomfortable to be writing what seem to be one-sided stories, especially when the reporter knows that there are details that would make for a more balanced story. These might include actions the cleric has taken to facilitate the accuser's healing or work the minister has done to resolve his or her own issues even beyond the requirements of the plan for rehabilitation.

When I first began writing about allegations against clergy, I didn't talk to the accusers. Some were not reachable or had moved. After awhile I began to interview accusers when possible because I thought it important to have them say what they were after, what they thought they needed. Some were very clear about this, and some didn't know what they wanted.

Another dilemma arose when an accuser whose name had not been made public approached me with information alleging that one cleric had abused people in more than one parish. The cleric's name was already public. The person calling me was now willing to go public and provided documentation of contact with the denomination. I considered the "more than one parish" aspect of this story to be critical, and we ran it. All kinds of entities end up being judge and jury, and reporters may be among them whether they want to be or not.

One of the toughest situations for a reporter involves cases that have been only partially publicized. What if the accuser reaches a settlement with the Church, then volunteers the story but not the name of the accused? What if the media is led to discover the name? Just as sticky is the scenario of the legislative hearing. A public forum on a bill to change the statute of limitations on molestation of minors is sure to draw some of those who have already gone public with their stories. What does the press do with the testimony of someone who names a dead minister who has not been the subject of public allegations? A national wire service has used such a name; I have not.

More Tough Decisions

Even after making the tough decisions, writing the story is not all there is to any of these situations. A reporter's usual concern over editing and headlines only increases when such a sensitive subject is involved. I much prefer the term "accusers" rather than "victims," unless guilt has already been established.

When a church official is interviewed, on-the-ball editors will avoid using that person's picture if readers are likely to mistakenly presume that the official is the one accused.

Most readers are unaware that reporters don't write their own headlines and don't decide where and how their stories are played. Still, I do on occasion put a note at the top of the story reminding the copy desk of words I think we should avoid in the headline, or some other point. Or I may ask an editor whether an acquittal or other action that is favorable to the Church is going to get the same "play" as the original allegations.

Reporters and editors are familiar with using the right-to-know law when dealing with governmental agencies. Not being tax supported, Churches can keep many things private, unless cases make it into criminal or civil courts. So then the question of how far the media pursues each non-court situation comes under ethical rather than legal parameters.

I often have to make these decisions. I don't print everything I know or even everything I can prove or properly attribute. However, I have tried to follow through on some of these cases so that parishes and the Church at large can know the status of a particular cleric. There is a particular dilemma when the name— or the whole situation—has gone unpublished. If an offending cleric remains in the community, with knowledge of predatory behavior limited to members of his or her congregation, people can remain at risk without the knowledge they could have gotten from the local newspaper.

As a newspaper, we tend not to use the names of children who have been abused. When cases of abuse by any adult have occurred in a small town, I have encouraged editors to try to take particular care to help safeguard identities. But no matter how careful a newspaper is, that probably will not stop townspeople from sharing names indiscriminately.

When those abused are now adults who have come forward voluntarily and approached the press, I believe that they have to accept full responsibility for making their own names public. If they expect to be offering their names for a one-time use only, that needs to be discussed because most media would not agree to it. Once published, that name is on microfilm and in computers of libraries forever. A newspaper that publishes it locally usually has no way to keep it from being picked up by a wire service, where it is then available to the newspaper Mom and Dad may read in Florida.

I have had the experience of dealing with a person who sought out newspapers and television stations several times in the course of a year but then claimed to be "revictimized" because I used his name in a story as the person who had made public allegations about a cleric. He did not get the published apology he wanted.

I have also made extensive efforts to cover some stories discreetly or on occasion not at all when it was obvious that a speaker intended to share an experience only with a small audience—not thousands of readers. Stories that focus on the recovery process rather than on allegations against a particular individual might refer to the abused person by a pseudonym.

Where congregations are willing, I would like to do more writing about the healing process. I think it could be done in a respectful way that might really offer some guidance to congregations who don't realize there are things they might do to help the process. By not treating this aspect, we may be missing a golden oportunity to educate the wider community.

What the Church Can Do

The nitty-gritty question, of course, is how should the Church deal with the media when allegations are made. The following suggestions should be helpful:

- Be proactive. If a congregation or denomination can be up front about a problem, it will help. If some official has a good working relationship with the media, perhaps that should be the person who speaks on the Church's behalf.

- Do more than answer the questions that are asked. Offer the media a copy of the Church's policy on misconduct and any background that may be helpful. Provide the names of experts the reporter might consult.

  Keep in mind that many newspapers may have a variety of reporters writing about any one issue. You may have to start at square one with each of them.

- Limit the legalese. Of course you may have to work with lawyers, but watch that their careful attention to detail doesn't take the "church" out of church statements or church activities.

- Keep the media apprised of the positive action the Church is taking. You may not invite reporters to sessions that are intended to further the congregation's healing, but you can let them know it happened.

  At a New England convention of a Lutheran denomination a few years ago, delegates were brought up to date on a situation in one of their congregations. This was the first case to have gone through the denomination's revamped disciplinary process. Those attending offered the congregation their support and wishes for healing during prayers and through a resolution. The case made the papers in the state where it occurred, and my coverage of the convention mentioned the supportive follow-up.

- If coverage is unbalanced, offer information in a constructive way that may help to correct that. Even if the reporter does not feel able to do a follow-up right away, there's a good chance he or she will keep your concerns in mind the next time.

- If your points really aren't getting across in the media, try an opinion column or letter to the editor.

- Offer resolution. Even if the Church cannot release details of its findings on a particular case to the public, it can still provide information that gives people something to deal with and a way to work through their own feelings. In a public case remember that the parish where the abuse was alleged is not the only parish where people will be hurting.

- Last, I would remind congregations and denominations that when the responsibilities for covering stories of alleged abuse belong to one reporter, that person is subject to being as overwhelmed, desensitized, and burned out as any of the church officials or other people involved.

All involved are human beings. That's what makes journalism so difficult—and so rewarding.

Part Three:
Intervention and
Long-Term Healing

Living Through the Crisis

Nancy Myer Hopkins

The Crisis Stage

The Chinese character for the word "crisis" is made up of two characters together, one for danger, the other for opportunity. This is a perfect concept to keep in mind while managing a case through the congregation's crisis phase. This phase usually lasts at least six months or even longer, depending on a number of variables that will be enumerated later in this essay. Most people in leadership positions facing clergy sexual misconduct for the first time are well aware of the dangers inherent in the situation and will frequently feel overwhelmed with worry that a wide variety of people will react negatively to disclosure. The impulse to keep things as quiet as possible is common and perhaps inevitable, given our culture's penchant for secrecy. However, we know now that disclosure is far preferable to secrecy. We can also identify many predictable responses to disclosure, and knowing what to expect is half the battle.

There is at the same time great opportunity presented in squarely facing up to a case of sexual misconduct. A congregation is in a unique position to examine its common life and to deepen relationships within the community. Individuals will often be encouraged to face their own family-of-origin issues and also to confront a wide variety of abusive situations in their personal lives. A process for healing can address much more than just the presenting problem, and an intriguing by-product for the congregation is often spiritual renewal. By modeling a new openness for the wider community, the potential for building a societal change of behavior and attitudes is also there.

The crisis phase for the congregation begins at the moment they find out there has been sexual misconduct on the part of either clergy or other staff or even key lay leaders. The most orderly way for this to happen is a determination by an investigating body that misconduct has occurred, appropriate discipline has been decided on, and a decision has been made to disclose this fact to the congregation.

These cases seldom proceed in such orderly steps. A typical scenario will have the accused suspended from congregational duties immediately after charges have been made while an investigation takes place. Such an investigation can take a long time, leaving a congregation in a kind of excruciating limbo until resolution is achieved. Other cases will wind up in the civil or criminal courts; when this happens, the congregation is usually thoroughly traumatized, especially when legal advisers say that nothing can be talked about until resolution is achieved.

People known to be victims but unwilling to press charges can be supported and encouraged to do so, but they must never be pressured because making a charge involves great risk for them. A guilty cleric who chooses to take the case to trial will most likely be advised by his lawyer to use tactics similar to those used with rape victims, namely, impeach the character of the victim. These cases that end up in ecclesiastical or civil court are unfailingly nasty, brutal battles in which nobody wins, and this includes everyone in the wider Church but most especially the congregation.

There are a number of ways that a congregation may arrive at the point when clergy sexual misconduct must be faced. The most traumatic situation probably occurs when a cleric currently serving a congregation is discovered to be out of bounds with parishioners in the recent past. Other cases can involve older infractions but a new charge, or older cases when there was an old charge and either some discipline or the "geographical cure" took place, but it was only disclosed to very few laypeople, if any. "Father was just spirited away suddenly without any explanation" is an all-too-familiar refrain. While the latter scenario is not so dramatic and immediate, often congregations that experienced "the mystery move" will have developed unhealthy ways of being in community precisely because a major secret has been kept. With that secrecy usually goes many of the attendant additional behaviors so characteristic of closed systems.

The concept of closed systems has been well articulated by William White.[1] White has examined the common life of many nonprofit organizations and discovered that they have frequently become dysfunctional systems as they have become progressively closed. His theory is that the inevitable result of progressive closedness is sexual involvement between members in the system. I have adapted his criteria for use with a congregation and put it in a form that can be used as an assessment tool either by consultants for their own understanding as they begin their work or, toward the end of the crisis phase, with clerical and lay leaders.

Characteristics of Open and Closed Congregations

	Open	*Closed*
Theology and worship	Tolerant of some differences in theology and worship but willing to engage over hard issues.	Narrow theology, nearly everyone must believe and worship the same way.
Social makeup	Heterogeneous mix of class, race, types of family structures. Located in a relatively open community with a variety of housing options. Staying in a community with changing demographics.	Nearly everyone from same race or class.
Social activities	Moderate amount of socialization among members outside of church. Clergy able to have outside contacts and social lives, give	Much socialization among members outside of church. Clergy largely limited to socialization with congregants (no time to

[1]See William White, *Incest in the Organizational Family: The Ecology of Burnout in Closed Systems* (Bloomington, Ill.: Lighthouse Training Institute, 1986).

	own family life precedence.* Living in own home.	do otherwise). Expected to put in long hours in both church and social settings.* Clergy living in church-owned housing, especially if adjacent to the church.
Outside influences	Cooperation with other denominations, local congregations, and life of the diocese or conference. Welcoming input from outside. Significant outreach, some requiring person-to-person activity.	Tendency to act as a lone entity in community and conference or diocese. Little receptivity to consultants or other assistance. Little outreach.
Clergy tenures	Tenures of senior clergy not overly short (under 5 years) or overlong (10 years). Young assistants move on after a reasonable time. Leave without guilt.	Long-tenured clergy. Assistants becoming senior pastors.* Clergy burning out, acting out, or having to leave precipitously.
Lay members	Power spread evenly throughout the lay leadership.	One or two people controlling events. Some people behaving destructively.
New members	A plan to attract and incorporate new members. New members attracted because of congregation, not primarily because of personalities of clergy.	Having rhetoric of wanting new members but no plan.

*Only applicable if other indicators exist or if housing is a source of conflict.

Boundaries	Healthy boundaries between members. Clergy getting intimacy and sexual needs met in appropriate ways outside the congregation. No secrets. Flexible internal and external boundaries.	Too-loose internal boundaries between all members, but rigid external boundaries. Clergy violating boundaries with congregants. Clergy overworked and thus having feelings of entitlement: I deserve this.
Talk rules	Openness about problems. Working through conflict as it arises, then moving on.	"No talk" rules. Secrets being kept by those in power. Conflict ridden or conflict shut down.
Loyalty	Loyalty to members and clergy tempered by need to hold people accountable.	Blind loyalty leading to failure to hold people accountable.
Intimacy and feeling	Members able to be present for each other as they face life's changes. A lay and clerical pastoring approach.	Dependence on clergy to do all the pastoring. Superficial and polite interactions between members.

If the concept of openness and closedness is introduced too soon, however, while people are still reeling from their intense feelings generated by the betrayal of trust, they are likely to reject it out of hand. Later it may be helpful as a way to get congregants to take a good look at themselves and to begin to be able to see that they may have somehow contributed to the situation. There comes a point at which people should be able to move beyond the presenting problem and begin to look at the larger picture.[2]

[2]See Mark Laaser, "Long-Term Healing," p. 232 of this volume.

Breaking the News

It is best to break the news to a congregation by letter ahead of any possible press coverage. The letter can be timed to arrive several days before weekly services so that the people can begin to deal with their shock collectively when they gather for worship. The letter should be relatively short and to the point, telling the bare outline of the situation, inviting people to a congregational meeting, and stating that considerably more information will be available at that meeting. Congregants can also be told that there will be some education about issues raised by the situation and that they will have an opportunity to express their feelings generated by the news together at that time.

Sometimes the offending clergyperson who has been disciplined may ask to say goodbye, either in person or by letter. We strongly advise against having that done in person. This is because usually a clergyperson who has been out of bounds has poor boundaries in many areas and has no idea of how his or her behavior has impacted others. It will take long years of therapy to bring one who has acted out to the point at which he or she would be able to say goodbye appropriately. Sad to say, sometimes this never happens, primarily because the clergyperson does not choose to do the hard, intensive, and ongoing work of therapy.

Frequently, however, a goodbye letter is possible, provided that congregational and denominational leaders have veto power over what is said. I have seen some examples of good letters, some not so good, and some terrible. A good letter will be short, express regret and sorrow for the damage done to people in the congregation, and say goodbye. A not-so-good letter is often self-serving or excessively self-flagellating, putting a kind of reverse grandiosity of the writer to work at becoming the absolutely most abject person on the face of the earth. The worst letter I have seen quoted St. Paul from prison, equating the writer with Paul under unjustified persecution.

The first one or two Sundays after notification are best used to help people just to get used to the idea that a major piece of very disturbing news must be dealt with and that they will be offered a carefully designed process to take place within two to three weeks of hearing the news. We do not do the congregational meeting any sooner than this, because many people will need to get over their initial shock before they can do any serious work on their feelings in a small-group setting.

Sermons and talks by church leaders will focus on acknowledging that yes, this is very difficult for all of us, but openness about what happened is important, and we have a plan to face this together. At this point it is well to avoid getting into long explanations about what happened. Instead, tell people that this information will be available at the congregational meetings to come. The reason for this is that people need to have equal access to the story at the same time, to be followed up immediately with an emotional debriefing together in a safe and structured way. Spend a lot of time explaining what will happen at the congregational meeting, but do not get drawn into arguments about the case. A pastoral presence demonstrating care and concern is what is required. Often, a visit from the bishop or district superintendent will be greatly appreciated, and he or she should also avoid getting into the details of the case prematurely. Make the point that it is hoped that everyone will come but that this is an optional meeting. Stress that the meeting will last four hours and that everyone should be prepared to stay until the end.

The reader will notice that Chilton Knudsen has a different approach to timing and methodology when it comes to breaking the news to a congregation.[3] There are undoubtedly drawbacks and advantages to either approach, but we are in complete agreement on the essential elements of congregational intervention. It is amazing, in fact, that we have independently developed strategies yet do agree on so much.

It is also premature to speak about reconciliation or forgiveness at this juncture. Sometimes in religious settings these are the first comforting phrases that leap to our lips. However, in cases of a major betrayal of trust, this either can be a mask for denial or it can fuel the anger of those who are feeling very traumatized by the news. Reconciliation is a hoped-for outcome, yes, but it will not appropriately come until much hard work has been done by all parties affected. Recognize that people will be in very different

---

[3]See "Understanding Congregational Dynamics," p. 75 of this volume.

places relative to grief throughout the process; some will be deeply affected, many will be troubled, and some may not be very much affected at all. This point will be made many times during the entire healing process.

Expect a lot of sidelong reactivity, either positive or negative in nature. One congregation we have worked with was in a setting where incest and child sexual abuse was endemic in the local culture, and the offending cleric's behavior had been widely known but never acknowledged. The congregation had dwindled to a handful of people. On the Sundays after the leaders were told the truth and a plan for helping the congregation face the news was accepted, attendance jumped dramatically each successive week.

Other forms of reactivity are probably manifestations of displaced anger. Common targets of such anger are church officials, any pastors left on the scene, key lay leaders, and victims. Or there may be sudden and intense symbolic fights over seemingly trivial matters.[4]

There may be a marked absence of direct conversation with clergy remaining on staff about the case even after the first letter has gone out. This is probably because many congregations that experience clergy sexual misconduct, being already relatively closed systems, have firm "no talk" rules well in place. To some extent they seem to close ranks against the clergy, at least until the congregational meeting breaks things open. The parking-lot conference is a common occurrence during this period.

The Press

During the initial period it may be advisable to consider using the press to help tell the story. When I have suggested this move to most church leaders, I have usually gotten stunned looks, as their natural response is to view the press as the enemy, not to be trusted. However, our experience has been that a careful nurturing of the press can yield beneficial results. If a proactive stance is taken and press releases are offered rather than reporters having to drag details out of reluctant and withholding church officials, then it is possible to establish a working partnership with

[4]Nancy Myer Hopkins, "Symbolic Fights: The Hidden Agenda When Clerical Trust Has Been Betrayed," *Congregations* (May/June 1993).

the press that will serve the needs of the wider community as well as of the congregation.

Sometimes members of the press will want to be present at the congregational meeting. We do not permit this for a number of reasons. We make it clear that this meeting is for members of the church only. We are very selective about who the invitations go to. If a member of the congregation happens to be also a member of the press, we ask that person either to come and consider everything they are hearing "off the record," or if they are not able to do that, not to come. People will be doing their own work on very difficult issues, and they must feel safe.

The articles on the press cover this subject in much more detail.[5] In the crisis phase at the congregational or judicatory level it is well to have one person designated to be spokesperson, to offer well-thought-out releases, and to negotiate for sensitive coverage that does not use sensationalist headlines and gives equal coverage to the healing process the congregation and community will be offered. That the Church has changed its way of dealing with these cases is in itself newsworthy.

Planning for the Congregational Meeting

Often it is helpful if smaller groups of lay leaders and/or staff members have a chance to experience the process prior to the congregational meeting. Then some of those people will be well prepared to be small-group facilitators for the larger meeting. It may be necessary to offer more than one congregational meeting, depending on the size of the congregation.

Can victim-survivors be present? As a general rule I advise caution in having direct victims present. If a victim is a member in good standing, however, it may not be possible or even desirable to discourage him or her from coming. Some questions to ask about the wisdom of having victims present are (1) How long has he or she been in recovery? (2) How strong is the person? (3) Can the person face the possibility that his or her credibility or character may be attacked by another member of the congregation?

---

[5]See Mary Lou Lavallee, "Communicating with the Wider Community," p. 173, and Roxanne Moore Saucier, "One Reporter's Story," p. 184.

In any case, a direct victim should be accompanied by a support person, and if the intent is to reveal his or her experience with the abuser, some parameters for doing that should be established beforehand. In old cases, particularly, a victim will often have worked hard and will have become a survivor; granting a request for a hearing from at least the lay leaders may be an appropriate way to respond because this action represents a powerful tool to assist in the continued healing of the survivor. Likewise, hearing the survivor's experience can do a lot to break down some of the most intractable denial that may still be present in the congregation. In one case a woman stated that she had been unable to believe a priest's behavior for over ten years, until she heard directly from a victim what had happened to him.

Sometimes family members of victims want to be present at a congregational meeting. In many cases family members will be even angrier than the direct victim, especially if that person was a child at the time of victimization. Many of the same caveats listed above apply to family members, as does the potential for better understanding of the victim's pain on the part of everyone else. Each case needs to be decided on its merits.

Can family members of the offender be present? This is where things get really sticky. Spouses of offenders typically are either highly defensive and protective of their mate or are extremely angry at him or her, at the church, or both. Much resistance toward the idea of opening the case in the congregation may come from those who are feeling protective of the cleric's family.

We usually make the point, sometimes *ad nauseam*, that the presenting problem here is the cleric's offending behavior, not the telling of it. There may also be a deeper problem with the congregation as a dysfunctional system, but we are not going to deal with these issues very much until the immediate betrayal of trust is worked through. However, spouses of offending clergy may have had a very different picture of the congregation, and their anger at the congregation may be to some extent justified. Also, spouses will be very angry especially if the family is losing its primary income and residence.

In some cases, the spouse of an offender may exhibit some of the same symptoms of those women who have been identified as suffering from battered-wife syndrome. There may or may not be physical abuse present, but years of severe emotional abuse may create a very similar response. An explanation for the puzzling tendency of some women to remain in abusive marriages is given by Elizabeth Waites:

> Female victims may be especially prone to ambivalence, particularly when the abuser is a family member. Victims are often unable to leave an abusive relationship because of practical difficulties or threats, but it is the love-hate characteristic of the relationship that sometimes leads the victim to cling to it in spite of ongoing abuse. Although the victim experiences many losses—loss of trust, loss of a good parent or spouse who has now turned destructive, loss of illusions about the safety and dependability of significant relationships—occasional indications of love or even the memory of loving behavior may enable the victim to avoid confronting the clear evidence that love has been lost.[6]

Another framework for understanding the spouse who hangs around in spite of the continuing damage this does to her is that of codependency, or the idea that we can be addicted to certain relationships.

> Codependency is a devastating disease. If we remember that the co-dependent woman is really a tiny child living in a woman's body, trying desperately to hide from the terrible emptiness at her core, her behavior becomes more understandable. Clinging to an abusive relationship feels preferable to letting go and falling into a terrifying abyss.[7]

In recent years, however, the concept of codependency has been questioned by some feminist writers. Many have pointed out that women in our culture are socialized to be codependent—enablers, nurturers, responsible for relationships. To have such behavior then characterized as pathological creates a tremendous double bind:

> The codependency movement therefore represents a brilliant compromise for some women entrapped in difficult relationships. It gives them permission to think more about their own aspirations

[6]Elizabeth Waites, *Trauma and Survival: Post-Traumatic and Dissociative Disorders in Women* (New York: Norton, 1993) 10.

[7]Charlotte Davis Kasal, *Women, Sex, and Addiction* (New York: Harper & Row, 1989) 39.

and needs, without directly challenging those of others. As Harriet Lerner has noted, our culture dislikes and fears angry women, but it is not threatened by sick women meeting together to get well.

> . . . Women are so comfortable saying, I am a recovering addict; the problem is in me. They are so uncomfortable saying that the problem is in society, in their relationship, in their financial standing. Women get much more sympathy and support when they define their problems in medical terms than in political terms.[8]

Debate also rages over how much of these behaviors are due to socialization or to innate feminine traits. Or are they, as some suggest, merely the behaviors of people who are trying to survive as a member of a subordinate group? Deborah Tannen's work on linguistics examines male and female language differences in a descriptive way that rings true for many. However, she fails to point out that most of the language patterns employed by women are the patterns of those who are in a subordinate role.[9] Also, the hypervigilance noted to some extent in nearly all women is not so much a feminine trait as it is a trait of one who is "one-down" in the culture. At any rate, wives of offenders are deeply impacted by their husband's behavior, and it is no wonder that they frequently send conflicting and disturbing signals.

When I hear that a spouse is angry at her husband and that she has either temporarily or permanently chosen to leave the marriage, then I usually think there is the best potential for both husband and wife to make a more complete recovery. Bringing to the surface the spouse's anger at the offender really does seem to be a prerequisite for eventual healing in the marriage. It must also be said that there are cases where the marriage has stayed intact and become healthy through the hard work of both partners. Any treatment center worth its salt will provide significant treatment for family members as well as for the perpetrator.

Members of a congregation may need to be reminded that the cost of leaving a marriage, even temporarily, is generally higher

---

[8]Carol Tavris, interview with Harriet Lerner, quoted in Tavris, *The Mismeasure of Woman* (New York: Simon & Schuster, 1992) 203.

[9]Deborah Tannen, *You Just Don't Understand: Women and Men in Conversation* (New York: Ballentine, 1990).

for women than for men. Earning power is not as great, and the care of the children usually falls to the woman. Furthermore, not only must a clergy spouse deal with the losses of all other women in such situations, she must also face the probable loss of the family's primary support community and their home. "Out on the street" is not just a euphemism; it is often a reality.

The situation of the spouse can make matters more complex for the congregation. For example, in one congregation there was an incidence of a clergy spouse running out during a service in tears as an announcement was made of a congregational meeting. In another, a clergy spouse divorced her husband when she became aware of his behavior. She filed charges with the Church before any of his victims were willing to come forward. There have been many difficult cases of clergy spouses whose husbands did not tell them the truth about their clearly predatory behavior. They have therefore often been cruelly blindsided in the community when the cases have become public. Just to illustrate the variety of responses, there is another clergy spouse who remained a member of the congregation long after her husband, to whom she was still married, was deposed. Her continued presence was felt as intimidation by many in the congregation for over ten years. When the situation was finally opened, the wife was welcomed at the meeting but asked not to participate in a small group when feelings were being expressed. A firm decision had to be made not to let her presence continue to shut the congregation down. By handling this situation in such a way, the congregation was given permission to deal more openly with many feelings that had long been stuffed and to eventually make their peace with the wife, who continues to be a member of the congregation.

Some clergy spouses will appreciate expressions of support, some will not. At any rate, the Church must not abandon them. If a perpetrator needs help in leveling with his or her spouse, then that should be offered. In fact, it may be wise to build into official policy and procedure a meeting that the judicatory official will have with the couple, the primary purpose of which is holding the cleric's feet to the fire and requiring that he be truthful with his wife. At the very least, she deserves to know exactly what will be told to the congregation. Even when a spouse is angry at the Church, assistance in obtaining such things as housing and career counseling, therapy, or a return to school should be offered from time to time, even it is continuously rejected. The article by Ann and Derek Legg has more on the needs of the spouse.[10]

The children of offending clerics who remain in the congregation can also present a big challenge. In one congregation that also had an old case being opened, the divorced wife and two teenage children were still in the congregation. The Church provided a therapist for the family, which had already done a good amount of therapy, and they all participated fully in the congregational meeting. We also did some extra work with the peers of the teen-agers in the youth group. Family members of clerics who have been out of bounds have their own work to do. Often, breaking through the denial and the secrets in the family is necessary so that work can begin. Therefore, while opening these cases may be particularly painful for the family at first, it often provides the catalyst for the beginnings of recovery for families of the offender and also for the offender.

The Crisis Meeting

Preparation and Set-Up

The best place to have the meeting is the parish hall. Arrange round or rectangular tables so that six or seven people will be seated at each one. Direct people as they enter the room to sit thus at the tables. Choose enough small-group facilitators from the congregation so one will be available at each table you expect to fill. The facilitators can be trained one hour before the meeting to handle the work in small groups. If it is your practice to get people to sign up in advance for things, you may do so, but this is not necessary. Schedule the meeting for a time that is not part of a regular meeting time. Provide simple foods for breaks and a meal if necessary. Do not have food so elaborate that the usual kitchen crew will have an excuse to be absent from part of the meeting because of serving or cleaning up. Provide child care for at least four hours.

[10]See "The Offender's Family," p. 140.

The point of this set-up is so that people can move quickly from small group to large group with a minimum of fuss. Scheduling the meeting outside of regular times assures that people will have self-selected this meeting, the purpose of which they will know in advance. Some people will elect not to attend any congregational meeting, and this needs to be honored. I will discuss how to handle those who do not come after we have looked in more detail at the process of the meeting.

Make provisions ahead of time for any people who may become aware that they were victims of any kind of sexual abuse. Sometimes, too, people may recall an instance when they had knowledge they should have reported, and they may suddenly experience a lot of guilt. It is also possible that one might report his or her own out-of-bounds behavior. Do not promise not to report if that should happen; those facilitators who are ethically or legally mandated to report should make that clear at the outset. At the beginning of the meeting we always identify a man and woman who are present who have the skills to do crisis counseling and are willing to be thus used. These people should not be members of the congregation; they can be either local therapists or members of the response team. It is also advisable to research ahead of time and pass out a paper listing local therapists and a local hot-line number, if available.

Key Elements of the Meeting

The main components of the first congregational meetings are (1) truth telling, (2) sharing and validation of feelings, (3) education, (4) spiritual reflection, (5) asking the question Where do we go from here?

Schedule a break after the sharing of feelings, not before. We have found that the small-group work bonds people to one another and to the process, so they are then not likely to leave. On the few times we have varied the order and scheduled the small-group work after the break, we have lost some who were skittish about sharing feelings and who really only wanted to hear the details. This is damaging to the process and the eventual goal of community and trust building. This is another area in which we learned from our mistakes.

Truth telling. It is best if persons representing the denomination can be present for the meeting and have a primary role in the truth telling. Typically this will include significant denominational leaders and a lawyer. They will tell what the behavior was, what the status of the case is, and what measures have been taken to help any victims, and they will describe how the accused clergyperson and the family are being cared for and any discipline that has been imposed. If resolution of the case is not yet arrived at, church officials should be careful to use the term "allegations" whenever describing behavior. Under such circumstances one must be careful to speak of the accused and the complainant rather than of the perpetrator or offender and the victim or survivor.

When describing behavior, it is not necessary to whip out anatomical dolls or charts, but it is necessary to tell people enough about the behavior so they cannot minimize or deny what was going on. It is appropriate to use correct terms for sex acts and to give an idea of the scope and duration of the behavior. It may also be important to describe how the victims were vulnerable, if that can be done without revealing the identity of any victims who wish to remain anonymous.

After the presentation participants can be given a chance to ask questions for clarification. It is also possible at this time to invite anyone present who has *first-hand* experience of the cleric that they wish to share, to do so. Often this will elicit positive as well as negative observations. A surprising variety of experience frequently emerges from this session, often describing different kinds of abusive behavior, much of it not necessarily sexual, that people have experienced from the offender. Verbal abusiveness, financial irregularities, and substance abuse often seem to cluster with sexual abuse, but this is not to say that if a person exhibits any of these other behaviors, he or she is automatically out of bounds sexually.

It must be emphasized that the Church is not at this point conducting an investigation. If more information emerges during the process of opening a case with a congregation, that information may eventually provide part of the total picture of what happened, but the investigative process is totally separate.

Because the emphasis on disclosure represents such a radical change in the way any of the institutions in our culture operate, we expect a significant amount of resistance. The congregation will inevitably have members who are very uncomfortable with truth telling. There are a number of possible reasons why this should be so.

Resistance to Disclosure

Sometimes extreme discomfort with disclosure will happen because of rigid secret-keeping rules in a person's own family of origin. If one has an earlier and unresolved history of having been a victim, this may render any discussion of sexual abuse impossible for that person. Anyone who is out of bounds sexually is not likely to want similar problems to become a matter for common discussion; or the opposite can happen, and such a person may project his or her own difficulty outward, engaging in excessive and punitive search-and-destroy missions. Another motive might be that possession of the secret within the system represents power that will be lost when there is no longer any secret.

I believe that the only legitimate reason for not disclosing is that that the victim will be easily identifiable and wishes not to be known. Increasingly, though, victims are pushing for disclosure. This makes the practice evidently present in some regions and in some denominations of paying off victims in return for their silence a particularly disturbing and destructive one.

I would argue that even if the intention is to restore a clergyperson to ministry, this is no reason to keep silent about the fact that misconduct is a part of his or her history. In fact, I would suggest that it is absolutely vital that people who are going to be ministered to by this person should know, in order to be sure that the ministry be conducted safely. Furthermore, a person who is actively working on a recovery process can make a powerful witness about healing in a congregation that will invariably have many people in it who are struggling with the same issues.

Everyone in a congregation will be somewhat reticent about disclosure at first. Secrecy and cover-up are such cultural norms that none of us is immune. The combination of obsession and repression we bring to sexual matters also contributes greatly to this reticence. And yet we know that it is the act of keeping a secret that is so harmful, causing much additional harm and separation in any system, be it family, congregation, or the wider community. A major component of sexual abuse is the use of threat and intimidation by the perpetrator to keep the behavior secret. Unless we confront this head on, we will never recover from any kind of abuse in the many places it appears.

Church leaders may have additional reasons for resisting truth telling. Because they are charged with the care of the entire Church, they must weigh the interests of complainants and accused alike in order to arrive at a fair hearing that allows for due process. Judicatory officials tend to be much more closely associated with and sympathetic of the clergy and will therefore experience a great deal of ambivalence when managing these cases. If an investigation has determined guilt and officials do not fully understand the congregation's and the wider Church's need for disclosure, their natural tendency to protect the clergy may cause them to respond to pleas for privacy or confidentiality that may really be pleas for secrecy.

Another group that often advises no disclosure may be the Church's lawyers. Many lawyers think in adversarial terms and may be afraid of the possibility of suit from the accused cleric if anything is said at all. However, that outcome is extremely rare; I do not know of any cases where such a suit was successful. In fact, a suit from a victim because a case is not sensitively handled is a far more certain probability.

Sharing and validation of feelings. This step is basically a trauma debriefing and usually goes very well. When people finish, they express a great sense of relief. We hear comments like "It was as if a bomb was diffused," and "Now I understand a lot more about what has been going on," and "I no longer feel so alone." Those who have been very angry better understand those who have continued in denial. If we get resistance, it comes from some who may be very afraid of their own feelings or who fear that someone's (or their own) anger will get out of control. The method we use helps accommodate the former fear and prevent the latter outcome. People in groups of six are given verbal instructions and the help of a previously trained facilitator from the congregation to ensure they have a safe way to state feelings without getting into dialogue, discussion, or argument until everyone has had a chance to speak.

The validation of feelings is presented by a member of the intervention team. People are assured that all feelings are OK, and sometimes a visual model of the grieving process as it relates to congregational life is shown. We normalize the fact that many people will have very mixed feelings; they may well have positive feelings remaining about their pastor as well as feelings of betrayal. We ask people to give each other space to be wherever they may be relative to the grief process.

Education. Whatever education is indicated will be determined by the facts of the case. It is always important to address the issues of power abuse and to be especially thorough about that when adult exploitation or abuse has occurred. We have learned to make a distinction between the various origins of power that can be at play in a congregational setting. Sacred power is that which accrues to the priestly role; it is due to transference, projection, the embodiment of the divine in the person of the cleric, and the assocation of the pastor with a congregant's major life events. Much of this power is unconsciously given and unconsciously received. Secular power also gets factored in and is present in both the clergy and laity. Secular power resides in differences in age, class, race, wealth, and status in the community. The extent to which the laity have the power to hire and fire their clerics also influences the power equation.

In the cultural context in which this is occuring, gender power imbalance is so pervasive that we often do not recognize it when it is in play. We are beginning to suspect that the accrual of power to the clerical role may be quite different for male clergy than for female clergy. We are hearing many stories of female clerics who have been sexually harassed or abused during their vocational formation period by male clerics in mentoring roles, or who have been sexually harasssed by male members of their congregations and, in some cases, have been fired for calling those laymen on their behavior.

We do not have truly hard data on the gender distribution of sexual abuse—who abuses, who becomes victim—and statistics are always somewhat problematic. There are always concerns about underreporting, but it seems that in family settings, 20 percent of the abusers of children are reported to be women; in congregational settings involving clerical power abuse, 3 percent of abusers are reported to be women. Of the more than one hundred cases of sexual abuse that I am aware of, the three cases of women who abused involved victims who were one underage female, one woman, and one man whose wife considered herself the aggrieved party.

We must not ignore the gender power imbalance dimensions of the problem when we are educating the congregation. Understanding the power dynamics is a challenge, in part because of the paradox that clerics are most prone to abuse their power when they themselves feel powerless. The inappropriate crossing of sexual boundaries is nearly always precipitated by feelings of extreme neediness and entitlement on the part of the clergy.

It is also helpful to recognize that there are other forms of power abuse that are not sexual. It is possible for clergy and laity alike to traumatize vulnerable individuals in a congregation with angry outbursts of verbal abuse, misuse or theft of funds, and threatening excommunication or shunning, just to name a few common behaviors. Sometimes such behaviors cluster with sexual abuse, sometimes not. Substance abuse carries with it its own problematic set of dynamics and is a frequent accompaniment of sexual abuse.

The key to discerning if power abuse was present in any given situation is in deciding if it was possible for the person who got sexually involved with someone in a pastoral role to truly be able to give consent to that relationship. The sexual behavior per se is not the issue. In addition to all the other permutations of power imbalance discussed above are those pertaining to vulnerability. Vulnerability is present in anyone who has been a previous victim of any kind of abuse, is developmentally delayed or mentally or physically ill, is in counseling with the cleric, is in any kind of life transition involving loss, is under spiritual direction or being mentored.

There is considerable debate raging in the Church right now over the question if it is ever permissible for an eligible cleric to date an eligible congregant. Rutter,[11] Fortune,[12] and Peterson[13]

---

[11]Peter Rutter, *Sex in the Forbidden Zone* (Los Angeles: Tarcher, 1989).

[12]Marie Fortune, *Is Nothing Sacred? When Sex Invades the Pastoral Relationship* (San Francisco: Harper & Row, 1987).

[13]Marilyn Peterson, *At Personal Risk: Boundary Violations in Professional-Client Relationships* (New York: Norton, 1992).

all say, "Do not even think about it." Lebacqz and Barton[14] argue that clergy are most likely to find suitable mates who share their values in the congregation, and that dating may be possible if an eligible person is not vulnerable and if a strict and complete set of guidelines are followed to ensure safety in the relationship. The assumption is that the primary goal of such dating is to openly explore the possibilities of a commitment, not in having a secret sexual relationship. There are always cases with gray areas, but if we list the conditions under which it *might* be possible to date safely, then it will be easier to understand when the trust of the pastoral relationship has been betrayed. This is a list that does *not* have any optional elements:

1. Both parties are eligible.
2. The layperson is not vulnerable (see above).
3. The relationship is not secret; congregants and superiors both know they are dating.
4. The clergyperson is under regular supervision, which includes discussion of the relationship.
5. The congregant finds another pastor and, ideally, another congregation, until the relationship either stops or the couple commits to each other publicly.
6. The couple lets the sexual component of their relationship develop slowly, saving sexual intercourse for marriage.

This approach still carries an element of risk in today's Church. It will be noted that this was the way many clergy courtships were carried out in the days prior to the sexual revolution. In fact, it is the sexual revolution that has been partly responsible for bringing us to this point. Women understandably want to do away with the double standard, which traditionally made women responsible for maintaining sexual boundaries for both sexes. In learning to say yes to being sexually active, however, women found themselves still forced to bear the lion's share of the accidental consequences of sexual freedom, especially when pregnancy was a result. Then too, men grew accustomed to women who would increasingly say yes and then were puzzled when

---

[14]Karen Lebacqz and Ron Barton, *Sex in the Parish* (Louisville: Westminster/John Knox, 1991).

women realized that in order to say a genuine yes they also had to be able to say no. The alarming rise in incidents of reported date and marital rape may be one of the results.

It should be obvious that this is an extremely complex issue. If we apply the above considerations to a number of different situations we are aware of, it is possible to see that each case must be judged separately and that congregations have a right to be told the reasoning used by judicatory officials in determining what discipline was appropriate, based on the ability of the congregant to give consent and the degree of power imbalance present. I am also assuming that we are only talking about a clergyperson who has had a one-time slip. If there are more people making similar complaints, then there is a different and much more problematic pattern of behavior present.

Other possible educational needs for the congregation may be to have an understanding of pedophilia, sexual addiction and compulsivity, the issues around recovered memories, and some knowledge of multiple personality disorder, if these are part of a diagnosis for either victim or offender. In one recent case we were dealing with both of the latter topics, and we asked a psychiatrist to help us out with the educational piece because we recognized that we were in over our heads.

It may also be helpful to explain to the group how the Church is handling these cases differently now as opposed to even several years ago, as our understandings and knowledge have changed rather dramatically in a very short period of time. We know now of the severe trauma that clergy abuse causes to not only direct victims but secondary victims, especially the congregation. We also know that it is much more difficult than we thought for a person who is afflicted with sexual compulsivity or addiction to recover without intensive long-term group work and therapy.

If one is opening an old case, the congregational dynamics relative to closed systems and the keeping of secrets will need to be explored. Some congregations will need to look at the ways they have scapegoated the pastors who followed because of a virulent strain of anticlericalism present in the congregation.[15]

---

[15]See Darlene K. Haskin, "Afterpastors in Troubled Congregations, p. 155, and Nancy Myer Hopkins, "Further Issues for Afterpastors," p. 165, in this volume.

Spiritual Reflection. Participants will be asked to answer for themselves the question Where is God in all this? Alternate questions are What Bible story or hymn does this remind you of? and Where is the hope in all this? This can either be done in small groups or in the larger group, depending on the size of the larger group and the amount of time remaining.

In a sense, our entire approach to addressing clergy sexual misconduct is about empowering laypeople. One of the direct ways we do this in the congregational meeting is to ask people to do their own theology. This takes the risk, of course, of having some "bad" theology articulated. However, it has been our experience that when people struggle with this profound question together, they will often come up with some surprising observations; if one layperson says, for instance, that God is punishing us, another will have a different idea, and some helpful dialogue can occur. It is usually a good idea to have a clergyperson or lay theologian on the team to wrap this up, summarizing what has been said and then providing a concluding statement. This is the point at which the dangers of "cheap grace" and the issue of eventual repentance, forgiveness, and reconciliation can be addressed with the acknowledgment that much more work in this area will need to be done as time progresses.

Where do we go from here? The amount of time spent on this question during this first meeting will depend on the length of time allotted to the meeting and who is at the meeting. If a leadership group such as a vestry or parish council is meeting prior to a congregational meeting, this step would involve some planning for other meetings to come and could take a long time. If people are worn out from meeting at this point and need some time to process what has happened, it may be best to schedule this question for another meeting, merely raising it as unfinished work yet to be done. Often that is the way we handle this at congregational meetings that have been very intense and have possibly run late.

It is wise to appoint a task force for healing made up of people who understand that the process of healing is just beginning. Such a group can take responsibility at this point for assessing further needs and figuring out ways to address them. One way to get input is to send a survey home in the mail a week or two later with suggestions for follow-up activities as well as plenty of space provided for other suggestions and comments. It is often sufficient to make the point at the congregational meeting that while we are in the process of "putting this behind us" (a phrase heard often), we are not there yet, and there will be more work to be done.[16]

Who runs the congregational meeting? The meeting will always be run by people who come in from outside the congregation, sometimes known as a pastoral response team. They can be either consultants with specialized training in understanding congregational response to clergy sexual misconduct, or a team from the denomination that has been trained. A primary reason that anyone from the congregation should not be in a leadership role during the meeting is that everyone in the congregation has already been inducted into the system and is experiencing grief to one degree or another. All need to be helped to work together to heal. Furthermore, if clergy or lay leaders are in up-front positions other than doing introductions, the danger is that they will get scapegoated, becoming targets for free-floating anxiety and anger.

It is important to have both men and women represented on the pastoral response team. This is vital any time sexual abuse or exploitation is an issue. Men frequently hear other men better, and women may respond better to a woman leader. Having men and women sharing responsibility provides an important model for equalizing gender power, the disparity of which is a major underlying cause of sexual misconduct.

What about people who are unable or who choose not to attend? It is a good idea if there are shut-ins to visit them with the express purpose of bringing them on board, if they wish that. It may also be advisable to schedule later open meetings that will cover essentially the same ground if there are enough people indicating a need. Sometimes people will want to attend more than one such meeting. We have had people show up at three successive meetings with the same format and express appreciation for it each time. Occasionally, there will be a small group that related to the cleric in a special way, such as one with an intensely spiritual focus or a youth group, perhaps meeting weekly. These folks

---

[16]For more on this process, see Mark Laaser, "Long-Term Healing," p. 232 of this volume.

may be especially shattered and may need to do some additional work of their own.

In order to build on the change of attitude and new openness arising out of the congregational meetings, it is advisable to tell people who are there that they are free to tell others in the congregation who wanted to attend but were unable to do so and, *if they ask*, what they heard about the specifics of the case in the plenary sessions. Make it clear, however, that what was said in small groups by way of personal sharing remains confidential. Everyone going out of the meeting is, in some sense, an ambassador for truth telling and a new openness. Recommend that they give people a chance after hearing the details to talk about their feelings, much as was done during the meeting.

If a person has adamantly refused to attend a congregational meeting, this should be honored. Some people who have personal histories of sexual abuse may have enough self-knowledge to know that they will be terribly disturbed by such a meeting. Others may refuse to come out of ordinary cussedness. Under these circumstances it may be best to just let the matter drop, but be clear about not letting them scuttle the process for others.

Some Variables That Determine How Easily a Congregation Will Recover

The congregation: history, and how open or closed is it? At the same time consultants are beginning the crisis work, they will also start getting a picture of the way the congregation has operated together. It may become obvious that congregations have had unreasonable expectations of their clergy for many years, thus contributing to a string of incidences of clerical burnout. One of the first questions that should be asked is How have your other clergy left this congregation? Another clue that will cause consultants to sit up and take notice is a long history of conflict. Other congregations may seem depressed. This is quite common when the case is an old one that never was dealt with openly. All these things can be noted for people during the crisis period, but the real work on these more long-term problems will take place soon after the crisis phase, when the congregation should be more receptive to taking a good look at its history including an examination of patterns, both positive and negative, that have developed over the years.

Another variable is the degree of openness or closedness, mentioned previously. However, the fact that outside help has been asked for is in itself a sign of hope, especially for a system that is otherwise seen to be relatively closed. This brings up the obvious point that we never go into a congregation without the invitation of denominational leaders and the remaining clerical and lay leaders of the congregation, if the congregation is not completely autonomous.

Key lay leaders: how healthy are they? Very often a burden will fall on the shoulders of one or more key lay leaders when a cleric is removed, especially if the one removed was the senior pastor. Even the most "together" of senior wardens, elders, or council presidents will experience great distress while piloting a congregation through the rocky shoals of a major clerical betrayal of trust. Denominational leaders often seem to forget that these leaders volunteered for a very different job, and had they known what they would be getting into, they most likely would have run the other way. One senior warden I worked with for nearly a year writes:

> Of course, the Senior Warden could resign, but there are two reasons why I did not. One, I was naive; I had no idea of the complexity of the situation or the demands that would be placed on me. Two, I felt a responsibility; I felt some obligation . . . to see it through. I don't think I was unusual in that response; I believe most wardens would respond in the same way. Throughout the whole process the idea of resigning has been a comfort, knowing that I could protect myself if the situation was too intense.
>
> This has been a learning experience for me; I have grown in ways that I could not have imagined last April. It hasn't been pleasant; in fact, some of it has been unpleasant, and much of it has been a chore. But it has forced me to assess my own strengths and weaknesses and learn from the experience.
>
> I have tempered my theological knowledge of leadership with experience. I know that I have to seem confident in the future, even if I am not always confident. I know that I have to adjust my expectations of people and organizations; volunteer organizations may not always respond to my need for quick and responsive action. I have also learned how to trust and who to trust.

He goes on to say, "Don't be embarrassed when you start to feel that the people on the vestry and in the congregation start to be your 'flock.' Don't be concerned that you don't feel that way."

He also mentions meeting the needs of parish paid staff, for understanding the canons, and dealing with the almost inevitable but hopefully temporary drop in attendance and pledged income often experienced after new cases break. Planning the agenda for and conducting innumerable and seemingly endless vestry meetings also fell to him in the absence of the senior pastor, who had been removed.

One of the most difficult tasks lay leaders face, in many Protestant denominations at least, is that of negotiating severance packages with a pastor who has been removed. Leaders get caught in the squeeze between the demands and expectations of the offending cleric and the expectations of parishioners, who are often all over the map on this issue, depending on what their relationship continues to be with the offender. There are always many other details of the leave-taking that suddenly assume great symbolic value for all concerned, and feelings are typically intense.

If the cleric is so badly impaired that he has no sense of the effect of his behavior on others, he may try to put off the leave-taking and keep showing up at the church or at people's homes. Many who are disciplined do not seem to have any understanding of how their continuing behavior affects others. This is probably as good an indication as any of how ill they have really become.

Are there laypeople present who may be abusing their own power? This dynamic does not always become obvious to outside consultants during the early phases of recovery. Church people are often so unfailingly nice that they are reluctant to identify one or more of their members as having destructive behavior, especially to an outsider. It is often not until the recovery process gets stuck that the influence of other laity who are abusing their power becomes obvious. Some common behaviors we have identified are exercising rigid financial control through misuse of their own considerable resources, sexual harassment or even abuse, and indulging in verbal, abusive, angry outbursts. These behaviors frequently bear an uncanny resemblance to the offending behaviors of the removed cleric. Another common behavior of power-abusing laity is having knowledge of earlier congregational secrets and blocking the information sharing with the congregation when knowledge of the secret represents power. Not every congregation has these problems, but enough do so that the possibility needs to be considered.

How do we deal with such difficult people? Once the behavior is identified, a small group of well-chosen members will first attempt to confront the person about his or her behavior; sometimes this will be an elaborately planned intervention, sometimes not. It depends on the severity of the behavior. Some coaching from a person skilled in doing such confrontations will probably be necessary. This move is not only for the sake of the congregation but for the person being confronted. It is never helpful to a person to have people fail to call him or her to account for destructive behavior.

If confrontation fails to get the desired result, more drastic measures may be necessary. People will need to give each other support in not responding in the same old way to the behavior. If they do a good job of this, the person will either have to start changing or leave the congregation. Here again, church people seem to think they must put up with any kind of behavior because the worst thing that could happen is to lose someone. I believe that a community of faith has as part of its mission that of holding people accountable, both within and without.

Clergy remaining on staff: how healthy are they? Are they able to exercise a nonanxious presence and not take the inevitable reactivity personally?[17] Clergy in such situations will do well to be in therapy themselves, if needed. At a minimum they will be taking care of themselves and getting support outside the congregation. Denominational leaders will want to provide extra supervision and support. Often new job descriptions will have to be developed for those remaining on staff, and the timely addition of a good interim pastor can help a lot. One of the things we are discovering is that there is a drastic shortage of good, competent, mature interims who can step into these settings.

There are special difficulties if one is an afterpastor in a congregation that has been dysfunctional for a long time because of

---

[17]Edwin Friedman, *Generation to Generation: Family Process in Church and Synagogue* (New York: Guilford, 1985).

one or more cases of clerical power abuse or any kind of burnout of a clergyperson in a congregation's history.

Status of the offender. How effective was he or she in other ways in the congregation just prior to being disciplined? Often the profile of a clergyperson who has shown a predatory pattern of abuse of either children or vulnerable adults is that of a very charming, even charismatic, personality. He or she may have attracted a great many dependent people and may quite possibly have been an effective pastor. This type of offender is frequently responded to by people who are either temporarily or chronically needy for whatever reason. Therefore, when the discipline comes, many of these people will be either in deep denial or totally devastated.

Conversely, if the offending cleric was not functioning very well, perhaps even abusing his power in other ways such as in abusive angry outbursts or having progressed to serious substance abuse, people may well heave a huge sigh of relief when he finally goes. The initial trauma to the congregation under these latter circumstances may not be as great, but more subtle and just as problematic difficulties can arise later.

Was the discipline considered fair by a majority of the congregation? There will probably always be some in any congregation who feel that the discipline meted out to the offender was either too lenient or too harsh. However, if the majority are satisfied and given good, careful explanations, this should not be a long-term problem. There is always a tension felt between the need for compassion and caring for the offending cleric and the equally important need for consequences to happen. Consequences are important for the offender, too, as it is appropriately chosen consequences that may well determine how well the offender's recovery proceeds.

Is the offender still in the community and basically unrecovering? There is nothing worse for the congregation than the continued presence of an offender who "doesn't get it." Even if the cleric is no longer a cleric or attending services, as most are not, the possibility of running into that person locally puts many congregants in a continual state of apprehension and dread. Frequently, too, such clerics have trouble letting go of the congregation. It is not unusual for congregations to have to change locks or withhold final paychecks in order to get such things as church-owned vehicles back. Sometimes, offenders have gone into endeavors like selling insurance and have thought nothing of contacting all former parishioners in order to get clients.

It may be possible for some people in the congregation to maintain a friendship that has been of long-standing duration and provide support for a clergyperson who has been disciplined, but it must be made clear that this choice *always* rests with the congregant. Also, it will be helpful if a distinction can be made between giving support and enabling a person to stay ill. The decision to remain friends cannot in any way be a result of manipulation or coercion by the offender.

In those cases where a disciplined clergyperson continues to contact people against their will, it may be necessary for denominational leaders to issue what amounts to the ecclesiastical equivalent of a restraining order. Occasionally it has been necessary for individuals who continue to be harassed to get restraining orders from the courts.

Status of family members of both victims and offenders. Are there family members remaining in the congregation and causing difficulty either because they are highly defensive or are unable to let go of anger? We have discussed this issue relative to such a person's presence at a congregational meeting, but it can also be a problem over the longer haul. Sometimes it will appear that a person is attempting to sabotage a congregation's continued healing by shutting down the new openness achieved at the congregational meetings. It must be made clear to people that whatever they are feeling is OK, but others are feeling differently now, and we intend to do whatever it takes to continue with the healing process.

Are there known victims in the congregation? There is a well-known tendency in our culture to scapegoat victims, especially if they are women. This must be guarded against at all costs. It will probably be necessary to do much education around the issues of power abuse beyond whatever is done during the congregational meeting so people understand that there was never any possibility of this having been a relationship between consenting adults. Sometimes, too, people will tend to blame child victims, especially if they come from economically marginal or otherwise troubled families.

How helpful has the denomination been to the congregation? The availability of denominational input and assistance is a major variable in how well congregations will recover. Congregations that are relatively autonomous are sometimes at a disadvantage because there is not much help available to them from outside; at the same time, there may be less potential for a badly bungled denominational response. The best prevention of this latter outcome is to have in place before any trouble occurs a good relationship between denominational leaders and the congregations under their care. This is a two-way street and requires careful nurturing of the relationship so that mutual trust exists before any difficulty arises. I am constantly amazed that the congregation, which is made up of laypeople and is the basic unit of the Church, is often the least empowered of all when clergy sexual misconduct becomes an issue.

Strategies and models for the development of a good denominational response ahead of the need are emerging in most denominations. These are best if developed regionally and have wide input from a variety of sources. A collaborative effort during development along with good dissemination of the resulting policies and procedures will go a long way toward getting ahead of the curve. It is generally agreed that it is best to develop definitions and general principles rather than trying to anticipate every possible situation and write a rule to cover it. Anyone working on this must be able to have a systems view of the imapct of clergy sexual misconduct on the whole Church and not just be thinking narrowly about the needs of complainant and accused. In particular, I would stress, don't forget the needs of all those who become secondary victims.

Long-Term Healing

Mark Laaser

When someone like me goes into a congregation to help with the healing, the knowledge of my sexual misconduct in the past must be revealed. If this doesn't happen, there is the possibility that the healing process for some will be traumatized. The worst scenario that can happen is that people, most importantly victims of any kind, will find out after the fact and feel betrayed.

Congregations heal over time, one member at a time. In this volume we have tried to identify some of the healing needs of various individuals both inside and outside the congregation. Long-term healing strategies can't be cut from a blueprint and applied to every congregation. Individuals and individual churches must come first. Healing strategies must be tailored to each congregation only after the needs are understood clearly. Nancy Myer Hopkins has described how to come about understanding these in her article on the crisis stage. Any long-term strategy for the healing of a congregation must also recognize that not all members *will* heal, will *want* to heal, and that not all will do so at the same time or in the same way.

When Jesus confronted the paralyzed man at the pool of Bethesda, he had been ill for thirty-eight years (John 5:2-9). It might seem obvious that this man wanted to be healed. But the first question Jesus asked was "Do you want to be healed?" The man might have said, "What do you think, are you crazy? Of course I want to be healed." Instead, the man offered excuses as to why he hadn't been able to get into the pool. Imagine, in all that time he hadn't figured out how to ask for help!

The Will to Heal

We must remember that congregations may already have the resources to be in the healing process. They won't heal, however, if they don't want to. We are doomed to be frustrated if we don't recognize and accept that this may be the case. Whatever our level of training and access to resources, we can't help if we are not welcome to be helpers.

This means that when we conduct an interview with the leadership of a congregation we should assess this factor of willingness. I learned this lesson the hard way. A church in California had discovered that their pastor had sexually acted out with women in the church. One influential and wealthy member of the church paid my way to fly out and be with the board of the church. When I walked into the room there was an icy reception. They didn't know who I was and what I was doing there. They didn't want me there. They proceeded to have a four-hour fight-filled meeting. This was what they wanted. They wouldn't listen to anything I had to say.

What I should have done is interview the leadership before I ever got on the plane. There should have been a clear understanding of what my role and service was to be. This should not have been just for the weekend I was actually there but for a period of time. This is to ensure that denominational authorities have been informed of our work and are in full accord with our involvement. If we don't do this, we run the risk of offending competent people at the denominational level and perhaps having them be in conflict with us later.

In another situation, I was invited to speak at a specially called meeting of a congregation after the regular Sunday morning worship. Halfway through my talk a member stood up and said, "Will you get to the point? What is your point?" My point was how difficult the healing process would be. This man said, "We are not here to heal, we are here to ask for the resignation of the current board because they have forced our pastor to resign. We want him to stay." This man later led a faction of people out of the meeting. They formed a new church and called, as their first pastor, their old pastor who had just resigned. He was considered a wonderful preacher and leader. Many people in this church thought they could have a relationship in which things would be different. In short, they were looking for a hero to save them. They needed a hero and were not willing to let go of this image even though they knew the facts of the sexual exploitation.

Most of the people in the new church did not accept that the pastor had been at fault. They blamed the women for being seductive. They blamed his wife for not being available. They blamed themselves for not being there to listen to him. They wondered out loud why he had not come to them for help. One woman said, "I would have been the first to go over to his house to comfort him."

In this situation, even though the leadership of the church wanted help, the people in the congregation didn't. Often we will see that the leadership has been living with the facts for weeks and months. They have had time to react and to be together and process their feelings. They have been privy to private conversations and the revelation of facts that might not be appropriate for the whole congregation to know because they would injure victims. Leadership may be further down the healing path that the rest of the congregation. They may be tired and frustrated. They may just want to move on.

In the situation I just described, the congregation shouted members of the board down when they tried to tell some of the facts, which would have justified their position. Many people said, "Why can't we just forgive and forget?" Verses of Scripture were quoted. Tearful people talked of love and acceptance: "Don't we all have problems?"

I learned after I arrived on the scene that the potential for this kind of conflict existed. I would have served them better had I interviewed enough of the board to know that the timing of my visit was probably not appropriate. This church needed to proceed more slowly and gently. The board needed support to do this. The result was a permanently divided church. Now there are two churches, very close to each other, that will have negative feelings for each other for years to come.

We need to be sensitive to this kind of situation. We must not always be ready to rush in on our white horses with our resource manuals, lectures, and videotapes. In the beginning stages of the long-term healing process those who want to be healed may be a small number. From this small group, however, a process can be started that can eventually lead to a positive influence on the entire congregation.

It is also important to have denominational support. Many denominations are establishing sound intervention strategies and have national and local staff trained in handling these situations. The Parish Consultation Service has begun training programs to increase these numbers. We should always be alert to determining who is inside the system that may be able to help.

Some denominations and religious bodies are provincial in their feelings about helping themselves. When Jimmy Swaggert was exposed for involvement with prostitution, for example, the local Assemblies of God district superintendent was very clear that the situation was a matter for internal investigation and discipline. Some religious groups feel strongly about their own theological or biblical interpretation of the events.

In the early stages of our research-action project, two of us were invited to help a local congregation deal with the leave-taking of a pastor who had been arrested for soliciting male prostitution. Some of our recommendations were written up and presented to the healing committee of this church. Several of the highly educated professionals objected to bringing in outside help. We wound up providing a training for this religious group's local counseling agency. The agency's counselors then worked with the church.

The Long-Term Effects of Clergy Sexual Misconduct

Not all members of a congregation will heal at the same time. Grief reactions can be delayed for years. Some members will be in denial for short or long periods of time and later come to realize that they have stored up many emotions about the situation. It is possible, then, that we may be asked to work with congregations years after the events took place. Historically, no one was there for them to initiate any kind of healing process. We know that in the past many denominational leaders encouraged secrecy and "forgiving and forgetting."

In the first year of the Parish Consultation Service, we worked with a church in which a lawsuit had been filed against a pastor fifteen years after the sexual abuse took place. The newspaper publicity of the case forced the church and the denomination to finally deal with the situation. When we arrived on the scene, members of the church were finding out for the first time why their "beloved" pastor had really left years ago. The denominational officials were the only ones who really knew at the time. The emotions we encountered were as fresh as if the events had happened the day before.

There are many of these historically wounded congregations in which healing processes need to take place. One church sent out a letter to all graduates of the parochial school and their parents in which a sexually offending priest had taught. The letter sought to offer help to any primary victims who may not yet have been identified or any secondary victims whose trust and faith had been damaged. This letter was sent twenty-five years after the events took place.

We suspect that much church conflict over even petty issues can be traced back to unresolved issues connected with a major betrayal of trust. In another church in which the truth was not originally told, the pastor had not only been sexually abusive but in many ways had also been emotionally abusive. He ruled with an iron hand and enforced arbitrary discipline. He was very angry with women and occasionally preached from a sexist position. He especially treated female staff very badly. There were many people in this church who had been hurt by this pastor in a variety of ways. The feelings of anger and resentment had festered for years. Women were angry with men over what seemed to the men to be petty issues. Men were angry with women for being so angry. People were angry with one another for not being able to handle controversy that the old pastor would have dealt with swiftly. When these good people finally learned the truth and started talking to one another about their feelings and memories, it was a healing revelation.

Even if the facts are known initially, reactions may be delayed. We know that sexual trauma victims may repress memories for years. The same is true for victims of pastors. This dynamic also applies to secondary victims, those whose faith has been betrayed. Long-term healing strategies recognize that victims of the pastor who surface in the initial period may not be the only ones. The church must be ready to accept other victims, even years later, and be prepared to deal with them. Secondary victims may also have these delayed reactions.

Education should be provided to the congregation about what physical, emotional, and spiritual symptoms may be present in people who have suppressed or repressed reactions to trauma. Currently this is clinically described as post traumatic stress disorder. It would be wise for a church to ask a clinician acquainted with this condition to provide this education and to be available for additional needs that may arise.

This is important for another reason. In a typical congregation there are many sexual-abuse survivors of other perpetrators. If they have not dealt with their memories, the current events in the church may serve to trigger them. It has happened a number of times that when we teach about sexual abuse someone will start crying in the middle of the presentation because they have remembered something traumatic at the hands of a different perpetrator. We must be ready to deal with this not only during the crisis phase but throughout the healing process.

The Stages of Grief

When we do confront congregations and members who are ready to heal, we believe that long-term healing is a process of grieving. There are four stages of grief that can be identified in congregations. All of them are normal and must be worked through.

1. Shock

Shock is most prevlant in the crisis stage, which Nancy Myer Hopkins deals with in "Living Through the Crisis." It is a stage of disbelief; the mind and spirit prevent emotions from being felt. This is natural and protective. It is like the brain going into coma to repair itself from physical injury. A problem occurs if people believe that this numbness is a permanent reaction to their loss and that they don't have any feelings. Then, when strong emotions occur later, they can be misidentified. For example, anger that surfaces later about some relatively insignificant church matter might be thought to belong to that issue, when, in fact, it is part of the grief reaction to the earlier issue. Thinking that the numbness of the shock stage is going to be permanent can also create fear. People might think there is something wrong with them because they were "doing so well." Emotions that surface later may then cause panic.

Reminding people of the stages of grief and telling the truth repeatedly is the best way to help them out of the shock stage. The one-year anniversary of the events, for example, may be a good time to remind people of the loss. This is often a time when feelings will resurface. The same time of the year brings the same weather and annual events, which may trigger old feelings. It is a good time to provide opportunities for group support and the sharing of emotions.

2. Searching

When shock wears off, it is normal for people to not want to accept and deal with their sadness at the loss. The stage of searching means that people may wish that their pastor could return and that their trust level could be restored. This is often a time when congregations actually bargain with the pastor or the denomination to facilitate a return. Often congregations will be angry with denominational officials for not allowing the pastor to stay or for treating him badly. One dynamic that complicates this further is that the searching and bargaining phase is also simultaneously being experienced by the offending pastor, who may well be in contact with at least some congregants, who then can get stuck in this phase much longer than is normal.

Searching can be a time of denial. People may feel that the events really didn't happen, that such a good pastor really couldn't have done the things that have been alleged. Facts are ignored. Where denial isn't a factor, the minimizing process of "forgiving and forgetting" may be adopted. It does seem biblical and spiritual to be of a forgiving and graceful nature. This dynamic, however, is most often adopted for the purpose of avoiding feelings. We have often seen people ragefully angry at others for not being "forgiving."

Tragically, many victims can be disbelieved at this time and re-victimized in the process. Victims can also be blamed for the "seduction" of the pastor. People may need to protect the "perfect" nature of the pastor. He must certainly have been overwhelmed by some utterly beguiling person. It was not his fault. In one situation the parents of a child victim were blamed for being bad parents. It was thought that if the son hadn't been so needy and seductive, the poor priest wouldn't have done the things he did.

What is so hard for congregations to accept is the idea that their pastor is at fault. They need to protect their faith and their trust level. They need for things to stay "normal." Other people or factors need to be scapegoated. This is a major reason why so many afterpastors encounter so much anger. They are like the stepparent who tries to take the biological parent's place. When people are not ready to accept the loss, anyone who tries to remind them of it can face extreme forms of anger.

A final danger in the searching phase is that pastoral search committees, charged with the responsibility of finding a replacement, will often seek someone who strikingly resembles their former pastor physically, emotionally, and/or spiritually. Often congregations will search for the same type of charismatic personality, who they hope will lead them out of their depression. The potential here is that often this type of "heroic" charisma brings with it a histrionic and narcissistic personality, which leads to new trouble. It is no wonder that we have discovered congregations in which four or five successive pastors have sexually exploited congregants.

It must be recognized that there will be those who need a longer period of time to express deep feelings of loss and sadness. In the latter phase of healing this is probably best accomplished in a small-group setting. Modeling these feelings by those mature enough to express them can be helpful. Long-term healing strategies will identify people who seem to be handling their feelings in mature ways. These people can then be enabled and encouraged to express them in group settings. Using the same ground rules established during the initial congregational meetings[1] may be necessary to ensure that all are heard equally and all listen respectfully.

Beyond the disclosure that occurs at the initial congregational meetings, presentation of the known facts and any new developments can continue to be a part of ongoing meetings. We have

---

[1]See Nancy Myer Hopkins, "Living Through the Crisis," p. 201 of this volume.

often seen lawyers, church leaders, or denominational officials handle this well. Facts can be stated in ways that don't compromise the anonymity of innocent victims. The "forgive and forget" faction will possibly vehemently oppose such disclosures, but disclosure is essential to the healing process. Despite many people's fears, this is not harmful to the pastor because it helps him deal with his issues and reduces the possibility of a double life in the future.

Educationally broad-based information can be given at public meetings about the nature of sexual abuse and exploitation. Ideally, recovering victims from other congregations can participate in this by telling their own stories. This can be powerfully healing but requires maturity on the part of that person. Recovering victim-survivors can help a congregation see how damaging the abuse was. This forces people to acknowledge that their pastor did in fact abuse.

Recovering offenders can also be valuable in telling their story. This kind of honesty and courage demonstrates to members what true recovery looks like and illustrates the complexities and ambiguities inherent in clergy sexual misconduct. Even pastors who have been egregious offenders have often been effective pastors in other areas of ministry. People need to grieve the loss of that "good pastor" and to know that healing is a possibility for all. Attendance at meetings where these kinds of presentations take place should be voluntary. There will be those who aren't ready to deal with their feelings.

There are many other related educational activities that small groups can pursue during the long-term healing phase. Most educational tasks can be structured so there is an opportunity for people to continue the emotional process of healing. The following offerings have been beneficial:

Family of origin exploration. Individuals in a small group can be taught to do an extended family tree, called a genogram, which includes gathering personal data about all family members of at least three or four generations. This typically includes such things as divorces, premature deaths, alcoholism, familial patterns of abuse, secrets and traumatic events that reverberate through the family. Also, it is important to identify positive events, such as when family members have overcome difficult circumstances. It is also possible to examine relationships between people cross-generationally so that patterns of such things as extreme closeness, distance, or conflict can be identified. An intriguing question would be, "Why have you been comfortable (or uncomfortable) in this particular congregation?" There are books and computer programs available to help individuals do a genogram,[2] and a local family therapist would probably be glad to assist.

Doing a congregational genogram. There is now being piloted in several congregations a program designed to help people in small groups examine a congregation's history. This combines small-group process with research and is intended to have an end product that will then be presented to the rest of the congregation. The groups look at such things as the history of key lay leaders, clergy, important and pivotal events, triumphs and traumas. They also take a look at what they can learn from seeing their buildings through the eyes of someone who might be walking in for the first time. Just one of many questions asked is Whose pictures are on the wall in your buildings, and what does that tell you about who is important to this community? This is being developed by Nancy Myer Hopkins.[3]

Engaging the services of family therapists. Another, less structured way to do the work of looking at a congregation's history is to engage a team of therapists to help look at the church family's past as it impacts the present, but in a more freewheeling way. Two of our Parish Consultation Service consultants are family therapists, and they have developed this approach. Ann and Derek Legg, who have contributed to this volume, worked over the period of a year with a group in a congregation to help bring resolution to some very painful events that involved feelings of betrayal because of the actions of a number of clergy and diocesan staff. The members of the congregation also were able to acknowledge their own part in the problems, which became very complex, and there was enough misunderstanding present to go around for a good long time.

[2]Monica McGoldrick and Randy Gerson, *Genograms in Family Assessment* (New York: Norton, 1985); Randy Gerson, *MacGenogram* or *Genogram Maker,* write to: Humanware, 2908 Nancy Creek Road N.W., Atlanta, GA 30327.

[3]Nancy Myer Hopkins, "A Congregational Genogram," under development, publication pending. Write to: 2 Fox Run Road, Cumberland, ME 04021.

Toward the end of that year it was felt that the congregation as a whole, which had been continuously brought along with the small group's work, was ready to design a healing service. Because there were some lingering resentments that could never be resolved, it was decided that individuals would write letters expressing their feelings. Then those letters were burned. This was happening just before Lent. They hit on the idea of mixing the ashes from the letters with the ashes of last year's palms, a tradition in many denominations that have a rich liturgical heritage. Those ashes were used during the Ash Wednesday services, placed on each penitent's forehead with the words "Remember that you are dust, and to dust you shall return." The leftover ashes were mixed in the soil of small potted plants and given to the children at Easter. This certainly is an inspired use of ritual, but the point is, those ideas emerged from the community and were timely. They fit that congregation's particular circumstances and style. If such a ceremony had been gotten from a book and imposed on a group, it would have probably fallen flat.

There are a wide variety of twelve-step groups that a congregation could sponsor and provide space for. Victim's support groups are another possibility. There are programs available to do studies in sexuality, and a safe and respectful place could be provided for men and women to talk to one another about their gendered experience. Local rape crisis centers and women's shelters will be gold mines of materials and assistance in offering education about the issues of domestic abuse and sexual violence. There is a good program available to help people look at sexual violence in the media.[4]

It can be the job of a congregational advocate, someone from outside the congregation skilled in understanding the dynamics, to help a task force appointed from the congregation to plan for educational events and to work with search committees and others to find the most suitable candidates for the new pastor. It is the advocate's job to understand the family dynamics of the congregations and the personalities in it. An advocate is a gentle reminder of the truth and a model of effective leadership.

[4] *Study of Violence in the Media*. Write to: Center for Media and Values, 1962 Shenandoah, Los Angeles, CA 90034, or phone (310) 559-2944.

We strongly believe that the best way to survive the searching phase is to replace the pastor with an interim rather than a full-time appointment. An interim should be a person of substantial training and maturity in order to withstand the brunt of negative reaction and church conflict that will inevitably be a part of the first year.

3. Disorientation

Being without pastoral leadership always disorients congregations to some extent. However, a clerical vacancy following sexual misconduct can be particularly disorienting. People wonder how they will survive. Simple decisions become ominous. There are practical questions, from who will preach on Sunday to who will officiate at weddings already scheduled. More importantly, faith becomes disoriented. Pastors are parent figures who model faith, and often we identify our own faith with this modeling. Faith now seems hypocritical. What was preached was not practiced.

In the face of practical difficulties and confused faith, disorientation often produces a congregational level of depression. This is an atmosphere of potential conflict in which some search for black and white answers, others leave the church altogether, and some seek new and charismatic leadership. It can be a time of anxiety and anger, blaming and self-righteousness.

It may be necessary at this point in the congregation's development to take a good look at the structure. How clear have the internal boundaries been? Where has the power resided? Have there been historically unrealistic expectations of the clergyperson's role? Do new job descriptions for all paid staff need to be developed? How do we live our stated values about what it means to be part of a covenantal community? How will we know if we are violating those values? It will probably take a consultant to help sort out the structural questions. Doing this activity as the major response to sexual misconduct, however, without simultaneously and straight-forwardly tackling the truth of the betrayal of trust is pretty much wasted effort.

If conflict has reached mammoth proportions, then a consultant who is skilled in teaching people to manage conflict and also understands the endless complications of displaced anger generated by misconduct may be needed.

This is a time when the congregational advocate and/or the new interim must be at his or her toughest. He or she must be tough in gentle ways, "living reminders" of faith. It is not entirely clear that an interim in a basically pastoral role can avoid some of the dynamics of being an afterpastor. If this happens, another person such as an advocate may have to be the one who gets tough, and the two of them might, to some extent, play "good cop, bad cop." The presence of destructively behaving laypersons in the aftermath of sexual misconduct has been noted in a significant number of cases.

One of the ways to help congregations survive the disorientation of this phase is to model healthy boundaries and rules that any congregation should adhere to. There are several rules that, if followed, will help to build a new trust level in the congregation:

We don't deny the facts and we do talk. From day one of the crisis the truth has been told without harming innocent victims. No one has been allowed to cover up the facts. As new ones are learned, they are shared with the congregation. Regular congregational meetings are held as necessary to inform those who wish to attend. Various denominational leaders may participate in these. Lawyers may be called in to explain legal considerations. Psychologists, social workers, counselors, and educators may be sought to explain the dynamics of the situation as pertinent and to offer the resources for help that are available.

In other congregational meetings and business the facts are not ignored. They are openly discussed whenever they might affect the life of the church.

We do feel. Those who are able to model what their feelings are may be called on to share them in meetings of the congregation. Expressions of anger and sadness are openly tolerated and encouraged. In public congregational meetings the larger audience can be broken up into smaller discussion groups. Each one will have a designated leader who is mature and capable of leading group sharing of feelings. Recovering victims and perpetrators from other situations who are mature and in safe enough emotional places may be asked to share their stories. Congregational leaders can tell their stories of how the situation has affected them.

We don't minimize. The significance of the abuse and the damage done to both primary and secondary victims is openly accepted and discussed. We don't seek to create martyrs whose only job is to suffer, but we do wish people to accept the pain and consequences of the situation. This is also a place for primary and secondary victims, not necessarily of this congregation, to tell their stories.

We don't blame. The most damaging dynamic in any congregation is blame. In this volume various authors have discussed the forms in which blaming takes place. Victims, victims' families, congregational and denominational leaders, and new pastors may all be targets. Blaming occurs when nobody is mature enough to take responsibility for their own involvement in the situation. It is difficult to accept that which we may dislike about ourselves. It is also difficult to accept sinful and immoral behavior in others that we might be frightened of in ourselves. It is much easier to scapegoat others for our mistakes or be angry at someone else rather than ourselves. It may also be easier to keep our image of the pastor-abuser pure if can we can blame someone else for what he or she did.

A healing congregation learns to take responsibility for its role in the current crisis. As noted above, during the time of a search for a full-time replacement for the pastor, a good exercise is to take inventory of the dysfunctional dynamics of the congregation that may have led to the vulnerable situations of both pastor and victims. What were the unrealistic expectations of the pastoral role? What were the imbalances of power in the congregation? What is the role of men and women in the congregation? What are the age-old conflicts that never really get resolved?

4. Reorganization

The final stage is a stage of acceptance. The congregation accepts several key facts. Their pastor is gone and is not coming back. He was not perfect. Damage was done to many people. Nothing is completely black and white. No one is all wrong. No one is all right. And our God continues to be a loving and graceful God even though many negative and consequential things have happened.

For churches that are somewhat mature to begin with, reorganization may simply be a stage of accepting the loss, processing sadness, and returning to normal. For other, less-mature churches reorganizing will be more a matter of spiritual growth. Sadly, we have found that it is often immature churches that find immature pastors. As Richard Irons and Katherine Roberts have described, pastoral sexual dysfunction is more complicated that simply defining it as immaturity.[5] It is helpful, however, to know that in many ways immaturity refers to congregations and pastors who are "stuck" in adolescent development. There is a "heat-seeking missile" quality to this. Dysfunction finds dysfunction. Adolescent churches seek answers that are rigidly black and white and leaders who are heroic in adolescent fashion. Adolescent heroism is about high drama and rigid control, not faithful and courageous leadership.

It is the job of the congregational advocate and/or the interim to minister to this adolescence. In many ways he or she is being called on to model spiritual maturity. Moving beyond spiritual adolescence challenges people to search for their internal spirituality as opposed to external, rigid, black-and-white answers. The advocate and/or interim must be able to model this.

Churches that are able to move to a more mature stage of faith are able to become healthier families. One might prefer to call them "communities" of faith and not "families" of faith. There are several qualities about this health. Healthy communities have healthy boundaries. Love, affirmation, and nurturing is expressed in appropriate ways at appropriate times. Abuse does not take place. Boundaries are flexible enough to distinguish between being too rigid and too loose. For example, it might be too rigid to say that hugs are never permitted between a pastor and a parishioner. There are times when hugs are appropriately nurturing. It is also right to say that there are many times not to hug, when it is an invasion of people's physical, emotional, and spiritual privacy.

Healthy communities have healthy rules. People talk, share feelings, accept the reality importance of some issues, do not overly dramatize others, and accept responsibility for their own mistakes without blaming others. This also means that there is no enabling, that no one is trying to cover up for others.

[5]See "The Unhealed Wounders," p. 33.

In healthy churches roles are clearly defined, people accept certain responsibilities, and no one is made to be the hero—either all the time or vicariously for others. Even though a pastor and other church leaders accept responsibilities, all people are saints in the sight of God and all share in the division of labor. This means that there are no father or mother figures that people look up to with childlike trust. People's faith is placed with childlike trust in the hands of God. Work is shared, not dominated by a few religious workaholics.

I worked with a church that was in the reorganization phase of grieving. This church established a healing committee that functioned for several years after the event of sexual misconduct. It was a large committee with people of different skills and professions on it. Over the time of healing this group organized seminars in which they brought in lawyers and counselors to speak. Often at these public and voluntary forums, members of the committee would give a testimony of how they were doing with their feelings. They published lists of resources for victims. They devised a curriculum for their Sunday school and youth groups that dealt with sexual abuse and other issues.

During this time, their new pastor allowed these people the freedom to work at their own pace and direction while providing gentle encouragement and supervision. In the process of participating in the healing activities himself, he accepted his own alcoholism and went for treatment. He publicly acknowledged this and was warmly welcomed back when he finished treatment.

One of the last formal actions of this church was to invite their bishop to come and talk to them. During his talk this courageous man said several things that reflected his own maturity and pointed the way to final issues in the long-term healing process. First, the bishop said that he was sorry for what had happened. Even though he did not feel personally responsible for the sexual misconduct of the pastor, he acknowledged how painful it was and apologized on behalf of the national Church for it.

Second, he informed the congregation about what was happening with the former pastor, what the legal process had been, what treatment had been like, and what the future might be. Certain anonymous facts had to be protected, but within appropriate boundaries he told the truth.

Third, the bishop offered to help any victims who had come forward or who would come forward in the future. He said, "I *welcome* you to come to us." He described what would happen if they did. Resources were listed, anonymity was pledged, and financial help was offered.

Fourth, the bishop led everyone to the sanctuary where he celebrated a service of communion dedicated to ongoing healing and reconciliation. It was a powerful and extremely important moment, sacramental in nature, pointing to a healing and graceful God.

Ultimately, the long-term healing process is a process of reconciliation. A reconciling congregation is one that has moved through the grieving process, maturing in their faith. Trust has been restored in God, in ministry, and in one another.

Finally, what does reconciliation mean for victims and the pastors who have sexually offended against them? A number of us on the Parish Consultation Service have witnessed reconciliation meetings between clergy and one of more of their primary victims. I can't remember any other experiences that were as healing as these. Such an experience demands that the best interest of the victims is the primary concern. If such a meeting would be therapeutic, then it is an experience that should be considered. It can be important if a victim is to move on with life and become a survivor. This is not a matter of forgiving and forgetting and should not take place too soon. A victim must have time to work through anger and other feelings. A meeting of this nature assumes that justice has been done. Forgiveness, however, can be dramatically powerful for the victim. It is the final stage of healing.

Such a meeting can be equally powerful for the offending pastor. If he or she has come to a place of humility and genuine sorrow for the damage done, expressing this and asking for forgiveness can be extremely healing. We suspect that when such reconciliation meetings take place, both victim and perpetrator heal faster.

The long-term healing of a congregation and all the secondary victims in it might also benefit from such an experience of reconciliation. This has been extremely rare. In some cases a sexually offending pastor has been allowed to ask for the forgiveness of the congregation immediately after the events have been exposed. Jimmy Swaggert, for example, gave a tearful confession of his sexual sins to his congregation. He asked for their forgiveness. He then continued in his ministry and chose not to follow the discipline of his denomination.

Confessions like this can be for the purpose of manipulating forgiveness. I have known several pastors who preached eloquent sermons about forgiveness. This is not asking for forgiveness in humility. It is demanding forgiveness out of selfishness. This kind of pastor may even feel, "I deserve that you forgive me. You better forgive me or God will be angry with you." Some congregations are all too eager to have matters return to the status quo; their feelings of shock and denial will make them all too vulnerable to this kind of demand.

I have often been accused by congregations of not believing in forgiveness. As one who has dramatically experienced it myself, nothing could be further from the truth. I simply know that without consequences and justice, I and others would never heal. Consequences can be for the purpose of healing and restoration. They are a corrective. There are those who would deliver them out of anger, judgment, and a need to punish. Consequences motivated by these feelings are rarely helpful. It is true, however, that consequences and justice can be meted out with love.

I believe that a sexually offending pastor who is healing and is humble can genuinely desire an experience of reconciliation with his or her former congregation. Such a pastor might seek ways to make restitution. Some of us have tried, directly or indirectly, to pay for therapy for victims. Others of us try to teach and work with clergy so as to prevent abuse in the future. In the future there may be other creative strategies for making restitution.

There can be the possibility, in certain situations, that a public apology by the offender to the congregation might be a matter of reconciliation. Such a meeting should always be a specially called meeting of the church in which those who are ready to hear such an apology can come. Whether or not this appearance would be damaging to any victims in the church must be considered. This is never for the purpose of restoring the offender to the same church. If done at the right time and in the right spirit, however, such an experience can be reconciling.

Victims themselves may need to be reconciled to the congregation. As others in this volume have said, they are often revictimized by the congregation when they try to tell the truth. They are not believed. They are the recipients of anger because they have caused disruption. They have brought consequences to someone who was beloved.

In some official way, it can be appropriate for local congregations to apologize to victims and seek to restore them to fellowship. Victims may not desire this. It may be too painful for them to remain in the same congregation. Others, however, may find that it is part of their healing to come back. This may take months or years, but it can be powerfully important. Victims should always be welcomed to come back.

Ultimately, the long-term healing of a congregation is an act of reconciliation with God. Grieving may cause people to be angry with God for the terrible things that have happened. A healing congregation has come past these feelings and knows that the damage was caused by people and not by God. Reading the psalms will remind people that historically there have been many in covenant with God who felt abandoned and angry.

It is a pioneering time for long-term healing strategies. Historical silences, denials, and overt deceptions have prevented many congregations from experimenting with what works. At the present time we often are being led by what lawyers are telling us is safe to do rather than by what our spirits are telling us is right to do.

Finally, if we are to help we must be sure our own spirits are healed of past losses. Rare is there one of us who has not been affected by the situation of pastoral sexual misconduct. We must be sure that our angers and sorrows, our own grief process, is complete before we can help anyone or any congregation deal with theirs. When we are ready and able, we will be helping build healthy communities of faith.

Conclusion

When we began our research, we started with a number of questions. (1) What does a congregation need in order to be able to heal? (2) How can we meet those needs? (3) What can happen in a congregation when nothing is done? (4) What is the afterpastor experience? (5) Who else are secondary victims? (6) Where is the hope in all this?

Nearly every author in this volume has highlighted the need congregations have for knowledge. Information *is* power, as we are so often reminded in this, the information age. There is nothing more central to our work than that. Furthermore, congregations need much support from the wider Church and a chance to come together as a community to process the difficult truths they must face.

Several articles contained herein address the second question, how to provide for those needs. We have developed strategies to help congregations get what they need to heal, and we continue to learn new approaches. This is what makes the work both challenging and exciting.

When nothing is done, it is becoming increasingly apparent that congregations can evolve into very troubled settings. Evidence for this is provided most compellingly by the stories of afterpastors. They have been so hurt by their experiences in these congregations that many of them consider leaving ministry. The hopeful thing is that—in many cases—it is not too late to heal, even if the traumatic events happened years before.

This is the first time we have looked consistently at all those who become secondary victims. Common themes thread through their stories, too, the need to know and work with the truth foremost among them.

The Final Question

Where is the hope in all this? This is the question that surrounds and permeates all of the other questions, and all of our work. There are many times during the process when hope seems far removed. There have been some truly tragic events in which it is hard to see any hope at all. Those very rare occasions when false and frivolous accusations have been made come to mind. Even more disturbing have been those not-so-rare occasions when an accused and very likely guilty clergyperson has been able to stone-wall to the end, viciously attacking any victims in the process. Sometimes victims become so enraged that they get vengeance confused with justice. For them it seems that no amount of restitution will ever satisfy.

When people are polarized in anger, hurting, fearful, or defensive, it is hard to maintain a vision of hope. It is especially difficult when we are personally being attacked and can see no clear way to any immediate resolution of very difficult conflicting interests. Even so, there is hope. Justice is possible. We must be willing to take the long view, the goal of which is nothing less than transformation of a religious and secular culture.

It is not until a victim becomes empowered enough to find her or his voice and confront the institution that the healing for everyone involved becomes a possibility. In order for this first step to happen, the victim will have had the courage and fortitude to work with a therapist or support group in order to be ready to come forward. The next requirement is a receptive climate in the church and the willingness to do the extremely hard work of confrontation, discerning as fairly as possible where the truth lies and facing that truth squarely and openly. Then, recovery and eventual reconciliation for all parties—for the victim-survivor, the offender, the congregation, the wider Church, and even the wider community—becomes the essence of our hope.

Clergy sexual misconduct is only one form of power abuse. Yet when we begin to confront this form of abuse in the church, we automatically open ourselves to having an impact on all other forms of power abuse, beginning from within the church, and radiating outward to the wider community. Sexual abuse is related to the larger issues of racism and sexism; both "isms" are driven by the underlying belief that certain people can be objectified and used for the gain or gratification of those in power. It does not matter where we enter the system for the purposes of reform; all are connected, and justice achieved in one area will spill over into another. Any time we give voice to the voiceless we are justice making, and that is also where the hope lies.

The pain of sexual abuse has been silently borne by victims for centuries. When we begin to acknowledge that pain, it surfaces and gets shared. The total aggregation of shared pain is not necessarily any greater now than when it was so acutely felt by a few, but our intentional willingness to acknowledge and embrace that pain as people of faith is what eventually will enable us all to heal.

Contributors

Rev. Nils Friberg, Ph.D., is professor of pastoral care at Bethel Theological Seminary in St. Paul, Minnesota.

Darlene K. Haskin, M.A., is a counselor in private practice, a consultant, and a supervisor for victims' advocates. She serves on the boards of trustees of Seabury-Western Theological Seminary, Berkeley Divinity School at Yale University, and the Alban Institute.

Rt. Rev. Harold Hopkins is director of the Office of Pastoral Development of the Episcopal Church, U.S.A.

Nancy Myer Hopkins, M.S., is eastern coordinator of the Parish Consultation Service. She also works in clergy family wellness and prevention.

Richard Irons, M.D., lectures broadly about professional impairment and develops assessment programs nationally.

Rev. Chilton Knudsen is pastoral officer of the Episcopal Diocese of Chicago and works directly with congregations in the healing process.

Mark Laaser, Ph.D., lectures and leads seminars internationally. He has helped implement an intensive out-patient program for sexual addiction at the Birchwood Center in Eden Prairie, Minnesota, and is a consultant with several treatment programs nationally.

Mary Lou Lavallee is an Episcopal Church communicator and for seventeen years was lay canon for the Episcopal Diocese of Western Massachusetts.

Ann Legg, M.Ed., and Derek Legg, M.S., clinical members of the American Association for Marriage and Family Therapy, are family therapists in private practice who also work with families of offending clergy as part of the Ministerial Health Services based in Minneapolis. They also consult with congregations about clergy sexual misconduct.

Rev. Margo Maris, M.Div., is west coast coordinator for Parish Consultation Service. She works with victim-survivors, is co-chair of the National Committee on Sexual Exploitation of the Episcopal Church, and vice chair of the board of the Interfaith Sexual Trauma Institute.

Rev. Kevin McDonough is vicar general of the Archdiocese of Saint Paul and Minneapolis.

Rev. Katherine Roberts is an Episcopal priest in Atlanta, and works with the assessment and treatment of impaired professionals.

Roxanne Moore Saucier, a Roman Catholic layperson, is religion reporter for the *Bangor Daily News,* Bangor, Maine.

Phyllis A. Willerscheidt, M.A., is executive director of the Commission on Women of the Archdiocese of Saint Paul and Minneapolis.